The RCIA: Transforming the Church

A Resource for Pastoral Implementation

REVISED AND UPDATED EDITION

Thomas H. Morris

PAULIST PRESS
New York ■ Mahwah, N.J.

Dedicated to the memory of
Rev. James B. Dunning
(1937-1995)
Founder and Staff Member of
The North American Forum on the Catechumenate

Acknowledgment
The Publisher gratefully acknowledges use of excerpts from the English translation of *Rite of Christian Initiation of Adults* © 1985, International Committee on English in the Liturgy, Inc. All rights reserved.

Library of Congress Cataloging-in-Publication Data

Morris, Thomas H., 1956–
    The RCIA : transforming the Church : a resource for pastoral implementation / Thomas H. Morris.—Rev. and updated ed.
        p. cm.
    Includes bibliographical references.
    ISBN 0-8091-3758-5
    1. Catholic Church. Ordo initiationis Christianae adultorum. 2. Initiation rites—Religious aspects—Catholic Church. 3. Catholic Church—United States—Membership. 4. Pastoral theology—Catholic Church. I. Title.
BX2045.I553M67   1997
264'.020813—dc21   97-28822
                                                                                                        CIP

Published by Paulist Press
997 Macarthur Boulevard
Mahwah, New Jersey 07430

Printed and bound in the
United States of America

Contents

Part Two: Implementing the Rite

Part Three: Other Important Considerations

Abbreviations*

CIC   *Codex iuris canonici* (*Code of Canon Law*), 1983

EN   *Evangelii nuntiandi* (*Evangelization in the Modern World*), Paul VI, 8 December 1975

EACW   *Environment and Art in Catholic Worship*, USCC, 1978

GNLYC   *General Norms for the Liturgical Year and the Calendar*, 1969

GS   *Gaudium et spes* (*Pastoral Constitution on the Church in the Modern World*), Vatican Council II, 7 December 1965

MCW   *Music in Catholic Worship*, USCC, 1972

NCD   *Sharing the Light of Faith: National Catechetical Directory for Catholics of the United States*. NCCB, 1978

NS   *National Statutes for the Catechumenate* approved by the National Conference of Catholic Bishops on 11 November 1986

RCIA   *Rite of Christian Initiation of Adults*, US edition, 1988

SC   *Sacrosanctum concilium* (*Constitution on the Sacred Liturgy*), Vatican Council II, 4 December 1963

*All quotations from these official texts are in their approved translations, which may at times be non-inclusive.

Introduction
to Revised and Updated Edition

A farm family was forced to move to the city because of foreclo-
sure of their land. They had a five-year-old son named Johnny
who had lost his arm in a farm accident. Johnny's mother took him
to the parish school, and the teacher helped the children deal with
Johnny's disability by letting him tell his story. The day was going
well, so the teacher began to lead the children in a familiar activity, "Here's the church, and here's the steeple. Open the doors,
and..." Suddenly she thought, How is Johnny going to do this
with one arm? She looked over and saw a little girl reach across to
Johnny and whisper to him, "Here, Johnny, take my hand. Let's
build the church together."

At the time of the writing of this revised and updated edition of *The
RCIA: Transforming the Church,* twenty-five years have passed since Pope
Paul VI promulgated the *Ordo initiationis christianae adultorum (Rite of
Christian Initiation of Adults,* 6 January 1972); more than fifteen years since
more than 200 pastoral ministers gathered in Estes Park, Colorado for a work-
shop on Christian initiation during which The North American Forum on the
Catechumenate was born; and more than ten years since the late Rev. James B.
Dunning, founder and staff member of The North American Forum on the
Catechumenate, told Johnny's story at the end of a presentation he gave to the
National Conference of Catholic Bishops of the United States. At that same
meeting in 1986, the bishops approved several action items regarding the
implementation of the *Rite of Christian Initiation of Adults,* including the lat-
est edition of the ritual text with adaptations for use in the United States, along
with National Statutes for implementing the rite in the United States.

Indeed, much has happened in the last twenty-five years regarding the
implementation of the *Rite of Christian Initiation of Adults.* Yet there is still
some frustration and concern about the why and how of implementing the *Rite
of Christian Initiation of Adults.* It is not a question of good will. Team members work very hard. It may not even be lack of resources. Some team members have gone to week-long training institutes and bought the best books

available on initiation. Nor is it lack of conviction. Team members usually believe deeply in the power of the initiation rites to reform the lives of people, the initiated as well as the uninitiated.

No, for many parishes, the problem seems to be (to borrow an ancient and rich image) they are busy pouring new wine into old wineskins. Only one thing results from that—the bursting of the skins: confusion, disinterest, lack of involvement.

What are these "old" wineskins? Remember Johnny's teacher? "Here's the church, here's the steeple…" All of us have a particular understanding about sacrament and sacrament preparation that influences our pastoral practice. Like Johnny's teacher, we do what is familiar to us. So, when adults and children come to our community seeking initiation, we respond with what we know about Christian initiation: we put them in a group of peers and let them tell their story (just like Johnny). However, when things may be going well, we "forget" and use the more familiar models of sacrament preparation. We may use group process and the like, but underneath it all is a pattern of preparation very similar to what we have always known: sacramental preparation happening in the classroom, even when we disguise the "classroom" as someone's home or the parish center. This does not mean that elements of instruction play no part in the initiation process. Instruction, however, is not the dominant theme.

A RADICAL SHIFT

We need to shift the way we view sacraments and sacrament preparation, especially initiation sacraments: out of the classroom and into the assembly. The primary responsibility for initiation formation does not rest with catechists, books, or peer gatherings, all of which can be important components of an initiation process. The *Rite of Christian Initiation of Adults* is clear: "The initiation of catechumens is a gradual process that takes place within the community of the faithful" (*RCIA*, n. 4). "[T]he people of God, as represented by the local church, should understand and show by their concern that the initiation of adults is the responsibility of all the baptized." (*RCIA*, n. 9). These are not pious platitudes; rather, they are integral to an understanding and appreciation of initiation and the initiation process. It is the community of the faithful that bears the responsibility of initiation. The primary gathering of this community—the Sunday assembly—provides the context and direction for initiation formation.

The need to make this shift is even more compelling when we read in the ritual text that during the period of the catechumenate, we provide a suitable catechesis that "leads the catechumens not only to an appropriate acquaintance with dogmas and precepts but also to a profound sense of the mystery of salvation in which they desire to participate" (*RCIA,* n. 75.1). Yes, the information is important. We are not trying to hide people from the teaching of the community. The teaching of the community makes sense, however, when the inquirer experiences that teaching within the living, praying, serving community of the faithful. The Church responds to the questions of the catechumens less with instruction and more with an environment within which they can be open to experience the "profound sense of the mystery of salvation in which they desire to participate." Describing the period of the catechumenate—perhaps the most extensive period of the initiation process—the ritual text says "[it] is an extended period during which the candidates are given suitable pastoral formation and guidance, aimed at training them in the Christian life" (*RCIA,* n. 75). We are talking about a mentoring process that "must bear a markedly paschal character" (*RCIA,* n. 8): dying, rising, hope, new life, profound sense of the mystery of salvation…. We are talking about leaning over to Johnny and building church together, with our hands.

This mentoring process presumes that the process of becoming Christian is normative for remaining Christian. As with any apprenticeship, we give the catechumens the foundational skills for a way of life: the life of the Christian disciple. Therefore, the initiation process offers an important challenge to the community: be faithful to who you are. Perhaps it is this challenge that causes many parishes to opt for quick programs, thus avoiding the harder questions of how the parish is faithful to its call to discipleship.

WHY A REVISED AND UPDATED EDITION?

When the first edition of *The RCIA: Transforming the Church* was published in 1989, it was one of the few resources available to help initiation ministers with the implementation of the *Rite of Christian Initiation of Adults.* In the intervening years, much conversation has occurred in various circles on initiation topics. I have been fortunate to be part of many of those conversations in various capacities, including as executive director of The North American Forum on the Catechumenate since 1990. The fruit of some of these dialogues has emerged in presentations I have given across the United States, as well as in articles I have written in various journals, most especially *Catechumenate, Today's Parish, Modern Liturgy* and *Christian Initiation.* Often I found myself thinking, "I wish I had included that in my book." Well, after thinking that enough times, I thought it might be time to write a new book, a follow-up to *The RCIA: Transforming the Church.* But as I reread the text— and spoke with people using it—I realized there were many worthwhile items in it that would still be of use to people. Therefore, I decided to rework the original text and incorporate many ideas and insights that emerged since the first writing; hence, this revised and updated edition. If you are familiar with the original edition, you will find much new material in this edition to complement your earlier reading.

The purpose of this resource is the same as the original work: pastoral.

> It shies away from being simply practical. *Practical* is too cut and dried, too matter of fact, too sterile. *Pastoral,* on the other hand, is creative, empowering, dynamic. The implementation of the RCIA in any setting that has become practical usually suffers from minimalism (catechetically, liturgically, ministerially). Such programs are often convert classes disguised in new clothes. This resource is meant to help move from such practical programs toward a rich and empowering process in the life of the parish community.
> (*The RCIA: Transforming the Church,* 1989 edition)

There are many changes to this edition. I have expanded Part One to include more information on the place of liturgy in the initiation process, including the process of liturgical catechesis. Also, there is a presentation that clarifies how to use the rite with children of catechetical age and baptized candidates, as well as guidelines for adapting the ritual text. I have expanded the format and content of Part Two to include a guided reading of the ritual text appropriate for each period and step, along with suggestions for implementation. Each chapter in Part Two concludes with a section on adaptation with children of catechetical age and one on adaptation with baptized candidates. Part Three includes an evaluation process that an initiation team can use. Overall, most of the resource is new while keeping the same direction as the original edition.

It is not my intention to present the only model for implementing the *Rite of Christian Initiation of Adults.* It is my intention, though, to help parish ministers know the ritual text and make appropriate pastoral applications. My recommendations do reflect my experience, which is not transferable in every setting. Yet the foundation of this book—a critical reading and understanding of the ritual text itself—is not limited to any one community. It is my hope that people from various community settings—rural, suburban, urban, campus, military—and various ethnic cultures—Hispanic, African-American, Native American, to name a few—will find most of this resource helpful for their particular setting to help them create appropriate adaptations for those settings.

HOW TO USE THE RITUAL TEXT

This book will not make any sense unless you have a copy of the *Rite of Christian Initiation of Adults* beside it as you read. Nothing—not even this resource—can replace working directly with the ritual text itself. Therefore, I avoid quoting the ritual text in this resource unless it helps to clarify the issue discussed. Rather, I direct you to the part of the ritual text I am referencing so that you can read it along with my commentary. I am using the 1988 edition of the *Rite of Christian Initiation of Adults,* approved for use in the dioceses of the United States by the National Conference of Catholic Bishops.

Whenever you read references to "the rite" or "the ritual text," I am referring specifically to the *Rite of Christian Initiation of Adults* as a whole. Whenever I am referring to a specific rite within the *Rite of Christian Initiation of Adults,* I will indicate that directly, such as the rite of election. Since the ritual text uses a structure similar to this book (parts, chapters), whenever I refer to another section of this revised and updated edition of *The RCIA: Transforming the Church,* I note that the chapter reference is to "this resource."

If you are new to using ritual texts, allow me to explain a few items to ease your handling of the ritual text. Since Vatican Council II, Roman Catholic ritual texts are initially promulgated in Latin (what is called the *editio typica*) and then distributed to the various national conferences of bishops for translation. The English-speaking countries receive their translation from a group called ICEL (International Committee on English in the Liturgy), which the national conference of bishops then reviews and approves. Thus, once the bishops approve a translation (which then is confirmed by the Apostolic See), it becomes the official translation of the ritual text. Because various publishers distribute the text (and use different layouts of the text), the ritual text (and for that matter, most official Church documents) is referenced by numbers that can be found in the left margin of the text (most editions print the text numbers in red). Usually, these numbers introduce a paragraph, though many paragraphs may be associated with a single number. Therefore, references to the *Rite of Christian Initiation of Adults* will not be given as page 5, but as *RCIA,* n. 23.

If you look carefully at your ritual text, you will notice in the right-hand margin small numbers. When the provisional translation of the *Rite of Christian Initiation of Adults* was revised for the current edition, the decision was made to reorder certain parts of the text to make it easier to follow. Thus, the small numbers in the right margin refer to the corresponding text in the *editio typica.* When you see USA (see for example *RCIA,* n. 58), it refers to an adaptation approved for use in the United States.

*   *   *

ACKNOWLEDGMENTS

Many people contributed to this revised and updated edition of *The RCIA: Transforming the Church,* either directly or indirectly. These include candidates and catechumens, initiation teams, members and staff of The North American Forum on the Catechumenate, students at the Institute of Pastoral Studies at Loyola University in Chicago, and many women and men whom I have met and talked with at workshops, presentations, and institutes all across the United States. Thank you to all of them for helping to shape my thought. I wish to extend special thanks to my editor at Paulist Press, Maria Maggi, who, with good humor and a skillful eye, brought this project to completion. I am also grateful to *Catechumenate, Today's Parish,* and *Modern Liturgy* magazines and the *Christian Initiation* newsletter for giving me the opportunity to write about much of what is contained in this revised and updated edition. Many of those articles are reworked into this book. I would also like to thank Steve Roszel for his assistance with the section on annulments in chapter 12.

Now that the work is completed on this revised book, I realize more clearly the care my family and friends extended to me throughout the process. They gave me the necessary support that enabled me to put aside many things—including sometimes spending time with them—to provide this resource to you. In doing that, they modeled in real life what I write and talk about on initiation: people and communities that struggle to live discipleship. To them, especially my dear friends Don Cammiso and Marguerite Stapleton, I am deeply grateful.

Thomas H. Morris
Lent, 1997

Part One

Foundational Issues

1

Understanding Christian Initiation

Once upon a time, a young monk was pondering many of life's questions. He found himself perplexed by a key one: "Why are some people faithful, and others not?" Eager to discover the answer, he raced to his master-teacher, a wise elder monk. The elder monk responded to the question with a story:

> One day, a dog chased a rabbit. The rabbit ran fast and the dog, chasing after it, barked and barked. Soon the barking caught the attention of other dogs. So they, too, joined in the chase. What a noise they made! Eventually, as the other dogs began to get tired, they fell off from the chase and went home. Finally, the only dog left was the first dog, still in pursuit of the rabbit. Up and down the roadways they ran until the rabbit eluded the chasing dog. Once the dog realized he could not catch the rabbit, he returned home, ever watchful for the next time and the next chase.

The young monk remained silent for a respectful period and then said to the elder monk, "I don't get it. What does that mean?"

The elder monk smiled and simply said, "The first dog was the only dog actually to see the rabbit. Those who remain faithful must see the vision."

With that, the younger monk went off to ponder his new learning.

(Source unknown)

WHAT IS THE *RITE OF CHRISTIAN INITIATION OF ADULTS?*

The *Rite of Christian Initiation of Adults* is the result of the directives of Vatican Council II for the restoration of the catechumenal process (*SC,* nos. 64, 66). Its promulgation in 1972 by Pope Paul VI marked a significant shift in the practice of initiating adults in the Catholic Christian community: the local community forms men and women, responding to an often inexplicable call, around the word of God. Together they discern and welcome God's invitation to embrace life in the Catholic Christian community. This leads to serving the mission of Jesus in the world today.

The *Rite of Christian Initiation of Adults* is a restoration of the ancient practice of initiation in the Church. Focused on conversion, candidates entered an extended period of formation and probation. The community ritually celebrated the conversion at various points on the journey, culminating with the celebration of baptism, confirmation and eucharist at the Easter Vigil. An extended catechesis followed this to help the newly initiated to live the commitment they made: lives of justice, service and charity as witnesses of the reign of God.

Initiation into the Christian community is not concerned about programs that come and go. Rather, Christian initiation is concerned with the fundamental values of the Christian way of life. That is why the *Rite of Christian Initiation of Adults* is not a program but a sacramental process. Though we celebrate the *Rite of Christian Initiation of Adults* during a period of from one to three years, it reflects a sacramental attitude that is at the heart of all Christian living: conversion. From this experience of conversion (and conversion means a "turning" of the whole person, not just the intellect), the Spirit empowers the believer to proclaim the gift received: liberation and redemption in and through the person of Jesus, the Christ.

The *Rite of Christian Initiation of Adults* is one rite divided into various periods that respect the individual's journey of faith. Community celebrations that serve as transitions or steps throughout the rite mark these periods of initiation formation. The periods of the *Rite of Christian Initiation of Adults* and their accompanying transition celebrations are as follows:

Rite of Christian Initiation of Adults
Period of Evangelization and the Precatechumenate
Rite of Acceptance into the Order of Catechumens
Period of the Catechumenate
Rite of Election or Enrollment of Names
Period of Purification and Enlightenment
Celebration of the Sacraments of Initiation
Period of Mystagogy or Postbaptismal Catechesis

These various periods are a process of *formation* to the gospel. The *Rite of Christian Initiation of Adults* helps facilitate the experience of God for those seeking full initiation into the community. This formation to the gospel becomes the seed for renewal in the parish community not only because new members come to the community, but because the actual formation team for the *Rite of Christian Initiation of Adults* is the parish community. The catechumens challenge the parish by asking hard questions: Why are you Catholic? What do you believe? Why do you believe? Why would I be happier if I joined your community? How is God alive here? The parish needs to ask and answer these questions of itself often. As the parish members witness to their sense of being ambassadors for God, they deepen their appreciation and use of God's gifts in the community. An active initiation process keeps the winds of renewal always current in the parish.

KNOWING THE VISION

It is very easy to lose sight of the vision of initiation and get caught up with all kinds of programs to "get people through," thus missing the mark when it comes to the how and why of initiation. Taking some time right at the beginning to look at the rite itself to discover anew the compelling vision it offers for Christian initiation is wise.

Surprisingly, some people implement the *Rite of Christian Initiation of Adults* without reading the entire ritual text. Perhaps they pick up an idea at a workshop, or read an article about a certain aspect of the rite. All of us can profit greatly by immersing ourselves (and our initiation ministry) in the vision the rite sets out for us. We do this for at least two reasons: (1) so we are faithful to the Church's intention when we initiate, and (2) so something bigger than the myriad of details catches and takes hold of us.

Where do we find this vision? All ritual texts provide this vision—what we call the theological foundations of the ritual text—in the "Introduction" (also known as the *praenotanda*) to the ritual text. This theological vision, found in the "Introduction," provides the groundwork for understanding and implementing the rites.

The introduction to this book notes that the approved translation in the United States is a reordered version of the *editio typica*. The editors moved much of the "Introduction" to other sections of the ritual text. For example, they have moved the part of the introduction that is pertinent to the celebration of the rite of acceptance into the order of catechumens to just before the text for this particular rite. Therefore, a thorough study of the "Introduction" of the *Rite of Christian Initiation of Adults* would not only comprise *RCIA*, nos. 1-35, but the introductory comments to each period and step. However, for our purposes here, we will limit our initial reflection to *RCIA,* nos. 1-35; we will discuss the remaining introductory notes when we address the particular period or step. To explore the theological foundations of the rite and get the most out of this reflection, the reader will need to have a copy of the rite, and to read the appropriate section of the "Introduction" before turning to the commentary.

THE "OTHER" INTRODUCTION

The *Rite of Christian Initiation of Adults* also includes a section called "Christian Initiation, General Introduction" which is found after the "Foreword" and before the ritual text for initiation. This "General Introduction" was written earlier as an introduction to the rite of baptism (used with infants); its primary focus deals with baptism. The editors include it in this edition of the *Rite of Christian Initiation of Adults* to complement the "Introduction." As with the "Introduction," this "General Introduction" provides key theological and liturgical foundations for understanding initiation. The reader is encouraged to review this section as well.

COMMENTARY ON THE INTRODUCTION

Introduction
Read RCIA, *n. 1.*

The major theme throughout the initiation process is conversion. This section provides a summation of the conversion process: we proclaim Christ, one seeks relationship with God because of this proclamation, and one enters into a way of life in response to the Holy Spirit. Clearly this is God's work well before it is our work. We cannot program such a response to the mystery of Christ. We also note that the rite as outlined is for adults who can respond in faith to God's call.

Recall, however, that for the purposes of initiation, the *Code of Canon Law* (*CIC,* canon 852) states that we treat children who are of the age of reason as adults. The *Code of Canon Law* does not presume we treat children as if they were adults. Rather, two things are at stake here: (1) the integrity of the full initiation experience as normative (as opposed to the separated model that we have with infant baptism and delayed confirmation-eucharist), and (2) the value and validity of children's religious experience.

Read RCIA, *n. 2.*

When we speak of Christian initiation, we are speaking of the entire process of formation and celebration. Thus, as indicated in this paragraph, we are talking about a whole repertoire of ritual action that necessarily is part of the initiation process. Implicit in this is the catechesis appropriate to prepare for such ritual celebration. Therefore, we need to think in holistic terms: The entire process is about initiation, not just the celebration of the sacraments of baptism, confirmation, and eucharist.

Read RCIA, *n. 3.*

While there is a foundational structure for this process of sacramental initiation (Part I), the ritual text also provides for adaptations of this structure for various pastoral circumstances. Note, however, that Part I provides the usual form. In other words, we cannot adapt what we don't really know.

Structure of the Initiation of Adults
Read RCIA, *n. 4.*

This is an insightful summary of the initiation process: It is gradual (not time-locked) and happens within the community of the faithful. Initiation is a journey in community. That is the starting point. The catechetical sessions are fine and good, but they are subordinate to life within the community. Therefore, we need to find ways to involve the community in the initiation process. Perhaps instead of creating new groups for the catechumenal process, we should look at what already exists in the parish community and immerse the candidates and catechumens into those experiences.

Furthermore, the community benefits from the initiation process because it deepens our awareness and commitment to discipleship. Therefore, all of the catechumenal events, especially the liturgical celebrations, need to happen in the midst of the community. The candidates and catechumens will come to know God primarily by the way we live the gospel way of life (our example) and the care and concern we offer to them (relationships). The primacy of the community provides a context for understanding the rest of the process.

The rite presumes (see, for example, *RCIA,* n. 75.2) that it is through the experience of the Christian community—our way of life, our example, etc.— that the catechumen is drawn to prayer. The emphasis is on the community's experience of God before an individual's experience of God. In fact, our discipleship only makes sense because of the community's identity as the Body of Christ. Yet it is the experience of most Catholics that personal piety precedes communal prayer.

Read RCIA, *n. 5.*

The language here is important: No programs are presented. There is not a program on the market that can do what this section describes: a spiritual journey (i.e., we cannot predetermine it), adult-focused (i.e., we take seriously the adult experience and the various ways to faith), accommodated to several variables (i.e., God's activity in the life of the individual, the free response to God's call, etc.). These variables are purposely vague to highlight the ongoing nature of the initiation process: Initiation happens all the time because God is calling and people are responding all the time and at different paces.

Read RCIA, *n. 6.*

Alongside this great respect for the individual journey of faith, as noted in *RCIA,* n. 5, the ritual text also directs the community to accompany the catechumens through its liturgical prayer (recall *RCIA,* n. 4). So, we mark the journey publicly because we are a public church. These rituals are liminal moments; catechumens cross over from one state to another in the conversion journey, and we ritually celebrate each of those transitions. Through this, we begin to tutor the catechumens in an important Catholic principle: We celebrate publicly our experience of conversion through our liturgical prayer.

Read RCIA, *n. 7.*

The text gives a short description for each period that precedes and follows the major steps in the journey (*RCIA,* n. 6). The opening sentence provides an important principle of liturgical catechesis: Whatever we do during these periods of formation should lead to the liturgical celebration. In other words, the ritual steps (e.g., rite of acceptance into the order of catechumens) provide the direction for initiation formation. If one wants to know the "content" of a period of formation, look at the ritual that completes that period of preparation. What are we celebrating? Therefore, what needs to happen to celebrate with authenticity?

Read RCIA, *n. 8.*

The reflection on the structure of the initiation process comes to a close with a reminder of what is critical about initiation: it is concerned with immersion in the paschal mystery. We are not about membership—if we were, then we could give people books and have them memorize answers and take the oral quiz and pass. No, we are about discipleship and a lifelong commitment of sharing in the paschal mystery. Furthermore, as this section highlights, we Catholics do this within the context of our liturgical life (e.g., notice the emphasis given to the primacy of the Easter Vigil). The way we initiate reflects what we believe about such discipleship.

Ministries and Offices
Read RCIA, *n. 9.*

The primary minister of initiation is the assembly (see *RCIA,* n. 4 above). This is often too easily lost when we start building initiation teams. Yet this section on "Ministries and Offices" says that the centerpiece of initiation ministries is the praying community as it embodies its commitment of discipleship. Throughout the remainder of this section the text gives directives for the full, active, and conscious participation of the assembly throughout each period and stage. It is from the basic baptismal responsibility that the other initiation ministries emerge.

Read RCIA, *n. 10.*

Sponsors are companions on the journey. Faith is not private. We share it with others. And it is with others that we nurture and nourish our faith. Right from the beginning of the initiation process we need to provide the necessary support and companionship for the catechumen to journey the terrain of faith. Sponsors not only serve to give testimony about the conversion experience of the catechumen (an important role), they also provide the necessary link to the community.

Read RCIA, *n. 11.*

What we have said about sponsors is also true of godparents—perhaps even more so—because the godparents are lifetime companions of the catechumen. Besides making the distinction between sponsors and godparents (though they can be the same person), this section highlights key insights mentioned earlier: the importance of the witness of lifestyles, how catechumens are drawn to God through the example of others, etc. Clearly, the ritual text moves us away from the cultural godparenting experience often associated with infant baptism.

Read RCIA, *n. 12.*

Initiation is clearly into the larger church, not just the local parish. The inclusion of the local ordinary and his role in the initiation process signals this point. Not only should the bishop be involved ritually in the initiation process, but he also appoints catechists to preside at particular rites of the catechumenate period.

In the United States, unless a diocesan bishop designates a different process, appointed catechists for initiation are deputed to preside at the celebrations of the word, minor exorcisms and blessings during the period of the catechumenate (see *RCIA,* n. 81ff.). This is noted in *Study Text 10: Christian Initiation* published by the United States Catholic Conference.

Read RCIA, *n. 13.*

The ritual text moves the particular pastoral care of catechumens to the local level. The pastoral staff members, along with the pastor, need to take an active role in the care and formation of catechumens. Additionally, they need to provide for an appropriate initiation practice. This, of course, presumes their own study of the ritual text.

Read RCIA, *n. 14.*

To maintain the integrity of the celebration of the sacraments of initiation, liturgical law gives the priest who presides at the baptism delegation to confirm. The text makes mention about the possibility of delaying confirmation, with reference given to *RCIA,* n. 24. We will discuss this option when discussing *RCIA,* n. 24. Suffice it to say for now that "serious reason" would be the only reason for such delay.

The misguided practice in some parishes of delaying confirmation for children of catechetical age until they are adolescents (to catch up with their teen peers) has no foundation in the ritual text. As we will see, if we delay confirmation, we are to celebrate it during the upcoming Easter Season.

Read RCIA, *n. 15.*

The ritual text notes the role of deacons in the initiation process here. If deacons have a solid formation in the ministry of the word, they should have key roles in this formation process since it is primarily a ministry of the word.

Read RCIA, *n. 16.*

Another key player in this process is the catechist. The ritual text reflects the restored place of catechesis in the community as a ministry of the word and a departure from a "catechism-instruction" approach to faith formation. That is not to say that instruction will not be part of the process. However, as *RCIA,* n. 75.1 clearly shows, that instruction is less fact-filled and more faith-filled. Here in *RCIA,* n. 16 we note the important links of an initiation catechesis: connection with liturgy, rooted in the word of God, responsive to the catechumen's life experiences, and incorporating the culture of the community.

Time and Place of Initiation

Read RCIA, *n. 17.*

This paragraph, while dealing with the practical issues of time and place for initiation, suggests a more central issue: the primacy of the rites themselves. Many parishes put the major focus on the "instruction" of the catechumens to the neglect of the ritual celebrations. Here in *RCIA,* n. 17, however, we see that the emphasis is placed squarely on the rites themselves: The rites set the agenda.

Notice that the importance of celebrating full initiation at the Easter Vigil gives direction to the rest of the process. This is helpful for many reasons, but most especially because it reminds us where this initiation process is headed. Thus, the guidance given here undoes our desire to align the initiation process with the academic year (begin in September and end in May). We give priority to the praying Church's liturgical calendar because of the importance of the rhythm of the liturgical year.

Always being pastoral, the ritual text does allow for exceptions to the guidance provided in this paragraph for serious pastoral needs. As we will explore later in chapter 3 of this resource, we should not take this lightly.

Proper or Usual Times

The following paragraphs provide guidance for the appropriate time to celebrate the major rites of the initiation process. What is of interest is the ritual text's attempt to hold in creative tension two needs: the needs of the community (as expressed in its liturgical calendar) and the needs of the catechumens on the journey of faith.

Read RCIA, *n. 18.*

Please note what the ritual text has not said in this paragraph about when to celebrate the rite of acceptance: It does not say to celebrate it on the First Sunday of Advent. Rather, the rite invokes the guidance of *RCIA,* n. 42 as the criteria for celebrating the rite of acceptance: initial faith and the first signs of conversion.

Simultaneously, the rite recognizes the need of the community to maintain its own rhythm of life (the liturgical year), and so it goes on to say that a few dates should be set aside as the usual time to celebrate the rite. Other principles need to be kept in mind when determining these dates: the primacy of certain seasons of the year in the liturgical calendar (e.g., the seasons of Advent and Lent already have their focus and we should not adjust it to include this rite), and the importance of celebrating this rite periodically.

Read RCIA, *n. 19.*

The season of Lent finds its origins in the initiation process. After the decline of the initiation process in the early Church, the focus of Lent shifted to reconciliation. The reforms of Vatican II highlighted both dimensions of Lent for today: initiation and reconciliation. Therefore, the ritual text places the rite of election at the start of Lent because the rite serves as a transition rite from the formal preparation (catechumenate) to the final preparation for celebrating the sacraments of initiation. While the rite gives a pastoral guideline for celebrating the rite at a different time, we need to maintain the normative nature of the Sunday gathering in the initiation process. Therefore, any deviation for celebrating any of the rites at a time other than the prescribed time (usually Sunday) needs to be done only if the reasons for such changes are as important (or more so) than the value of celebration within the Sunday assembly.

Read RCIA, *n. 20.*

The ritual text gives primacy for the celebration of the scrutinies during the Third, Fourth, and Fifth Sundays of Lent using the lectionary texts from Year A (see *RCIA,* n. 146). These scrutinies provide the foundations for the Lenten retreat for the elect and the community. The lectionary texts of Year A especially highlight the progressive reflection on the nature of evil and God's response in grace.

The directives are clear about the scrutinies: We are to celebrate three scrutinies. Deviation from this can happen only with permission of the diocesan bishop for serious reasons. If the bishop gives such permission, we are to celebrate one scrutiny minimally. A pastor cannot decide to eliminate any of the scrutinies without permission. The rite places such importance on these ritual celebrations that it, in effect, demands their celebration (and, therefore, demands we face the issues at stake squarely).

Read RCIA, *n. 21.*

The presentations of the Creed and the Lord's Prayer are also a part of the Lenten retreat and we celebrate them in the weeks following certain scrutinies. The problem here is celebrating these important ritual celebrations in the absence of the Sunday assembly. Many parishes gather during Lenten weeks for evening celebrations (e.g., evening Mass followed by a "hunger" meal), and they could celebrate the presentations at those times.

The rite also provides for anticipating these presentations in the period of the catechumenate. While this does diminish their place in the Lenten retreat, it does provide for the possibility of celebration at the Sunday assembly during the final weeks of the catechumenate.

Read RCIA, *n. 22.*

Notice that the text does not suggest the elect *may* "refrain from work and spend their time in recollection." It presumes it. Parish communities need to provide a way to allow the elect to spend this day in reflection and prayer in preparation for the celebration of the sacraments of initiation. During this day of prayer the parish celebrates preparation rites with the elect, presumably in the midst of the assembly (as with all other rites). If a parish celebrates Morning Prayer on Holy Saturday, they could integrate the preparation rites into that celebration.

Read RCIA, *n. 23.*

The Easter Vigil is the time for celebrating Christian initiation: baptism, confirmation, and eucharist. The rite does provide for celebrating during the Easter octave if the community is blessed with a significant number of elect. However, if that is the parish's problem (what a wonderful problem), then it is probably because the community takes the initiation process seriously and prays the rites with integrity. Therefore, why would the parish even want to celebrate initiation at any other time? Again and again, we return to the primacy of the Easter Vigil for the celebration of initiation. Note that if the celebration is at another time in the Easter octave, we use the readings of the Easter Vigil.

Read RCIA, *n. 24.*

Here we face the thorny issue of delaying confirmation. The rite suggests that if there is a serious reason for delay, we may postpone the celebration of confirmation until later in the Easter season. It is difficult to imagine what serious reasons—at least theological reasons—would cause the delay of confirmation in this celebration. Presumably the same reasons would delay the celebration of the eucharist as well (since confirmation precedes eucharist). Departing from the liturgical norm of celebrating baptism, confirmation, and eucharist risks tampering with the deep structure of the ritual celebration and what we proclaim when we celebrate (see *RCIA,* n. 215).

If, however, a serious reason (emphasis on serious) does cause the delay of the celebration of confirmation, noting that the delay is only until another time in the current Easter season is important. Thus, if the "serious" reason is for a child of catechetical age to "catch up" with his or her peers who celebrate confirmation at a later age, we find the rite does not support this. We must resolve any delay within the current Easter season. Why? One concern for the rite is an attempt to hold together the integrity of the sacraments and the important proclamation they make to the Christian community regarding Christian discipleship. The adolescent confirmation issue is a deviation from this norm for sacramental initiation and should not dictate the celebration of these rites.

Read RCIA, *n. 25.*

The initiation process does not end at the Easter Vigil. Mystagogy occurs during the Easter season at the Sunday celebrations of the eucharist. This should cause us to reconsider the energy we place on "midweek" meetings during mystagogy (for reflection on the Sunday readings, etc.—important, but secondary), often to the neglect of the Sunday assembly.

Outside the Usual Times
Read RCIA, *nos. 26-30.*

The rite always takes into account pastoral situations that might prevent the celebration of the *Rite of Christian Initiation of Adults* within the normal liturgical time. While those pastoral situations are rare, the rite does prescribe some guidance for when to celebrate outside the norm. However, the rite is clear: Those seeking initiation have a right to the best we can provide. Shifting from the norms expressed throughout the rite, therefore, should be done carefully and infrequently. (Note: Read *RCIA*, nos. 27-30 within the context of *RCIA*, n. 26.)

Place of Celebration
Read RCIA, *n. 31.*

Normally, we celebrate the rites with the Sunday assembly at its normal gathering place, i.e., the parish church. This is important because the rites are not just for the catechumens and elect—they are for the whole assembly. The entire people of God have a responsibility for the initiation of adults and children (see *RCIA*, n. 9); therefore, the celebration (and the preparation) of initiation during all of its periods and steps needs to happen in the midst of the community.

Adaptations by the Conferences of Bishops in the Use of the Roman Ritual
Read RCIA, *n. 32.*

The local conference of bishops, speaking as a body, has the authority to make appropriate adaptations to the ritual text in keeping with the needs of the church within the jurisdiction of the conference.

Read RCIA, *n. 33.*

Besides particular adaptations, the ritual text indicates specific decisions the conference of bishops can make (as noted in other sections of the ritual text).

Where applicable, the ritual text also indicates the decisions made by the National Conference of Catholic Bishops in the United States. Noting these decisions in the appropriate places in the ritual text is important. These decisions help clarify our understanding about certain underlying issues of initiation.

For example, subsection 4 deals with the issue of the giving of a new name in the rite of acceptance into the order of catechumens (*RCIA,* n. 73). The U.S. bishops decided against giving a new name, while allowing the local ordinary to approve such a practice depending on other local circumstances. This decision not to give a new name (except in particular circumstances) reaffirms the emerging theology of the communion of saints.

For reference, subsection 1 deals with the period of the precatechumenate, subsections 2-5 and 8 deal with the rite of acceptance, subsections 6-7 deal with the period of the catechumenate, and subsection 8 deals with the celebration of baptism. Review them and note the decisions in the appropriate sections of the ritual text.

Adaptations by the Bishop
Read RCIA, *n. 34.*

Initiation is not into a particular parish, but into the Christian community. The role of the bishop serves as a symbol of the universal nature of the initiation process. It is the bishop's responsibility to provide the necessary leadership and direction for the full implementation of the rite. He should also provide guidance in those extraordinary circumstances that require some departure from the norm. The text presumes that the diocesan bishop, as chief liturgist of the diocese, knows well the ritual structure and the ritual text.

Adaptations by the Minister
Read RCIA, *n. 35.*

The presider needs to make responsible and intelligent adaptations of the ritual text that remain faithful to the theological vision of the ritual text and are in keeping with the community gathered for prayer. Too often, we equate adaptation with personal whim or accommodation. Neither is appropriate. Liturgists and presiders need to be careful in making ritual adaptations, lest what we pray suggest something other than what we believe (and what we hoped to pray in the original text). Repeatedly ritual planners and celebrators need to ask "why and what" when deviating from the ritual structure. Why are we shifting? (What pastoral or theological value are we honoring?) What are we proclaiming when we do shift? (What do we believe through this prayer?) Both the why and what should be of such a nature as to bear the deep structure of the ritual prayer (and that presumes knowledge of that deep structure).

WHAT COMES NEXT?

The work of coming to a better understanding of the underlying theology of the *Rite of Christian Initiation of Adults* does not end here. In fact, it is important to note again that in the later sections of the ritual text there are introductory comments preceding the rites themselves. These, too, need to be explored.

In so short a space we have started to map out the terrain of initiation. Key themes emerge repeatedly: the centrality of conversion and the paschal mystery, the non-programmatic nature of initiation, the importance of all the periods and steps as a whole initiation process, the diversity of ministries emerging from the primary ministry of the assembly, the importance of the liturgical calendar as normative, and the importance of adapting the ritual text to particular communities (without diminishing the vision of the ritual text).

2

Underlying Theological
and Pastoral Issues

Before moving to questions of pastoral implementation, there are significant theological and pastoral issues that emerge when exploring the *Rite of Christian Initiation of Adults.* These issues provide a wider context for understanding the rite and its implementation.

EVANGELIZATION

"The preaching of the gospel to the men of our times, full as they are of hope, but harassed by fear and anxiety, must undoubtedly be regarded as a duty which will redound to the benefit not only of the Christian community, but of the whole human race" (*EN,* n. 1). Pope Paul VI's exhortation in *Evangelization in the Modern World* is a call to all the baptized to continue to live faithfully the mission of Jesus, the Christ. This mission is the proclamation of the reign of God, which is the in-breaking of "liberation from everything that oppresses men, but which is above all liberation from sin and the Evil One" (*EN,* n. 9). Such liberation, this salvation from our God, is at the heart of preaching the gospel.

Evangelization—from the Greek *euangelion*—means to "proclaim good news, to bear glad tidings." It is neither proselytizing nor moralizing. Rather, it is the witness of those men and women who have been grasped by the "good word" proclaimed in the Christ event, the paschal mystery: human liberation and salvation in and through Jesus, the Christ. An essential dimension of evangelization is witness.

Evangelization is necessary for Christian initiation. Men and women hear the gospel proclaimed, by word and deed, and come to a particular Christian community because of this initial stirring in faith. The process by which adults both hear and respond to this gospel in the Catholic community is called the *Rite of Christian Initiation of Adults.*

THEOLOGY OF REVELATION

We root a Catholic understanding of evangelization in a dynamic theology of revelation, which is affirmed in the *Dogmatic Constitution on Divine Revelation* from Vatican Council II and rearticulated in the *National Catechetical Directory* and the *Catechism of the Catholic Church.*

Revelation is not extrinsic, that is, something outside us. A static notion of revelation holds that it is "information," truth locked away that we need to uncover. When we discover the right combination, we will have all the truths revealed.

Rather, revelation is God's self-communication with us. It is God's desire to stand in union with us, to share life with us, to offer the gift of loving presence. Through this process of revelation (i.e., God inviting us into communication with God's very self), one comes to a heightened and more intense awareness of God's presence and love. The Christian tradition holds that the fullness of God's revelation—the ongoing and fresh gift of God's self to the community—is most complete in Jesus, the Christ, and that it is in and through Jesus that we come to know God: the God who creates us, redeems us, sustains us, and chooses to become intimately involved with us. The incarnation affirms that a primary place of God's revelation is in relationship with creation, especially humanity. Revelation is dynamic and ongoing. God is continually in relationship with us.

The Catholic community also holds the scriptures and the tradition as sources of God's revelation, thus offering a complement and fullness to the revelation of God in Jesus and in creation.

If we look to the early Christian community, we can see this dynamic sense of revelation in operation. The followers of Jesus experienced in Jesus new possibilities, a new way of life. After his death and resurrection, they began to name this experience of freedom and reconciliation with themselves, others, creation, the cosmos, and God as salvation. Initially, the earliest communities preached the reign of God as proclaimed in Jesus. They preached *what* Jesus preached. Eventually, though, as they reflected on their experience, guided by the power of the Spirit, the community came to affirm that it was precisely in Jesus that they experienced this reign of God. The preaching and belief shifted from what Jesus preached to *preaching Jesus.* Jesus became the preached good. Eventually, this reflection and struggle to name God in their midst (the symbols of the community) became formulated into creedal formulas and eventually into doctrine. Yet the first level was the experience of God, followed by appropriate reflection and internalization, followed by articulation, followed by formulation. Doctrine, in its best sense, is the articulation of the community of faith. It is the Church expressing its experience of God reconciling and saving us in and through Jesus the Christ. Doctrine, as an expression of revelation, is dynamic. It flows from the faith of the community.

This is not to say that doctrine is the product of consensus, opinion, or whim. Rather, doctrine is the formulation of a community's symbol system that authentically empowers the community to a deeper and more integrated response to God's call. Doctrine is an expression of faith. The important point here, however, is that doctrine flows from the religious experience of God in our midst.

Considering this, the initiation process helps individuals begin to name God's manifestation in their lives and to correlate their experience with the living tradition of the Catholic community. This correlation is a dynamic process of questioning, challenging, searching, resolving. During the precatechumenate, we are beginning to equip the journeyer with the basic skills to learn to seek God in their lives. During the catechumenate period—and throughout the Christian life—the task will be to remain faithful to the dialogue for true self-knowledge and a sense of mission.

Such a dynamic sense of revelation, therefore, suggests that there are not two types of experience—secular and religious. It does suggest that from *within* human experience we can come to meet and know the living God.

HUMAN EXPERIENCE

Are all human experiences revelatory? Do all human experiences—precisely because they are human experiences—serve as vehicles for the manifestation of God? All truly human experiences have the potential of being the bearers of God's manifestation in the world, of God's epiphany.

Experience is a fuzzy word for many. We often invoke it to include everything that happens to an individual—from the intense excitement of a basketball game to the passive resignation of being shuffled about in a crowded subway car. In our discussion of experience, however, we need to be more focused. To speak of human experience presumes some level of conscious interaction by the individual or group with an object (i.e., a person or an event). The person or persons are aware and in dialogue with the object. For example, a father and mother are sitting in the auditorium watching their daughter in her first dance recital. Most probably they are not aware of themselves sitting in the auditorium seats, or of many of the people around them, or even of the temperature in the room, unless any of these is a distraction (an uncomfortable chair or a cold room). They are focused on their daughter and her dancing. Being in the chair is not a human experience because there is no active and conscious encounter with the chair—it's probably taken for granted. The human experience is the encounter with their daughter, her dancing, each other as they sit there, and the feelings that are emerging throughout the performance (that is, the feelings they acknowledge). In another section of the auditorium, another parent is watching his daughter dance also. However, other things preoccupy him: for example, a crisis at the office that may result in the loss of his job. While the dance goes on, he feels restless and squirms in his seat, repeating in his mind possible scenarios at the office. He feels tired, and the darn seat is so uncomfortable. Suddenly there is a burst of applause and the dance is over. He was looking at the dance but not seeing the dance. For this man, his daughter's dance recital was not a human experience in that he was not consciously present or aware of the dance. His human experience focused on his job, his feeling tired and restless, and the uncomfortable chair. In order for an experience to be a *human* experience, it requires some level of conscious interaction between a subject (the individual or group) and the object (the dance, the chair, the daughter, the restlessness, and so on).

There are two basic dimensions of human experience. The first dimension is the level of the ordinary, the level of the sensory. One has a visible, sensible encounter with the world. The chair is uncomfortable, the dance is lively, the woman is cold, the iron is hot, the tree stands tall. This first dimension of human experience encounters things and people as they are.

The second dimension of human experience is the depth dimension, the level of interpretation and meaning. One shifts to move behind the sensory to possible meanings of the interaction. The fidgeting in the seat may mean the person is preoccupied, the tree standing tall may inspire values of truth and beauty, the touch of the beloved may inspire love and affection. The depth dimension of human experience breaks one open to a new level of awareness; it is a disclosure situation. Because of it, one enlarges his or her basic world vision or horizon. New levels of meaning emerge that are interpreted from a variety of perspectives. One interpretation or perspective is the religious dimension.

The religious dimension of the secondary level of human experience is the particular way of viewing these depth experiences that opens one up to seeing within these moments the mystery we call God. There is the recognition of an invitation to a new relationship with the Holy. We then allow that experience of God to come to stand within the community's tradition for verification.

When we move from the sensory to this secondary level of human experience—when we name beauty, truth, hope, love—we discover that the depth and immensity of the experience far exceed any words or phrases we can use. Depth experiences bring us to the limits of human language. So we use rich and multifaceted symbols to express, however inadequately, the depth experience. In the section on symbols, we will see how this symbolic discourse both appeals to the whole person and yet is unable to exhaust the meaning of symbols.

Thus, there are not two types of experiences: secular and religious. Rather, there is the religious dimension of human experience. Technically, talking of religious experience is inaccurate unless we have nuanced it to mean the religious dimension of human experience.

Every depth experience, therefore, has the potential of being a religious experience. If one can interpret the experience within the framework of a religious tradition, one can come to a new sense of meaning and a mediated encounter with the Holy. This mediated encounter—there is never a direct experience of God—affirms the sacramental and incarnational dimension of the experience of God.

This is very different from an understanding of religious experience (or the religious dimension of human depth experience) lacquered over life. There is no depth, no meaning. Rather, there is the polishing off of every experience with religious language. This rather facile use of religious language leads one to a private and individualistic expression of religious experience, and therefore God. God, in this context, stands outside human history and human experience.

One task of evangelization is to help people articulate levels of meaning in their life and then to enter into dialogue with the Christian tradition's expression of these same meaning-makers. Therefore, we need to proclaim the truth of the gospel to provide a credible and meaningful challenge to the contemporary man and woman's interpretation of their depth experience. Then the gospel can serve as invitation.

CONVERSION AND THE DEVELOPMENT OF FAITH

The *Rite of Christian Initiation of Adults* is not a program, but a sacramental formation process that prepares individuals and communities for a particular way of life. Conversion is at the heart of that way of life. The *Rite of Christian Initiation of Adults* facilitates the conversion experience.

Conversion is a turning around, an about-face. In a variety of ways, the individual encounters a transformation of values that empowers that individual to turn from what is inauthentic to embrace the truly authentic. In religious terms, conversion is the surrender of oneself to the all-loving God, who calls us to fullness of life. It is God asking us to give what we thought we could not give.

Authentic conversion is transformative. Not only does it result in a radical change in the individual, but it informs and affects every dimension of the individual's life. Furthermore, there is a qualitative change in the individual's manner of life that rings true.

One experiences an empowerment to move beyond self to a new sense of self, the process of self-transcendence. While one can be open to this experience, and can facilitate the possibility of self-transcendence, one cannot "do" it. As a dimension (and result) of conversion, self-transcendence is a dynamic openness to full and authentic human living. Ironically, it is in the very process of not seeking self-transcendence that one enters this transformative process. One finds self only in losing self. Losing self—embracing the path of conversion—is not about self-destruction. Rather, it is about entering into life in intelligent, rational, and responsible ways, thus allowing values for their own sake to be the driving force of life. The shift is from individual satisfaction to the values that promote the vision of the reign of God. One can recognize a new identity: self in relationship with God.

The Hebrew scriptures express the notion of conversion within the context of the covenant relationship. Over and again, God is inviting God's people simply to allow God to be their God, to accept God's gift of life and relationship. The Creator God desires to give life. Without this life, one lives in isolation and bondage. Acceptance of the covenant with God is what can deliver them from their bondage and isolation precisely because acceptance of the covenant is allowing God to be God—thus imparting the gift of life and relationship. The response to the covenant is a penitential heart (i.e., a heart that is open to hear God's saving word and available to receive the very life of God). Conversion is turning around from sin (i.e., the way of those not in true relationship with life) to a personal and loving relationship with God as expressed in the covenant.

The Christian scriptures develop this notion of conversion further with the radical acceptance of Jesus as the one who brings life. *Metanoia,* the Greek word most frequently used to convey the message of conversion, is a change of direction: from a way of life that fosters death to Jesus, who brings the fullness of life. We experience conversion within the context of the proclamation of the reign of God and the demands the reign of God makes for transformed living.

Conversion, then, is the change that happens when we allow God to love us enough that God reforms us, refashioned into men and women who value each other and our relationships in self-sacrificing love. The conversion manifests itself in different ways (e.g., intellectually, morally, affectively), but it is always a radical shift from one way of being to another. There is a breakthrough...a new vision.

The transformation effected by conversion comes at a price. The old dies so the new can live. Therefore, we can liken the conversion process to a grieving process. The literature on death and dying suggests a series of steps toward acceptance of death: denial, anger, bargaining, depression, acceptance. The significant point here is not that one becomes resigned to death, but that one accepts death. This acceptance can only happen when one realizes that the experience of dying is itself meaningful and the person willingly embraces the experience.

The encounter with God's unconditional love that results in conversion is similar: an encounter with God's love (usually mediated through others), the grappling to understand and accept, the struggle to discern the true and the real, the ongoing conversation and questioning for the true and the real, the emergence of an awareness that sees things as they are and the willingness to embrace them, the immediate change that results because of this embracing, and the subsequent changes that occur on every level of life because of the transformation.

The catechumenate process is helping people awaken to the stirrings of God to a renewed life, a turning to a more authentic embrace of life. We name the process conversion. The language that helps articulate the invitations of God is the language of symbol.

SYMBOL: THE LANGUAGE OF THE HEART

Talking about certain experiences is difficult. Words seem to fail us when we try to express our love and affection for someone. They seem even more inadequate when we try to explain the depth of our love for our beloved to a third party. The reason for this is that these experiences—love, pain, fear, hope, and others—are packed with meaning. Nothing we say or do can exhaust the meaning of the experience; there is always something more. These experiences, however, are common to all of us and we have found a manner of speaking about them that respects the depth of the message while still conveying the basic meaning and message we want others to know. The language we use is the language of symbol.

Symbols are the language we use to speak of the richness of reality. Symbolic discourse is the most common form of communication we have with each other. Daily we express our fears, sentiments, hopes, and dreams to each other through symbolic gestures: a kiss of welcome, a supportive hand on one's shoulder, an embrace for the sorrowing, slamming the door in someone's face, or a smile—whether it is a warm, inviting one or a cold, cynical one. All these symbols communicate a message to the other.

Symbols are different from signs, though some signs can also be symbols. A ring can be a sign of marriage. It can also be the symbol of the love and commitment behind that marriage. Symbols point to the inexplicable and help create the very presence of that to which they point. The encounter with the symbol evokes and actualizes a wealth of meanings. Because of this wealth of meanings, symbols evoke a response from various dimensions of a person, not just the intellect.

Symbols, therefore, affect the whole person. One moves from fact (what is seen or encountered) to meaning (the interpretation of the symbol). One's history with the symbol will influence this experience of symbol (or the meanings evoked by the symbol), and also the culture's experience of the symbol. For example, the experience of the symbol of bread broken and shared will necessarily include the individual's previous experience (or personal history) of shared food or bread, such as the memory of grandmother baking bread on Sunday after-noon and the sense of care and security that such a memory elicits. Additionally, the individual will be opened and exposed to the culture's experience of food, or as a staple of life. Not only is the individual affected by his or her own interpreta-tion and experience of the symbol, but the symbol also carries the wealth of meaning that a culture (and the history of that culture) has both experienced with and invested in that symbol—broken bread as symbol can be sharing in the life of each other, fostering care and support, and embracing the needs of the poor.

Thus symbols help communicate the inexplicable, the profoundly eva-sive, the simplest of truths. Bread ripped, oil smeared, wine poured—all speak of a world being transformed and our participation in that very transformation. There is a radical new presence in this transformation: God-present-with-us. As little as we can explicitly name and point out the experience of love in con-crete and final terms, how much less can we name fully the real presence of God in our midst. Symbols are religious language.

Since symbols evoke a response from the whole person, from every level of our person, then symbols have the power not only to transform the world, but to transform our lives. When we awaken to the power of symbols in our lives, the possibility occurs for new life, for transformation, for conver-sion. The language of conversion is the language of symbols.

We both experience and express faith in God through symbols. We root the sacramental life of our community in the power of symbols to evoke and heighten our presence to God's mystery. Eventually we formulate this experi-ence—because it is too great for us to encounter fully—into statements of faith and belief. Our creeds and doctrines are symbolic summaries of a rich and pro-found history of the experience of God as salvation through Jesus.

Since faith is articulated and experienced through symbols, the *Rite of Christian Initiation of Adults* becomes an important experience of naming and experiencing the symbols of our community. As one becomes immersed in the power of the symbols of our faith, one is opened to the possibility of transfor-mation, of conversion. Then there is a qualitative change in one's life. One becomes a disciple.

RITUAL PRAYER

People remember images and actions more than they do words, and they affect people more than words. It is not only what we say, but how we say it that makes an impact.

This is especially true for ritual prayer. Ritual prayer is a combination of various activities: movement, gesture, speech, symbol, and song. Ritual mak-ers (especially those of us responsible for leading the community in prayer) need to be sensitive to the various dimensions of the prayer—and to integrate those elements—if we hope to express authentically the intention of the prayer and the praying community.

Ritual makers need to spend careful time exploring all the dimensions of ritual prayer and make decisions on how to integrate those various dimensions in a way that expresses the best intentions of both the larger community (e.g., the Roman Catholic Church) and the particular community (e.g., St. Rose of Lima Parish).

Ritual structures and patterns emerge within the larger community to respond to the various needs of the praying community: thanksgiving, intercession, rejoicing, and mourning, to name a few. We then intelligently adapt these ritual structures for the particular community because we do not celebrate ritual in a vacuum—these are real people with real needs and intentions gathered for prayer.

The tradition summarizes these insights in an ancient axiom: *Lex orandi, lex credendi.* The law of prayer directs the law of belief. In other words, our communal prayer (all the dimensions of it, not just the words) gives expression to our communal belief.

We hope that how we pray will be consistent with the community's theological tradition, but that is not always the case. For example, what does a sloppy reading of the scriptures from a missalette say about our belief that the scriptures are the word of God? Or what does a posture of penitence (kneeling) during the eucharistic prayer say about our belief about this thanksgiving feast?

How we pray (action, symbol and words) forms people more deeply than all those lectures and classes. How we pray forms people's deepest structures of belief. Thus, it is imperative that ritual makers take the time to study and prepare the ritual prayer of the community. Preparation is not simply reading the texts. It means bringing the varying dimensions together to help express the community's deepest beliefs. Ritual makers need to ask of the ritual prayer: What is it that this expresses and how do we structure the prayer so it can express it?

This is especially true of the initiation rituals. Their relative "newness" in the community demands that ritual makers take the necessary time to prepare these rituals so that they not only express the intention of the rite, but that they include the whole assembly in the prayer.

More important, though, is that initiation rituals help define the fundamental identity of a community: Who we are is expressed in rituals that make people a part of us. Initiation rituals say for all of us: This is what we believe, this is who we are.

THE LITURGICAL YEAR

Vatican II does not give us a new definition of sacraments. However, it does give us a particular way of talking about sacraments: the language is relational; it situates the celebration of sacraments within the context of the community of the faithful. The celebration of the sacraments, therefore, must respect the rhythm of life of the community. One important aspect of that is the liturgical rhythm or the liturgical calendar.

The liturgical calendar sets out for the Christian community a way of viewing time that is different from that of the standard calendar. The liturgical calendar situates Christian life within the context of the saving life, death and resurrection of the Lord Jesus and the gradual unfolding of that mystery within the community. Echoing the insights of the *Constitution on the Sacred Liturgy,* n. 102, the *General Norms for the Liturgical Year and the Calendar* states: "By means of the yearly cycle the church celebrates the whole mystery of Christ, from his incarnation until the day of Pentecost and the expectation of his coming again" (*GNLYC,* n. 17).

This, however, is not to suggest an historical approach to the mystery of salvation (birth to death). Rather, the calendar revolves around the two great poles of the Christian confession: the saving death and resurrection of the Lord and the incarnation and future glorification of Christ. Whenever one immerses oneself in this rhythm of prayer and proclamation, one is exposed to the story of salvation.

The *General Norms for the Liturgical Year and the Calendar,* furthermore, presents a hierarchy of celebration in its listing of the principal feasts of the liturgical year: Easter Triduum, Easter Season, Lent, Christmas Season, Advent, and Ordinary Time. Ordinary Time does not refer to the "ordinariness" of the season, but rather refers to ordinal or counted time. This document elaborates on each season, pointing out the distinctive quality of each. While for many of us the initiation focus of Easter time and Lent is clear, the *General Norms for the Liturgical Year and the Calendar* can illumine our understanding of Advent and Ordinary Time.

The *General Norms for the Liturgical Year and the Calendar* states that Advent "has a twofold character: as a season to prepare for Christmas when we remember Christ's first coming to us; as a season when that remembrance directs the mind and heart to await Christ's second coming at the end of time. Advent is thus a period for devout and joyful expectation" (*GNLYC,* n. 39). Concerning Ordinary Time, it states that "apart from those seasons having their own distinctive character, 33 or 34 weeks remain in the yearly cycle that do not celebrate a specific aspect of the mystery of Christ. Rather, especially on the Sundays, they are devoted to the mystery of Christ in all its aspects" (*GNLYC,* n. 43).

The challenge for our communities is to remain faithful to the rhythm of the liturgical calendar even, and especially, when it stands in contrast to the standard calendar with its feasts and images: the Easter Bunny, Santa Claus, summer vacation, the school year and the like.

Implications for Celebrating the Rites of Initiation

When should we celebrate the rites of the *Rite of Christian Initiation of Adults?* For some celebrations, guidance is clear: the rite of election at the opening of Lent (*RCIA*, n. 118); the scrutinies on the Third, Fourth and Fifth Sundays of Lent, using Year A readings (*RCIA*, n. 146); the preparation rites on Holy Saturday (*RCIA*, n. 185); the celebration of the initiation sacraments at the Easter Vigil (*RCIA*, n. 207); and mystagogy during the Sunday Masses of the Easter season, using Year A readings (*RCIA*, n. 247). What about the other rites?

Pastoral wisdom—knowing the *Rite of Christian Initiation of Adults,* the community, the dynamic and rhythm of the liturgical year, the shift to liturgical theology—is needed in making the decisions when to celebrate the other rites. Keeping in mind the *General Norms for the Liturgical Year and the Calendar,* we can explore these various rites and the appropriate time to celebrate them.

The Rite of Acceptance

Does it not confuse the focus of the Advent season when we celebrate the rite of acceptance on the First Sunday of Advent, especially with Advent's strong focus on the second coming of Christ? Have we struggled sufficiently with the rite itself (including the suggested lectionary texts) to understand what it is that we are celebrating: call, promise, cross, word? Are we not historicizing the mystery of salvation by insisting catechumens must begin formal catechesis with the Advent season because it is the apparent beginning? Would Ordinary Time be a more appropriate time, both for the community and the catechumens, to celebrate this rite—perhaps a few times during the year (cf. *RCIA*, n. 18.3)? Might not the Feast of the Triumph of the Cross or a Sunday when we read a gospel concerning the calling of the disciples better accord with the rite?

Period of the Catechumenate

Could liturgical catechesis—drawing theological and catechetical meaning from the celebration of the liturgy—be the means to lead catechumens into a "profound sense of the mystery of salvation" (*RCIA*, n. 75.1), using the whole repertory of the liturgy (the lectionary, the orations, the primary symbols) over the course of at least a year? Recall that the *General Norms for the Liturgical Year and the Calendar* says, "By means of the yearly cycle the church celebrates the whole mystery of Christ" (*GNLYC*, n. 117). Why couldn't catechetical gatherings take seriously the syllabus of the liturgical year and its rhythm (and, thus, liturgical catechesis) rather than an "outline of Catholic teaching," however well intended? Why not "train them in the Christian life" (*RCIA*, n. 75) through the pattern and rhythm of the order of the faithful: the liturgical year?

The Rite of Election, Period of Purification and Enlightenment, Celebration of Initiation Sacraments and Period of Mystagogy

Given the markedly paschal character of the Lent-Easter cycle and the celebration of initiation, why would we want to consider celebrating election at another time of the year? If someone is not ready to celebrate the sacraments this Easter, why would we resist inviting him or her to allow the community to immerse him or her in its liturgical prayer, companionship and apostolic life for another year? Is someone's readiness in October for initiation a sufficiently "unusual circumstance" (cf. *RCIA*, n. 26) to prompt the decision to celebrate the sacraments then? Or is the centrality of the paschal mystery as proclaimed and celebrated at the Easter Vigil of equal or greater importance, thus persuading the community to delay initiation while continuing to surround the catechumen with the essentials of the period of the catechumenate? Does not discernment for celebration have as much to do with the community as it does with the individual?

LITURGICAL CATECHESIS

The initiation process has explicitly claimed the close link between catechesis and liturgy that has always been part of Catholic sacramental formation (either explicitly or implicitly). Basically, liturgical catechesis places the liturgical celebration of rites at the center of initiation catechesis. Liturgical celebration is concerned with all three spheres of time: past, present and future. Regarding the past, the celebration brings to expression the community's experience of the presence of God (and the experience of the individual within the community). The ritual prayer helps give voice to our experience of God who is faithful, merciful, gentle of heart, holy.

Regarding the present, the celebration is an active engagement with the community right now. Not only do we remember our lives with God, but we are attentive right here and right now to the marvelous presence of the Holy in our midst in word and sacrament.

Regarding the future, the celebration provides both a direction and a mandate for our lives: Go, and serve! Thus, any liturgical celebration sums up our past, situates us in our present and thrusts us into a salvific future.

Therefore, to celebrate the liturgical prayer of the community with integrity, there needs to be a correlation between our history and the celebration. In effect, the task of liturgical catechesis is to help make explicit our awareness of the presence of God celebrated in the liturgy. It does this as a *catechesis for* liturgical prayer. We can say the same on the other end of the celebration: A *catechesis from* the liturgical prayer offers us direction for discipleship so we can embrace our role as the Body of Christ in the world.

To do this, liturgical catechesis gets its "clue" from the liturgical prayer itself. With a myriad of symbols, gestures, words, objects and the correlation of these with the gathered people, liturgical prayer articulates the Church's understanding of what it means to be a disciple of the Christ. Thus, catechesis for liturgical celebration looks to these various pieces of the prayer for the direction of the catechesis.

Exploring the Meaning of the Liturgical Event

Good drama captures the imagination. Good drama captivates and holds our attention. Good drama has the potential to disturb our lives delightfully. This is analogous to the way many people experience the initiation rituals in our communities. There is often a sense of power in the experience, with people saying, "It was moving." "I felt the presence of God." "I knew something important was happening." When celebrated well, liturgy is evocative. Good liturgy catches people up in the experience.

However, for many people, they leave the experience with a limited interpretation of the ritual action. Moreover, for some, the interpretation is exclusively personal and, therefore, incomplete. Extending the same level of interpretation we would provide for scriptures to our experience of liturgy and its meaning for us is important.

In other words, preparing candidates or a community for the celebration of the initiation rites without providing some interpretive experience for them is inadequate. Similar to the interpretation of scripture, that interpretative experience needs to view the ritual text (and its performance) from three dimensions: the meaning behind, the meaning during and the meaning in front of the experience. Another way to speak of this interpretive experience is liturgical catechesis: letting the rites themselves direct the catechesis.

Meaning Behind the Ritual

The meaning behind the ritual is the hoped-for message the ritual intended for all celebrating the ritual. How will we ever know this?

Biblical scholars attempt to find this literal sense of the text (i.e., what the author intended) by using accepted applications on the text, tools such as literary, form and redaction criticisms. Using the tools of their profession, scholars attempt to understand the specific terms, the history and culture of the times, and the use of the text by the purported author. Thus, while we may never fully know what the author of the text intended, we can have an understanding that resembles the meaning for its time. This is helpful; this is also incomplete.

The same is true for a ritual text. The writers of ritual texts carefully chose language, images, movement, symbols and scriptures to help capture particular meanings for the praying community. For those of us using the translation, we are one step further removed from the actual text. With the help of scholarly commentaries by liturgists, we can begin to piece together the various dimensions of the ritual and come to some understanding of its meaning as proclaimed by the Church.

We must be aware of some cautions at this point. As we need to be careful not to reduce the word of God to the words on the pages of the Bible or lectionary, so too we need to be careful not to reduce the living prayer of the Church to the words in the ritual text. Ritual is ritual when prayed. The performance (in its technical sense) will be very important for an appropriate interpretation of the ritual event.

Thus, liturgical catechesis must take into account the meaning ascribed to the text by the Church as encoded in the ritual text. How do we do this? There are various ways to approach this; following is one method.

Begin with the Ritual Text

All rituals have their own code comprising words, actions, gestures and symbols. Part of our task is to come to some understanding of this code. We need to do this in two ways: the individual parts of the code, and the code in total. Let us look at the rite of acceptance into the order of catechumens as an example.

When one reviews the rite of acceptance, there are numerous pieces of the rite that need to be addressed independently: people inside and people outside, contents of the opening dialogue (regarding the candidates' desires at this time), the first acceptance of the gospel, affirmations by the sponsors and the assembly, marking candidates with the cross on their bodies, invitation to the celebration of the liturgy of the word, proclamation of the word and homily, optional presentation of a book of the gospels, intercession for the prayer over the candidates, and the ritual dismissal. Within each of these "parts" there are sub-codes (e.g., the specific proclamations at each signing of the senses or the specific prayers of the intercession).

Consult Other Resources

The ritual planners and the catechists need to explore each of these pieces and tease out its meaning in the larger Christian tradition. For example: What is our history and experience of the cross in the Church? What does it proclaim in our tradition? What are the promises made in our Judeo-Christian heritage? Here is when we consult the various resources available to us—commentaries, theological dictionaries, liturgical resources, etc.—to come to some understanding of the pieces within the lived history of faith of our community.

This is not enough, however, because the authors have put these various pieces together in a particular order to convey particular meanings. As if they were various pieces of a mosaic, each piece has been placed to create this piece of art called the rite of acceptance. With sufficient research into the background of the various pieces, we now look at the ritual as a whole. Perhaps the first thing to do (before reading more commentaries) is to respond to these questions: Given the order and placement of these pieces, what is the rite proclaiming? What does the ritual say is important?

Having answered these questions, reading what was the hoped-for meaning of the rite is helpful. We can find that in two places. The primary place is the introductory notes to the rite itself. For example, in the rite of acceptance, we would review *RCIA,* n. 41f. A secondary resource would be specific commentaries written by competent liturgists who have studied the rite itself.

The individual rituals, however, do not stand on their own (just as the individual pieces of the ritual code do not). Therefore, similar work needs to be done with the ritual structure overall: What is the meaning of the ritual process of initiation?

In effect, our work so far has brought us to some understanding of the meaning behind the ritual within various contexts: the Judeo-Christian heritage, the current placement of all the pieces to create the rite itself, the theological-liturgical commentaries on the specific rite, and the order of Christian initiation of adults as a whole.

Ask the Catechetical and Liturgical Questions

Now—only now—is the time to begin to ask the catechetical and liturgical questions.

The catechetical questions: What needs to happen to celebrate this rite with authenticity? How do we construct catechetical gatherings that lead candidates to the point where they can celebrate this rite with integrity and some knowledge? From this vantage, we can construct gatherings during the precatechumenate that are moving toward the rite of acceptance. Then there is no need to rehearse rites. Instead, we lead people to the celebration of the rite.

The liturgical questions: How will we celebrate this rite? What are the needs of this community as we celebrate this rite? How do we best adapt the rite to correspond to those needs? Why do we make these adaptations?

Meaning During the Ritual

The second dimension of liturgical catechesis concerns the celebration of the rite itself. Besides the meaning behind the rite, there are new meanings that arise in the celebration of the rite. Here we are concerned with issues of performance of the ritual.

Perhaps this experience is familiar. The initiation team has worked hard with the candidates in preparing them to celebrate well the rite of acceptance. Due to some unfortunate circumstance, the presider is someone who does not know the candidates—and, worse, does not really know the rite of acceptance (except the printed words in a ritual book). It seems that the celebration is a disaster.

But then the team talks with the people gathered—members of the community, candidates, sponsors—and finds out they had a rich experience. Something carried the ritual despite our attempts to manipulate it. This is part of the performance dimension of the rite.

The rite is truly the rite of acceptance in the actual praying (performance) in the midst of a particular community at a particular place and time. The rite both shapes and is shaped by this community in prayer. There is an evocative dimension in that performance—for better or worse, the very performance of the ritual action affects people's world views.

Therefore, it is very important that those responsible for the ritual enactment be careful with environment, space, movement, fullness of symbols and preparation of the assembly. All the pieces of the code noted earlier now come into playful exchange with each other to reveal something profound and holy. The actual enactment of performance of the ritual needs to be of such a quality as to truly bear the weight of that revelation.

Knowing the meaning behind the ritual can give fuller expression to the meaning during the ritual. In many ways, the meaning that emerges during the ritual is normally an unreflective meaning. That is, we do not stop and analyze the meaning in the experience; we let it happen. In that posture, something new can emerge. A dialogue can take place between participants and the ritual experience. In such a dialogue, both the people involved and the ritual itself are changed. Of special interest to pastoral leadership is whether the meaning emerging during the ritual enactment is remotely related to the meaning intended by the original architects of the ritual.

Meaning in Front of the Ritual

The third dimension is akin to mystagogy: reflecting on the experience of the mysteries. The ritual serves as a window through which we can see behind it (meaning behind the ritual—the intention of the creators of the ritual for use in public worship) and also in front of it. The "in front of" meaning emerges from the performance of the ritual.

Unfortunately, this dimension is often lost because we have not given people the opportunity to reflect critically on their experience. Sometimes it is the way we ask the question that is problematic. Other times, it is due to the hectic schedule most people keep that prevents them from reflecting upon much of life's experiences.

But if the ritual enactment was a powerful revelation of the divine in our midst, it warrants critical reflection by both the individual and the community. Our own interpretation does not stand in isolation. Those reflections will be in dialogue with the previously discussed dimensions of the rite. Yet at the same time, we need to validate people's experience of the ritual enactment.

Thus, we invite people—candidates, sponsors, the community—to respond to questions such as: What was it like standing outside while the rest of the people were inside? Talk a bit about your experience of being marked all over your body with the cross. What did that mean to you? What was your experience of being in the pew as the candidates stood in the aisles while we prayed over them? What is different for you now?

The insightful catechist will then begin to weave together the various dimensions of meaning of the ritual during the dialogue. Knowing the history and construction of the ritual, the catechist can turn back to that to clarify and connect the experience of the individual. Making explicit links will serve as both a corrective and an illuminator to the participants and to the rite. Having lived the experience of the rite, does the rite truly say what we think it says?

CHRISTIAN REMEMBRANCE: ANAMNESIS

There are at least two forms of memory: memory that returns to the past to live that past again, and memory that retrieves the past to move into the future. We know the first form of memory as nostalgia. The second is called *anamnesis.*

Nostalgia is similar to recollection: It wants to get back to "those good old days" and create again life as it was. Such memories are vivid and often very emotional. There is a sense of well-being in those memories—ah, if we could only live like that again. And for fleeting moments, nostalgia can be worthwhile.

The problem with nostalgia, however, is that it forces us into denial: Instead of moving forward in life, we want to retreat. Instead of claiming our future, we want to manipulate it. Instead of trusting the mystery of life, we feel robbed by it. Eventually, a life focused on nostalgia is weary, lifeless, and without hope (for hope demands the possibility of a future).

Anamnesis comes from the Greek that loosely translated means calling to mind or remembrance. This remembrance is active: It makes present the memory from the past. It not only recalls (as vividly if not more so) the memories as nostalgia does, but the memories can make a claim on us to live into the future. The memories give us hope and direction for the future because they tell us something about ourselves. It is interesting that the word amnesia comes from the same Greek root word as anamnesis. Amnesia—a loss of memory—often includes a loss of identity.

Christian Memory
Throughout the Jewish-Christian tradition there is an honored place for holding up the memories of the community. We remember (anamnesis) to recall the great deeds of God and to give thanks and praise. We remember

(anamnesis) to be hopeful in our future because our God walks before us into that saving future. For the disciples of Jesus there is a Christian memory. We hold in memory the saving acts of the Lord Jesus—his passion, death, resurrection, glorification, and coming again.

Mary Collins notes in *Contemplative Participation* (Liturgical Press, 1990) that our Christian use of the word anamnesis rises from a perception that there is a disorder analogous to clinical amnesia that plagues the human community. At the level of our spiritual identity we do not remember for long who we really are. Those ultimate relationships that give us our spiritual identity slip from memory and consciousness all too easily, and we lapse into a lack of comprehension about our deepest identity.

Initiation as Training in Memory

Part of initiation formation is training in the Christian memory. Perhaps that is the marked difference between those initiation experiences that "fail" and those that "succeed" (as if we could even use such categories).

Many of us struggle between models of information and formation when talking about initiation. On the one hand, we know that facts are not salvific (and sometimes our presentation of the facts is downright boring). Yet we know that information about the Christian way of life is important. On the other hand, we become equally disillusioned by endless discussions and sharings that may be a bit self-focused ("What did I experience in the scriptures?") without the necessary links to the tradition. Perhaps both models have overlooked the importance of memory. Memory can serve as the integrative dimension between information and formation.

How To Keep Memory Alive

How might we train inquirers and catechumens in this Christian memory? The *Rite of Christian Initiation of Adults* already gives us this guidance; it is simply a question of reviewing that material with this new question in mind. The factual answer, though, is rather straightforward: We model living the Christian memory. Initiation formation is an apprenticeship; we need to make more explicitly that which has become implicit for us.

Keeping alive the Christian memory involves keeping several variables in creative tension: people's individual lives, the varieties of ways people experience life (e.g., cognitive, affective, intuitive), and the Christian mystery held in active memory and lived out today. One means to bridge these variables is art: oral, visual, tactile, and auditory.

Story: Convincing, Compelling, and Challenging

Clearly, the primary component of any initiation catechesis is the great story of God's presence in the world: specifically through creation, through the witness of the people of Israel, through the life, death, and resurrection of Jesus the Christ, and through the ongoing life of the community of believers. Of primary place in this great story are the Hebrew and Christian scriptures that form and reform our imaginations. Here we encounter God's saving and reconciling work in our time.

The retelling of those stories, however, needs to be convincing, compelling, and challenging. Convincing in terms of authenticity: We have grappled with the stories in our own lives and made them part of our lives. Compelling in terms of the quality of our telling: We invite the hearers into the stories so that something new can emerge. Challenging in terms of the offer the story makes: the possibility of new life, a changed life. A significant factor in retelling the ancient stories is to help make explicit connections between these stories and the contemporary stories of all gathered. We need to listen to the life stories of our inquirers and catechumens and also those of our world so that God's story can be in dialogue with them.

These sacred and ancient stories lay a foundation for the telling of how our community has struggled to embody those stories through teaching and action: what we believe and how we live (doctrines and precepts). However, the quality of those stories (of doctrine, precepts, etc.) needs to be similar to the telling of the sacred stories, but with an additional quality: connection to the sacred stories. Our teaching and life practice as Christians are rooted in the sacred memory of God's story throughout time.

Enriching with Art

The great cathedrals and churches are testaments to the value of informing the Christian imagination (and, hence, training in Christian memory) with visual art: the great stained glass windows, the magnificent sculptures nestled in alcoves, the evocative paintings that once graced the homes of nobles and now are available to all of us in museums and cathedrals, the prayerful and penetrating images of icons, and the rich array of tapestries, vestments, hangings—all inviting the viewer to participate in the very object she or he beholds and to discover something (someone?) new.

Our catechumenal gatherings are impoverished when visual art is absent. In addition to the great symbols of our faith, such as the cross and the word, we need to allow art in its various forms to both enlighten and challenge. In addition to the art that should be a permanent part of the gathering space for catechumenate sessions, we can bring in photos and slides of great pieces of art to help form the imagination of Christian disciples (including ourselves).

One caution: Just as there are tepid ways of telling stories and downright boring ways of giving teaching, there are also tasteless and unimaginative representations that call themselves art. When all else fails, turn to the classical pieces for guidance and inspiration.

The use of color is also a way of helping catechumens keep time with the community. The liturgical colors can be part of the environment, as well as other sacred signs and symbols of the liturgical season (e.g., Advent wreaths).

Memories and Ritual Gesture

Forming catechumens for a liturgical community includes forming them in ritual gesture. Touch is essential in a sacramental church: laying on of hands, embracing in peace, sharing a meal. Recognizing appropriate limits, we invite catechumens to use their bodies in appropriate gestures for prayer and reflection: standing, kneeling, hands outstretched in blessing, hands turned upward in surrender, to name a few. Invite catechumens to use their bodies to help express the meaning in their encounter with God. At the same time, recognize that using our bodies to express ourselves (in an intentional way) is often considered, at best, odd in our day and age. Be careful not to be contrived or force the issue. Simply invite people to use their bodies to bless and receive blessing and other forms of praise.

The rite provides ample experiences of ritual prayer that include gesture in the various blessings, anointings, celebrations of the word, and exorcisms found in the ritual text. All gatherings of catechumens should include ritual prayer. And ritual prayer needs to use the body in some form.

Music and the Sacred Story

Music has the power to transform the heart. Music also has the capacity to tell a good story. Think of the numerous times someone started singing an old ditty from way back that you immediately joined in on, remarking afterward, "I haven't heard that in years. I can't believe I still remember it."

Music is also essential for passing on the sacred memories. Both listening and singing help heighten one's awareness of the sacred story—in history and in our time now. Just as a well-crafted love song can evoke powerful emotions, so too hymnody and sacred music can lift the heart in prayer.

Catechists should use recorded music only to bring great classical pieces to the gathering or to provide background music for reflection times. Simple chants, antiphons, and acclamations should become a part of the ordinary repertoire along with psalmody and simple hymns. Then, during the week, the catechumens can center and focus themselves by returning again to these familiar refrains.

Weave Together a Memory

Think back on Thanksgiving dinner when you were a child. Perhaps it was at your grandparents' home. Relive the experience: Smell the fresh bread and the roasted turkey; hear the delightful screams of children playing while the food is being prepared; see the colorfully decorated table with the embroidered napkins and tablecloth; feel the warmth of the home from the fireplace against your face, cold from playing outside; remember the warm welcome of your grandparents as they embraced and kissed you. Keep alive those memories of significant moments that shaped your life.

It is this art of memory-keeping, of keeping alive the sacred memories, that is so essential for Christian living and, therefore, catechumenal formation. We are not trying to pretend that we walked with Jesus. But when we tell the stories, we need to evoke sights, sounds, smells, tastes, and touches that stir us to believe.

When we tell the stories of the tradition—our teaching—we need to weave them in a way that is rich in images and sounds. Why can't we teach the great Christian truths through story, art, gesture, and music? For example, in exploring Christology, why not tell some great stories of Jesus' identity: the washing of the feet, the feeding of the multitude, the meals with sinners, to name a few? Include with those stories images of Jesus throughout history: reproductions of great pieces of art or icons or the stained glass windows of the church building. Weave throughout antiphons and acclamations or a hymn or two (e.g., "I heard the voice of Jesus say, 'Come unto me and rest'") that open further an understanding of who Jesus is. Include postures and gestures used by Jesus: washing, touching, holding, forgiving embrace. Couch all of this in ritual prayer: blessings or anointings. Would that not leave a lasting impression on the whole person-catechumen? Would that not somehow do something to reshape the imagination regarding Jesus for this person? Would not the Christian memory—in some small way—be more accessible to this person because he or she now has stories, sights, touches, and sounds to associate with the question, "Who do you say that I am?"

Our Task as a Community

Methods are not the primary answer. They are helpful. But methods can be as dry as the next technique if that is what they are. Instead, relook at the initiation process as part of the memory-keeping task of the community of believers. We need to keep the memories alive and pass them on for our sake and for the sake of the world. We need memories that are alive with images, color, sounds, and touch, memories that both invite and disturb enough that we realize we are no longer remembering but are actually part of the memory. We remember. We celebrate. We believe.

3

Getting Started in a Pastoral Setting

INTRODUCTION

One of the greatest obstacles to effective initiation formation is that too many parishes keep falling prey to academic models. These usually fall into one of two types: those that are primarily information-giving or those that are less structured but betray an "academic" environment and underlying attitude—the kind of model that involves a classroom (even one well disguised by chairs in a circle), a major presenter (a catechist?), activities (small group sharing?), a syllabus, and a particular calendar (start in September, end in May or June). This is especially true if sacramental preparation in the parish takes place in similar settings: baptism preparation classes or first eucharist, confirmation, and reconciliation preparation in the religious education or Catholic school programs.

Perhaps these models are so popular because they seem so manageable. While a bias toward such academic models has not caused major harm to the church, they have helped to compromise both our understanding and our celebration of sacraments.

By placing such formation in a strongly "academic" setting, we risk losing the vital link with the primacy of the liturgical celebrations. We give people an appropriate understanding of the sacrament(s) in question—in effect, we tell them the meaning of the sacrament—and then, perhaps as a reward for perfect attendance, we "give" them the sacrament. If you come to the five sessions, we will baptize your baby. If you finish your workbook and answer a set of questions, we will give you first communion....

These pastoral situations may be a bit of a caricature. Nevertheless, they at least should cause us to stop and ask questions about the where and what of sacramental preparation.

THREE BASIC PRINCIPLES FROM THE RITE

We need to explore three significant principles from the *Rite of Christian Initiation of Adults* that are critically important for our initiation practice. These reflections concern themselves with formation for initiation, but they are applicable across the board for sacramental formation.

Non-Programmatic Conversion

One cannot talk about initiation (or sacraments) without talking about conversion. Whatever metaphors we use to help explain conversion—death to life, new life, falling in love, turning around, change—fundamentally, conversion begins with God's gracious invitation to us and includes our full-bodied response. Conversion is not about intellectual acquisition (though information can be a part of it) or emotional conviction (though affect also is often part of it). Conversion has everything to do with life with God now because we know life with God. For the Christian, living with God now is living faithful to the mission of the reign of God as proclaimed in the life-death-resurrection of Jesus, the Christ (see *RCIA,* n. 1).

We cannot program conversion. (See *RCIA,* n. 76: "Nothing, therefore, can be settled a priori.") We can say the same about being in love. One cannot plan it; one can only respond to the invitation. This does not mean that this is a purely passive encounter (though it is humbling to know that God takes the lead here). Just as discovering the possibilities of love with another is very active—dating, conversations, arguments, shared times, private moments—so is the journey of conversion.

Thinking that somehow everyone's journey in conversion will begin to take form when we happen to be ready with our initiation program in September is naive. Or that everyone will walk the same road of conversion as the one we have planned. As companions of those in initial "explicit" conversion (because, after all, who really knows how long this person has been in the throes of conversion before ever meeting us?), we provide a setting that allows one to negotiate the conversion experience to come to a decision. That setting is the community of believers.

The Community of Believers

It takes many people to bring about this event we call initiation. Think of the birth of a child and all those involved on different levels: parents, siblings, relatives, medical professionals, other care givers, neighbors, the church. The same is true for initiation. This "birthing" in our community requires the time and energy of the entire community. Yes, there will be particular ministries of service (bishop, presider, catechist, sponsor, for example). Yet those ministries only make sense because of the larger call of the entire community to be present in this action of God giving life to the community.

The rite says it clearly in *RCIA,* nos. 4 and 9: sacramental formation happens in the midst of the community and is the responsibility of the whole community.

Formation and Guidance

When describing the period of the catechumenate, the rite states: "The catechumenate is an extended period during which the candidates are given suitable pastoral formation and guidance, aimed at training them in the Christian life" (*RCIA,* n. 75). The remainder of that section outlines the components of such a formation and guidance: catechesis, community, liturgy, and service. What is important here is the recognition that the journey of conversion in initiation is about providing the fundamental skill for living the Christian way of life. It is a mentored and apprenticed model, not an academic model. One learns the Christian life by living the essentials of the Christian life with Christians. Again, here is that essential link with the entire community of believers.

Now, here is the good news. God's work of conversion is just that: God's work. We cannot cause someone's conversion, so relax and stop trying to do just that. On the other hand, it is our responsibility to provide an environment in which one can become more attentive to and freely respond to the promptings of the Spirit. We mentor and tutor in the Christian way of life, providing a full breadth of all that is part of the foundation of Christian living (as outlined in *RCIA,* n. 75).

It would be foolish and naive of us to assume that all we do in initiation is for membership or to build up our parish community (both, however, might be benefits we do achieve indirectly). We do it to remain faithful to Christ's mandate that we all share in his mission: the mission of the reign of God. For Catholics, this mandate takes on particular meaning within the context of our sacramental-liturgical life, but only if we allow it to grasp us and give us a new future. Initiation is about preparing people for such a way of life. We need to be careful not to sanitize it lest the compelling vision of the gospel get lost.

BEGIN WITH THE END IN MIND

Recent literature in leadership and management gives us an important principle: Begin with the end in mind. In effect, the recommendation is to look at the outcome of any project to decide the best way to cause that outcome.

This is good, practical advice. In fact, the more one thinks about it, the more one realizes how essential this principle is in implementing any program or process. Knowing where we are going helps us steer in the basic direction.

It does not mean that there is an inflexible route to take; rather, we know where we are going and we know the basic tools we need to get there. Inevitably, we will need to change the routes we map out along the way—but we still know where we are going.

The "Where To" of Initiation

Begin with the end in mind. This is good advice for those of us involved in initiation ministry. Knowing the "where to" of initiation can help us in the "how" of initiation. Our understanding of the goal of the initiation process helps clarify all the various elements of preparation.

The beginning of the *Rite of Christian Initiation of Adults* defines the "where to" of initiation: "Thus the three sacraments of Christian initiation closely combine to bring us, the faithful of Christ, to his full stature and to enable us to carry out the mission of the entire people of God in the church and in the world" (*Christian Initiation: General Introduction,* no. 2). Echoing the insights of Vatican II's *Dogmatic Constitution on the Church,* the rite situates the initiation process in the middle of the mission of the reign of God.

For many, the goal of the initiation process is the celebration of the sacraments of initiation. To some degree, that is true. We are preparing people to celebrate the sacraments of baptism, confirmation and eucharist. However, if we end there, we are not embracing a full vision of sacraments. Sacraments are not ends in themselves; rather, they are thresholds to mission for the reign of God.

In and through the celebration of Christian sacraments, we encounter—and are encountered by—the living God so we might be the same for the world. Sacraments have less to do with what we get and more to do with who we become in relationship to the Holy.

2 Peter echoes this: God calls us "to become partakers of the divine nature" (2 Peter 1:4). God invites us to live the very life of God, to enter into relationship with God, to be united with God. Saint Athanasius reminds us that God became human so that humans might become God. Sacramental initiation brings us into that relationship. Our continuing participation in the sacramental life is one way of nurturing and deepening that relationship.

The End at the Beginning

The focus of the period of mystagogy is to enable the newly initiated to live the life of those who have become "partakers of the divine nature." Such a gift brings with it an equally compelling responsibility: If we embrace life with God, we must embrace God's work. This work is the mission of the reign of God lived by Jesus and offered to all disciples of Jesus—not only offered but mandated.

The period of mystagogy brings together the various threads of initiation preparation and celebration into the fabric called "disciple." Now the hard work of living the Christian life is of concern. The period of mystagogy helps in the transition from becoming a Christian to living (and remaining) a Christian.

The rite is clear in its expectation for this period: The newly baptized and the community enter this period in order "to grow in deepening their grasp of the paschal mystery and making it part of their lives" (*RCIA,* n. 244). How? Through meditation on the gospel, sharing in the eucharist and doing works of charity along with the community of the faithful (*RCIA,* n. 244).

There are no surprises here. The ritual text explicates the agenda of catechumenal formation (*RCIA,* n. 75) as the agenda of mystagogy. But there is a difference. During the catechumenate, we are in the process of forming or making disciples; we are providing the primary skills for living the Christian way of life. During mystagogy, our concern is to focus those skills so that both the neophytes and the community will be faithful to the disciple's way of life.

Getting There

Perhaps the problem lies in how we approach initiation overall. Many of us are so focused on getting people to the sacraments that we miss a key element noted earlier: Sacramental celebrations, including initiation, are not ends in themselves. Sacraments are thresholds for mission for the reign of God. It is in and through the celebration of Christian sacraments that we encounter and are encountered by the living God, who is both the source and the fulfillment of our lives. Through Christian sacraments, the Holy is made tangible, present and accessible through familiar objects and gestures—such as bread broken and water poured—so we may be that very holiness for a world crying out for freedom and reconciliation. Sacraments have much less to do with what we get (our consumerism approach to the Holy) and more about who we become in relationship with the Holy. Who we become, again and again, are disciples on mission.

Thus, when our sacramental preparation is predominantly focused on getting to the sacrament, we become concerned with getting people ready for that event. More often than not, that means some form of instruction about the sacraments (even if that instruction takes the shape of "lectionary-based catechesis"). Even with the best learning models, we tend to isolate the catechumens from the rest of the community through our weekly gatherings. We make few explicit links with the larger community, even on Sunday morning. The real work of initiation seems to happen in those gatherings after the dismissal of the catechumens.

From Preparing for Sacraments to Preparing for Discipleship

But what if our concern were preparing catechumens for becoming disciples on mission? What if the celebration of the sacraments—indeed, important moments in the life of the catechumens and the community—served as a threshold or passageway into a new way of life focused on mission? Then the real work of initiation would happen in the midst of the community, and everything else we do will enhance that experience. Catechetical gatherings would expand on the primary experience of gathering with the assembly, resulting eventually in a new identity for the catechumens as one of the assembled. One could then learn that the assembly is most faithful to its identity as the Body of Christ when it both gathers and is sent. When we send catechumens from this assembly (the dismissal), it is to reflect critically on their place in this assembly and on the responsibility of members of the assembly. Then, whatever form of catechesis emerges will not be to "teach them about Catholic life" but lead them to a profound sense of the mystery of salvation (see *RCIA,* n. 75.1). This will disrupt their lives profoundly and call forth the gifts and skills for living as a Christian. We will help develop those skills (see *RCIA,* n. 75) for a lifetime of Christian discipleship.

MODELS FOR IMPLEMENTATION

Given all of this, what does the *Rite of Christian Initiation of Adults* "look like" in a parish? How is it implemented? At least three basic formats or models—with nuances and variations that respect local need—have emerged as people begin the pastoral task of implementing the initiation process. Each model builds on insights gleaned from the previous model.

Model One: Initiation by Classes
In the first model, the primary work and concerns about initiation belong to the catechist—often a priest. The format is lectures or presentations with information about the Catholic Church. They do not follow the various periods and steps of the rite. Or if they are, they follow them in name only. The image is that of a classroom presentation.

This is an inadequate model. In fact, it runs contrary to the spirit and vision of the rite. This model clearly gives the message that faith is predominantly—if not exclusively—information. Receive this information, show good will and true desire, and we will baptize you. The one person giving information symbolizes the Church passing on its faith. While this may be comfortable and familiar to many of us, this is not sacramental catechesis as envisioned by the rite.

Model Two: Nine Month Initiation
Model two relies on an awareness of the periods and steps of the *Rite of Christian Initiation of Adults,* as well as recognizing the differences in focus and catechetical methodology. This model is a very popular and common model, especially for parishes beginning to implement the rite.

Model two recognizes the need for a period of precatechumenate that is informal and may be focused on story telling. Perhaps the gatherings are at the parish center or in parishioners' homes. After recruiting, advertising, and interviewing people, the precatechumenate sessions begin in September. After about eight gatherings—and the necessary discernment for readiness—the candidates celebrate the rite of acceptance (often on the First Sunday of Advent) and begin the period of the catechumenate. A series of presentations and reflections on basic Catholic issues (that may include dismissal catechesis based on the lectionary) usually characterize this period. This continues until the approaching Lenten season. Throughout this time, the catechumens and candidates have been journeying with the support of a sponsor, as well as celebrating various blessings and anointings.

After discerning readiness to celebrate the Easter sacraments, the catechumens and candidates celebrate the rite of election, enter the period of purification during Lent, and celebrate the initiation sacraments at the Easter Vigil. The whole initiation process reaches its peak at this moment of celebration. The neophytes continue to meet with the team, usually during the week, and often with less regularity. This continues until Pentecost. During the summer months, the team regroups, does some training modules together, and begins the process of recruiting and interviewing prospective candidates for the approaching September's precatechumenate gatherings. (See Figure 1.)

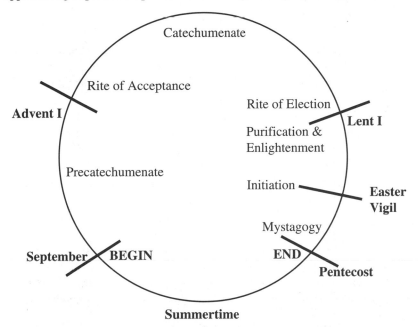

Figure 1: Model Two

Model two is the way many of us begin to implement the rite. And as a beginning, it has some merits. There is the recognition of the various periods. The structure such a calendar provides helps keep the process well organized and functioning. But the longer people try to implement the rite using model two, and the more time and energy teams exert in getting to know the dynamics and vision of the rite, the more inadequate they find their experience with model two. Basically, model two does not reflect the dynamic sense of the *Rite of Christian Initiation of Adults*. In fact, there are some real problems with this model with its very strong overtones of an academic calendar:

(1) The Spirit is not bound to the academic calendar. Men and women come seeking more information about the community at the time

appropriate for them. Sometimes it is because of a crisis, other times because of an upcoming marriage, or because of someone at work who inspired them, or a nagging need to belong, or . . . the list is endless. What is common to all these experiences is that they happen when they happen, and not on September 1. We do a disservice to people to send them away and ask them to come back in September, giving them a book to read while they wait.

(2) Each person in the initiation process has a unique story of conversion. Some people will need an extended time in the precatechumenate, while others will have had a great deal of exposure to the community already. And the length of the catechumenate itself will vary for each person. Model two forces people to conform to our time schedule for conversion, thus refusing to respect the uniqueness of each person's experience of God.

(3) The *Rite of Christian Initiation of Adults* is directed toward mystagogy: reflection on the mysteries that empower us for mission. The celebration of the initiation sacraments at the Easter Vigil, while a very special and sacred moment in the journey, is not the end of the process. The *Rite of Christian Initiation of Adults* is designed to bring one to mission. The entire process needs to be focused on mystagogy—the style of life of the initiated (servants of the reign of God). For many parishes, the goal of initiation is the Easter sacraments, with little care for mystagogy. In that model, sacraments become ends unto themselves.

In light of these concerns, many parishes implement the *Rite of Christian Initiation of Adults* using a different kind of "scheduling"—model three.

Model Three: Year-Round Initiation

Model three involves a year-round initiation process. In effect, it says that the community is always about the work of initiation, just as the community is always about the worship of God. Since the parish so intimately links initiation with the praying Church, it is modeled after the pattern of the praying Church: all year long. Look at Figure 2 to get a visual look at Model Three.

In model three, the period of the precatechumenate has two unique qualities about it regarding time: It is always available, and it is ongoing. Throughout the year—all year long—the precatechumenate or inquiry team is available to gather with interested persons. And they continue to gather for as long as the inquirers need to do so. The shape and personality of the inquiry group will change throughout the year as people move in and out. Later chapters will explore just how to do this. The important thing to keep in mind is that whenever someone comes to the community to discover more about the community,

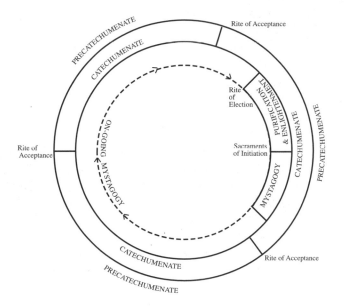

the parish staff (and, hopefully, the parish itself) knows where and when the inquirers are gathering that particular week.

When the individual discerns a desire and readiness to enter the community, they celebrate the rite of acceptance into the order of catechumens. If the parish has provided gatherings throughout the year for inquiry, then it is safe to assume that not everyone will discern readiness to enter the Church simultaneously, much less the First Sunday of Advent. Yet at the same time, the parish does not want to be celebrating this rite so regularly that its importance and its significance lose their impact on the community. An option is to plan three Sundays during the year when the parish would celebrate the rite of acceptance into the order of catechumens. Such a model respects the individual's journey in faith (various times of celebrating the rite helps people to more honestly discern their readiness), while helping to establish a liturgical rhythm in the community. The times of celebrating the rite can also vary to provide greater participation by the parish community. Depending on the readiness of the candidates, the parish may or may not celebrate the rite at all at the scheduled times. It follows, then, that some inquirers would remain in the precatechumenate during this time.

During the period of the catechumenate, the catechumens meet regularly to grow in their awareness of God's invitations to them of conversion and community. The shape and structure of these gatherings, which we will discuss later, will vary with each community. But it seems reasonable that the catechumens will meet weekly for an appropriate period of formation—usually a year (cf. *NS*, n. 6).

The bishop presides at and celebrates the rite of election on the First Sunday of Lent at the cathedral with the other catechumens of the diocese. The parish community can celebrate a rite of sending of its catechumens to the cathedral liturgy, which may include the enrollment of the catechumens into the Book of the Elect. The period of purification and enlightenment follows for the elect during the Lenten season. Catechumens who did not celebrate election would continue in the catechumenate.

The sacraments of initiation—baptism, confirmation, and eucharist—are celebrated during the Easter Vigil. Because of the centrality and importance of the paschal event in connection with sacramental initiation, we should celebrate the initiation sacraments at other times than the Easter Vigil only in extraordinary circumstances. The decision to move the celebration of the initiation sacraments to another time of the year should not be made lightly.

The period of mystagogy continues through the Easter season. The neophytes (newly initiated) continue to gather with the community at Sunday worship, but now there is no dismissal because the neophytes are full members of the community. However, the catechumens continue to gather for Sunday dismissal and catechesis. Many parishes provide additional opportunities for the neophytes to gather to continue to reflect on the scriptures and to explore the meaning of the mysteries they have celebrated (the sacraments), as well as to discover more fully their call to mission. While the formal period of mystagogy ends at the Pentecost festival, the U.S. bishops note that parishes need to provide ongoing mystagogy until the anniversary of initiation (cf. *NS,* n. 24).

Model three respects the vision and demands of the rite while providing a pastorally sensitive and workable model for pastoral implementation of the *Rite of Christian Initiation of Adults.* Parishes will nuance and adapt the insights of this model in ways that work best in their particular situation. Some people will find the development of this model difficult at first—especially if they are just beginning the implementation of the *Rite of Christian Initiation of Adults.* This model is one possibility of how a parish can implement the rite. This does not mean a parish will begin here— though there is no reason not to start with the full implementation at the beginning.

A parish may need to begin with some adaptation of model two. What is critical, though, is that the parish recognizes what it is doing: striving to develop a richer pastoral expression of the rite that is faithful to the spirit and norms established in the rite itself. Model three provides a jumping board for such an implementation.

Throughout the remainder of this resource, the process of initiation suggested in model three will be operative.

MAKING DISTINCTIONS

The *Rite of Christian Initiation of Adults* is divided into two parts, and it contains three appendices. Part I of the ritual text (*RCIA,* nos. 1-251) outlines the process of Christian initiation for adults who are unbaptized. This is where most of the conversation about initiation happens: explaining the foundations to create (or recreate) initiating communities. Part II provides guidance and direction for adapting the initiation process for particular circumstances.

Guidelines for Understanding Part II

A few guidelines will help in understanding how to implement part II.

1. Part I of the Rite of Christian Initiation of Adults (RCIA, nos. 1- 251) provides the foundation and vision for initiation. One cannot understand any of the adaptations in part II without being well versed in part I.

Unfortunately, many people turn immediately to part II, especially when working with children, and then they try to "do what is there." The result is at least confusion (there are pieces missing) and, more often than not, distortion of the vision of initiation embodied in the ritual text.

The operative principle in applying the adaptions in part II is very simple: One cannot adapt what one does not know. All the adaptations in part II of the ritual text presume knowledge of the full process of Christian initiation as outlined in part I. It is only with this understanding that one can then begin to adapt for particular circumstances.

2. When there is confusion about something in part II, return to part I for guidance. There are some sections in part II that are inconsistent with the vision outlined in part I. This sometimes occurs because the authors of the document attempted to make general pastoral decisions rather than leaving such decisions to the local community. For example, in various places in the section on children's initiation, we read that the rites are to be celebrated with a small group representing the parish community apart from the primary gatherings of the assembly. This contrasts with the vision of part I that calls for the public rituals to be celebrated in the midst of the liturgical assembly. In this instance, my advice is to return to the vision of part I: of course we celebrate the public rites for children with the community.

3. When something is missing in part II, presume that the directives in part I apply. Part II provides the particular ways of adapting part I to various circumstances. When reading the different sections of part II, however, some pieces may be missing. For example, there is nothing written about the period of the catechumenate for Christian initiation when someone is in danger of death. Nothing is missing, of course. In that circumstance, the rite requires no period of catechumenate.

In the section on children, however, there also is nothing written about the period of the catechumenate. That circumstance requires a catechumenate period, and so it appears to be missing. But it is not. In this case, part II offers nothing on the period of the catechumenate because the process described in part I applies. The adaptations in part II are specific to the sections to which they refer. Thus, in the section on children, the absence of information on pre-catechumenate and catechumenate does not mean that they should not be done; it means that they are done according to the directives given in part I.

4. *Interpret the directives of part II in light of the National Statutes found in appendix III of the U.S. editions.* The National Statutes give pastoral advice and direction for implementing the initiation process for both part I and part II.

With these guidelines in mind, we will look at each chapter in part II. We will spend much more time with chapter one (on children) because it has many more significant adaptations.

UNBAPTIZED ADULT	CHILDREN OF CATECHETICAL AGE	BAPTIZED, UNCATECHIZED CATHOLIC	BAPTIZED, UNCATECHIZED CHRISTIAN	BAPTIZED, CATECHIZED CHRISTIAN
Part I	Part II Chapter One	Part II Chapter Four	Part II Chapter Four	Part II Chapter Five
RCIA, nos. 1-251	*RCIA*, nos. 252-330	*RCIA*, nos. 400-472	*RCIA*, nos. 400-472	*RCIA*, nos. 473-504

Chapter One: Christian Initiation of Children Who Have Reached Catechetical Age

Chapter one of part II deals with the adaptation of the initiation process for children of catechetical age. For purposes of initiation, canon 852§2 of the *Code of Canon Law* mandates that we use the same directives for children who have attained the use of reason (completed seven years of age, cf. *CIC*, canon 11) as we do with adults. Thus, the primary intent of this chapter is to provide ritual texts with language appropriate for children according to their age and ability (see *RCIA*, n. 253). It also outlines some shifts in the process of initiating children. A few things about this chapter merit mention.

First, the initiation of children of catechetical age follows the same pattern as the initiation of adults, including full sacramental initiation: baptism, confirmation and eucharist at the Easter Vigil (see *RCIA*, nos. 8 and 256; *NS*, n. 18). The rites that are missing from this section (e.g., presentations of the Creed and Lord's Prayer) are to be celebrated as outlined in part I.

Second, the process adapted for children takes seriously the social world of the child—family and peers—and incorporates them into the initiation process. In fact, the language is very strong: "The children's progress...

depends on the help and example of their companions and on the influence of their parents. Both these factors should therefore be taken into account" (*RCIA,* n. 254, emphasis added). These peer companions often accompany the catechumens throughout the initiation process. Many parishes are including the peer companions in the formation process designed for catechumens, rather than including the child catechumens in their peers' religious education programs (see *NS,* n. 19).

Third, the celebration of the rites best occurs within the Sunday assembly. This is the vision of part I. In chapter one of part II, however, the text refers to celebrating the rites with children with a "small congregation" that "simply represents" the parish community (for example, see *RCIA,* nos. 257 and 260). Clearly, this is an adaptation that conflicts with the larger theology of the rite.

Fourth, avoid celebrations for "children only." A parish community celebrates the rite of acceptance into the order of catechumens with all the inquirers who are ready—adults and children together. We are an intergenerational community; separating people for these celebrations sends the wrong message. The liturgical rites should include and integrate everyone. The *Directory for Masses with Children* offers important principles and insights regarding the adaptation of liturgies to include both adults and children.

Fifth, the peer companions who have accompanied the catechumens throughout this process "may be completing their Christian initiation in the sacraments of confirmation and the eucharist at this same celebration," i.e., the Easter Vigil (see *RCIA,* nos. 308, 323). The inauguration of this practice may present difficulties in some parishes and dioceses. It is yet another shift in practice that we must explain to the parish community, but more problematic is that many bishops will not give delegation to pastors for confirmation in this situation. While the reasons vary, most are related to the current pastoral confusion of when to celebrate confirmation. Nonetheless, if the peer companions have indeed walked the road with their catechumen companions, and if the peer companions are ready for the completion of their own sacramental initiation, then the pastor can at least request permission to confirm.

At the end of each chapter in part II of this resource, comments will be offered for implementing the particular period or step with children of catechetical age.

Chapter Two: Christian Initiation of Adults In Exceptional Circumstances

Chapter two of part II provides an initiation process (both an expanded and an abbreviated form) for extraordinary circumstances, provided the bishop gives permission—on a case-by-case basis—for this adaptation (*RCIA,* n. 331). The ritual text outlines what those circumstances are: events that prevent the candidate from completing the initiation process (such as sickness or old age), or a depth of

conversion and religious maturity. Note that the National Statutes specify that
moving is not sufficient reason for an abbreviated catechumenate (*NS*, n. 20).

The directives for using this adaptation (*RCIA*, n. 332) prescribe great
caution: Its misuse could mean a spiritual loss for the candidate. As with the
other adaptations in part II, the directives highlight the importance and value
of the full preparation process for initiation. Only for pastoral necessity would
one want to tamper with the process outlined in part I.

In reviewing the ritual text (*RCIA*, nos. 340ff.), one discovers that it is a
merging of various rites: rite of acceptance, scrutinies, anointing with the oil
of catechumens, and the celebration of the initiation sacraments. Anyone who
has celebrated these rites separately with the community knows how powerful
and rich each rite is. It is a large task for one celebration to carry the weight of
all these rites. Hence the directive that one use this adaptation very cautiously.

Chapter Three: Christian Initiation of a Person In Danger of Death

Chapter three of part II deals with the celebration of the initiation sacraments with someone who is in danger of death. Yet even in these serious circumstances, the rite highlights the value of the entire preparation process. Not
only must there be evidence of conversion, but if the person recovers, he or
she is to enter a catechumenal process (see *RCIA*, nos. 371, 374). Without
downplaying the objective nature of baptism, the text affirms that ritual must
be an authentic expression of people's experience.

The ritual given is intended particularly for lay presiders. Normally,
priests and deacons are to use the ritual outlined in chapter two (*RCIA*, nos.
340-369). As with the adaptation in chapter two, there is the merging of various rites, such as the rite of acceptance and the celebration of the sacraments
(minus the celebration of confirmation if a presbyter is not presiding). The rite
does take an interesting turn, however, by incorporating the celebration of
viaticum (i.e., communion for the dying) from the *Pastoral Care of the Sick.*

Chapter Four: Preparation of Uncatechized Adults for Confirmation and Eucharist

Chapter four of part II will probably be one of the most used of these adaptations. It is concerned with adults (and children of catechetical age) who were
baptized as infants in a Christian community (including Roman Catholic, see
NS, n. 25) but did not receive further formation (see *RCIA*, n. 400). "Uncatechized" does not mean that these people lack information, but rather that they
have received little or no formation in the faith. The issue in this situation is
whether the person has appropriated the faith and is living in accord with it.

This process of formation is patterned on the one for the unbaptized,
with appropriate ritual adaptation that acknowledges their status as baptized

(see *RCIA*, nos. 402ff.). Just as the liturgical life and prayer of the community are at the heart of the preparation of catechumens, so it is with the preparation of baptized, uncatechized persons. And for both groups, we celebrate the completion of initiation at the Easter Vigil (see *RCIA*, n. 409). *NS*, n. 26, however, suggests otherwise when referring to uncatechized adult Catholics, and *NS*, n. 33 gives similar directives for reception into full communion. This probably reflects the growing concern in the United States that we often group candidates and catechumens with little or no differentiation. Recognizing that we would celebrate many of the rituals with both the baptized and the unbaptized, the U.S. bishops provide a series of combined rituals in appendix I.

The ritual text prescribes no ritual for the celebration of the sacraments in chapter four. For the person baptized in the Roman Catholic Church, we invoke the normative practice of the Easter Vigil: profession of faith, celebration of confirmation (presuming the bishop has given the faculty to administer the sacrament to the presider; see *NS*, n. 28 regarding the faculty to confirm Catholics) and celebration of eucharist (see *RCIA*, n. 409). The rite delineates the practice of receiving persons baptized in other Christian communities in chapter five.

Chapter Five: Reception of Baptized Christians into the Full Communion of the Catholic Church

Chapter five of part II completes what was started in chapter four. This rite of reception into full communion is not new. It was originally published in English in 1973 as a separate rite and then included in this edition of the *Rite of Christian Initiation of Adults*.

This section of the ritual text provides directives for baptized Christians—both catechized and uncatechized—entering into full communion with the Roman Catholic Church, and it therefore needs to be read very carefully (note the difference in practice prescribed for Eastern Christians in *RCIA*, n. 474). This is especially true in light of the common practice of having baptized Christians go through the entire initiation process (sometimes for more than one year) without an appropriate discernment of their need for formation (see *NS*, n. 30). With ecumenical sensitivity, the rite instructs that "no greater burden than necessary is required for the establishment of communion and unity" (*RCIA*, n. 473) and "any appearance of triumphalism should be carefully avoided" (*RCIA*, n. 475.2).

The key to understanding this section is the closing sentence of *RCIA*, n. 478: "In all cases, however, discernment should be made regarding the length of catechetical formation required for each individual candidate for reception into the full communion of the Catholic church." The presumption is that uncatechized Christians will need an extended period of formation comparable to the catechumenal process. Baptized and catechized Christians, however, may need only a short period of formation designed to incorporate them into the Catholic communion (see *RCIA,* n. 477) and its liturgical life. This instruction means the discovery of Catholic teaching within the liturgical community.

The celebration of reception into full communion can occur anytime during the year, preferably at the Sunday gathering of the community. This is especially true for the baptized, catechized Christian who may need only a short period of formation and preparation. The baptized, uncatechized Christian will probably be in the process for an extended period; reception may then take place at the Easter Vigil or at another suitable time.

There is a concern that by celebrating reception into full communion at the Easter Vigil, it may appear that we are treating these Christians as if they were unbaptized. That is why chapters four and five both take great pains to acknowledge the validity and dignity of baptism. We must make the appropriate distinctions throughout the process, both during liturgical celebrations and during formational gatherings. "Anything that would equate candidates for reception with those who are catechumens is to be absolutely avoided" (*RCIA,* n. 477).

Liturgical law delegates the presider to celebrate confirmation with the candidates during the rite of reception, "unless the person received has already been validly confirmed" (*RCIA,* n. 481). The current practice of the Roman Catholic Church is to recognize as valid only the confirmations celebrated by members of the Eastern non-Catholic churches who are being received into the Catholic Church (and, of course, of the Eastern Catholic Church). All other celebrations of confirmation are not recognized as sacramental for the purposes of initiation.

At the end of each chapter in part II of this resource, comments will be offered for implementing the particular period or step with baptized candidates.

Clarifications

There has been much discussion on whether the adaptations in chapters two through five apply to children of catechetical age. If we follow the directive of canon 852§1 of the *Code of Canon Law* as noted above, children indeed are clearly included in these adaptations. In a joint statement responding to particular questions on the initiation of children, the bishops of the dioceses of Illinois also came to the same conclusion (see *Response to Frequently Asked Questions on the Christian Initiation of Adults and Children of Catechetical Age for the Province of Chicago,* 1991, n. 15).

With all of our enthusiasm for a full implementation of the *Rite of Christian Initiation of Adults,* we may end up putting everyone through the same routine and pattern without the appropriate differentiation. Part II contains guidelines that will, at first, cause our initiation processes to be even messier than they are now. But eventually, once we learn the pattern in part II, it simplifies the initiation process for a parish community, making it more honest and integrative.

The crucial point is that we need to know the people who come to us, and we need to lead them along the path that provides the best experience of formation. It helps to know the various options.

	UNBAPTIZED ADULT	CHILDREN OF CATECHETICAL AGE	BAPTIZED, UNCATECHIZED CATHOLIC	BAPTIZED, UNCATECHIZED CHRISTIAN	BAPTIZED, CATECHIZED CHRISTIAN
First Period	Evangelization and Precatechumenate	Evangelization and Precatechumenate	Adapted & modified Evangelization and Precatechumenate	Adapted & modified Evangelization and Precatechumenate	Adapted & very modified Evangelization and Precatechumenate (if at all)
First Step	Rite of Acceptance into the Order of Catechumens	Rite of Acceptance into the Order of Catechumens	Rite of Welcoming the Candidates	Rite of Welcoming the Candidates	Rite of Welcoming the Candidates
Second Period	Catechumenate	Catechumenate	Adapted Catechumenate	Adapted Catechumenate	Adapted & Modified Catechumenate
Second Step	Rite of Election or Enrollment of Names	Rite of Election or Enrollment of Names	Rite of Calling the Candidates to Continuing Conversion	Rite of Calling the Candidates to Continuing Conversion	Rite of Calling the Candidates to Continuing Conversion
Third Period	Purification and Enlightment	Purification and Enlightment	Adapted Purification and Enlightment	Adapted Purification and Enlightment	Adapted & Modified Purification and Enlightment
Third Step	Celebration of the Sacraments of Initiation (baptism confirmation, eucharist)	Celebration of the Sacraments of Initiation (baptism confirmation, eucharist)	Celebration of confirmation (with delegation) and eucharist	Celebration of reception (profession of faith, confirmation and eucharist)	Celebration of reception (profession of faith, confirmation and eucharist)
Fourth Period	Postbaptismal Catechesis or Mystagogy	Postbaptismal Catechesis or Mystagogy	Adapted Postbaptismal Catechesis or Mystagogy	Adapted Postbaptismal Catechesis or Mystagogy	Adapted Postbaptismal Catechesis or Mystagogy

ADAPT, ADAPT, ADAPT

Seasoned ministers of initiation are familiar with a common cry when it comes to implementing the *Rite of Christian Initiation of Adults:* "Adapt! Adapt! Adapt!" However, a word of caution is appropriate here. The ritual text gives clear directives and guidance for pastoral adaptation throughout the rite.

Unfortunately, some people extend that liberty—often under the guise of "pastoral reasons"—to implement the rite in a way that is often less than faithful to the vision and intent of the rite.

The *Rite of Christian Initiation of Adults,* n. 5, gives the guiding principle for any adaptations. Here the text reminds us of the many variables that we need to take into account for Christian initiation: the many forms of God's grace, the free cooperation of the individual, the action of the Church and the circumstances of time and place. A prudent pastoral decision must take into account all these variables to be complete.

Furthermore, *RCIA,* n. 8 provides a foundation for understanding Christian initiation: the paschal mystery. Our participation (not membership, not information, not "catching up with peers") in the paschal mystery must be at the center of the entire process. The Church's worship supports this. Any divergence from the initiation process must keep intact the centrality of the paschal mystery and all its implications, such as conversion.

RCIA, n. 35 clarifies the parameters within which the minister of initiation can adapt. It encourages full and intelligent use of the freedom given in the rubrics of the rite and gives *Christian Initiation,* General Introduction, n. 34, as an interpretive text of how to use this freedom: "Taking into account existing circumstances and other needs, as well as the wishes of the faithful..." This is reaffirmed in *RCIA,* n. 35, when, "according to prudent pastoral judgment," the minister may accommodate the rite to the particular circumstance.

Principles for Pastoral Adaptation

It would be futile to guess the motivation behind some claims of "pastoral decisions" regarding implementing the initiation process, especially when such decisions seem to run contrary to the directives of the rite. If we can presume good will in all such decisions, it seems such contrary decisions reflect either an ignorance of the dynamic and theology of initiation or an ignorance of the juridical status of the rite. Concerning the first point, one can speculate that, faced with some pressing pastoral scenarios (e.g., what do we do with children who are seven when their peers are not confirmed until 14?), one chooses the path of least resistance without realizing that such decisions undermine some fundamental beliefs and structures in the Christian community. Concerning the second point, the revised liturgical texts are part of Church law and have the same authority and binding force as the canons of the *Code of Canon Law.* We should not decide to depart from the ritual structure and text casually.

A quick survey of the ritual text shows that adaptations that can be made due to "pastoral needs" or "pastoral reasons" (including serious and urgent ones) appear at least twenty times; "unusual," "extraordinary" or "special" circumstances appear at least six times; "serious reasons" appear at least thirteen times; and "circumstantial reasons" appear at least five times. Overall, the rite does not define these possible conditions, leaving the judgment to the appropriate person (or the conference of bishops). But the strong language (extraordinary, unusual, even pastoral) suggests that such decisions should not be made lightly.

Without exhausting all the possibilities, following is some guidance for making these pastoral decisions regarding implementing the *Rite of Christian Initiation of Adults*. In extraordinary circumstances, such as at a time of death, we will make important adaptations to the initiation process as outlined in part II, chapters 2 and 3 of the rite. The recommendations that follow apply to ordinary pastoral situations.

1. Be Clear About What Is a Pastoral Decision. Vatican II's *Pastoral Constitution on the Church in the Modern World* gives us direction here: "And so the council, as witness and guide to the faith of all God's people, gathered together by Christ, can find no more eloquent expression of this people's solidarity, respect and love for the whole human family, of which it forms part, than to enter into dialogue with it about all these various, different problems, throwing the light of the gospel on them and supplying humanity with the saving resources which the church has received from its founder under the promptings of the Holy Spirit" (*GS*, n. 3).

"Pastoral," therefore, involves a dialogue between the proclamation of the gospel (as encoded in doctrinal and liturgical principles) and contemporary human experience as a way of responding to these concerns of life. Both sides of the conversation are important and equal partners in the dialogue. A "pastoral decision" emerges in this conversation: What is the best response to this current situation that is faithful to gospel values and attentive to current needs?

2. Know the Dynamics and Structure of the Rite of Christian Initiation of Adults. One cannot adapt what one does not know. Coming to a basic understanding of initiation is prudent for all of us because it needs to inform our pastoral praxis in so many other areas of parish life. Indeed, if we took the insights from the initiation sacraments seriously, we would structure many aspects of parish life very differently than we do now. Who we are as Church and how we live faithfully the responsibilities of initiation would make new and challenging claims on all of us.

Especially critical, therefore, is a continual reading (and rereading) of the introductory notes and ritual texts in concert with supportive resources that help interpret the texts. While this will still leave one with an incomplete understanding of the ritual texts—it is in the very praying that another dimension of meaning emerges—this will provide a sufficient foundation for the dialogue with people's needs and situations that must occur to make a pastoral decision.

3. Assess the Current Situation. The ritual text provides room for adaptation because of the various situations in which we find ourselves. Recall *RCIA*, n. 5 and the variables that influence the initiation process. Which of these variables are of concern in this situation? And how does it compare with the other variables? "Not asking so much of the people" and "What would other people in the parish say if we confirmed an eight-year old when the other children are not confirmed until 14?" somehow do not capture all these variables. They may be real questions and situations we face, but they cannot be what drives our decisions.

4. *Weigh the Current Situation in Light of the Theology and Practice of Christian Initiation.* Earlier we noted that Christian initiation is about participation in the paschal mystery and conversion. If it were only a matter of membership, we could just "give" them the sacraments and move on. But so much more is at stake here. After assessing the pastoral situation in light of the variables noted above, we need to place that situation alongside the rite's concern for a full, pastoral formation that supports the journey of conversion and a full sacramental celebration of such an experience in the midst of the community. Pastoral leadership cannot ignore such foundational concerns.

5. *Consult with Others.* Having entered into conversation with the current situation and the theology and practice of initiation, make a preliminary judgment. Then talk it out with trusted colleagues. Name the situation and evaluate with them if things are as they appear. Clearly indicate the values at stake and why one set of values seems more pressing than another set. Listen to the feedback and allow it to challenge and broaden the initial decision. Usually, if we are resistant to talking out our preliminary decision with others, it is because either we have truncated the decision-making process (a snap decision) or we are not willing to hear another's opinion.

6. *Make a Prudent and Intelligent Decision.* Following these guidelines, one can then make a prudent and intelligent decision about a particular pastoral situation.

Clearly there are some "pastoral decisions" that we make immediately because of the circumstances at hand. One of the "serious reasons" that would prevent confirmation following baptism, for example, is being baptized in an emergency by someone other than a priest (only a priest can confirm). When we must make such decisions, we can only do the best we can do. But we can be prepared for such actions—and decisions of a less critical nature—by immersing ourselves in the dynamics and theology of the rite.

PLANNING THE RITUAL CELEBRATIONS

It is time to prepare the next rite of acceptance for the parish. Before beginning to "put on paper" the plan for the celebration of any of the initiation rites—really, any ritual celebration at all—there are a few ground rules we need to follow lest we fall prey to gimmicks and liturgical fads.

1. *Read the entire ritual text.* The whole thing? Yes, the entire collection of rites. Without the entire picture, we might end up highlighting pieces of the cele-

bration that are less important than others. Besides, being familiar with the entire context for all the celebrations is helpful. While there are some worthwhile commentaries on the *Rite of Christian Initiation of Adults,* nothing compares with reading the actual ritual text itself. Take the study edition and mark it up.

2. Know the particular rite. With the larger vision of the initiation rites, turn to a critical reading of the particular rite that will be celebrated. Not only do we want to know the particulars of this rite (who goes where and when), but the deeper issues within the rite. There is a basic Catholic principle that can be summed up as "we are who we pray." Our liturgical prayer is an expression of our deepest beliefs. Therefore, to celebrate this rite honestly, we can answer the questions "What is this rite celebrating? What do we believe when we celebrate this rite?" Besides personal reflection and conversation with colleagues, the various commentaries on the rites will be especially helpful here. (Part II of this resource is intended to help us at this point.) With this understanding, we can plan the rite to celebrate what is intended (with the appropriate emphasis where it belongs) rather than celebrating something else.

3. Know who will celebrate the rite. This principle includes not only the catechumens and candidates, but also the assembly. It is not enough to know the rite; we need to know who will be praying these rites. Many place almost exclusive focus on the catechumens and candidates when preparing to celebrate these rites, often to the neglect of the gathered assembly. The priority needs to be the gathered assembly; we pray sacraments as a community.

To help get a clearer idea of who will be celebrating, it might be helpful to take a piece of paper and draw a line down the middle of the sheet. On one side list the qualities of the parish community who gather for prayer (e.g., strong sense of social justice, no real catechesis on liturgy given in past) and in the other column list qualities of the catechumens, candidates, sponsors and catechumenate team (e.g., sense of excitement about scripture, willing to talk about relationship with God if they feel supported). Then consider all these qualities when preparing to celebrate the rite.

4. Identify the variety within the structure of the rite. A key principle for adaptation and celebration of ritual is: Know the rite and know the community. Having spent quality time doing just that, now it is time to look at the structure of the rite itself. Just as various forms of writing fill a newspaper—editorials, comics, sports reporting, world events, horoscopes—that do not receive equal emphasis, so the rite is composed of various dimensions: dialogue, movement and gesture, acclamation, symbol, prayer and intercession, exhortation, etc. It is important to identify each dimension to know how best to celebrate.

A helpful way to do this is to take a sheet of paper and begin listing in the margin the number for each section of the rite. Read the section and identify what is going on: Is this an acclamation of praise? Is there a procession at this point? Write the dimension of celebration next to the number, and follow with a short description. For example: *RCIA,* n. 54; Gesture/Touch/Symbol: Marking the entire body with the cross.

5. *Consider how to celebrate the rite.* Now, looking at the rite as a whole with its varied dimensions, consider the worship space, the needs of the community (remember: keep the focus on the assembly), and the rhythm of prayer. Explore the available options—there is no rule that says "Everything must happen up front in the sanctuary." Use the entire worship space. Keep asking: Why are we doing this part this way? If it is difficult (or impossible) to answer this question, go back to the reflection on the meaning of the rite. Be sure the way we construct the celebration is consistent with what the church desires to proclaim.

6. *Prepare the assembly to celebrate.* Many often overlook this step. And yet, the celebration of any of the rites is part of the prayer of the assembly. So prepare them: weeks before the rite, comment (verbally, in the bulletin, etc.) on the upcoming rite and its importance to the community; spend some quality time (even if a few moments) before the rite giving a context (not an explanation); make clear their role in the rite; invite people to gather after the celebration to talk about the rite.

7. *Celebrate the rite.* In order for the community to appreciate the initiation rites, we need to celebrate them well. Do the necessary homework. And avoid all the "cute stuff." The ritual is powerful in its own right, with appropriate adaptation.

8. *Reflect back on the experience.* Just as we will do with the catechumens, candidates, sponsors (and perhaps even the assembly), gather with those responsible for implementing the rite and critically reflect on what happened. What did this rite proclaim? What did we learn from this celebration for future celebration?

At first, these guidelines might seem like more work than they are worth. But they are not. The faithful preparation of the community's prayer is worth all the work and time they take. Use the time needed. The community will be grateful that we did.

GETTING STARTED

Parishes start to implement the *Rite of Christian Initiation of Adults* when people come seeking more information about the Christian way of life in this Catholic community. However, it is the rare parish situation that can immediately begin to implement the full rite. Normally, there will be stages of growth and development. Given all this, what are the essentials? Where does a parish begin?

There is nothing in the *Rite of Christian Initiation of Adults* that is not essential. However, with limited resources and limited staff, a parish can begin slowly. In this case, less is more. Following are some suggestions for getting started.

1. Form a catechumenate team. If the parish does not have people inquiring already into the life of the community, then it has the leisure of setting up an initiation team without the added pressure of an immediate catechesis for inquirers. Without delay, a wise coordinator will begin to seek out people who can serve on the team in a variety of capacities, as will be discussed in chapter four of this resource.

2. Recruit and train sponsors. An extremely important link in this chain is the sponsor. Often sponsors feel inadequate or incapable of serving in the ministry unless they are given some basic formation and insight into how the process works. Even if there are no candidates, begin to solicit sponsors now.

3. Choose inquiry households (or team) for inquirers. If the initiation team can begin with gatherings in parishioners' homes, it will make it easier to expand the precatechumenate in a full-year process.

4. Begin to prepare for dismissal catechesis. Even if there are no catechumens, spend time with the catechetical team on a regular basis unpacking the Sunday texts and highlighting the issues of Catholic life and teaching. Use this time for catechist formation.

5. Do some serious long-range planning. This does not mean making a schedule. It means tentatively planning a few rites of acceptance, deciding the best time for the rite of sending, and marking in the scrutinies, and determining when is the best time to celebrate the dismissal rite.

6. Begin to talk about it in the parish. Let parishioners know about the process of sacramental initiation. Highlight the importance of conversion and the development in faith for the parish community. Encourage preaching and teaching on the reign of God. Facilitate in whatever way possible the growth of the parish community so that it will be a community of the baptized that is willing to embrace and form men and women seeking our way of life.

4

Ministries in Initiation

INTRODUCTION

The challenge of official ministries in the Church is to hold in tension two important dimensions: remaining rooted in the ministry of Jesus while at the same time adapting and developing to meet the needs of a particular people in a particular time and place. The *Rite of Christian Initiation of Adults* offers a vision of ministry that attempts to do that. On one hand we have the traditional expressions of ministry, especially the ministry of baptism: bishop, presbyter, godparent. The *Rite of Christian Initiation of Adults* expands this vision of ministry—explicitly and implicitly—to include the ministry of the baptized community, the formative role of the sponsor, and the office of catechist. The "Introduction" to the rite explicitly calls for these ministries. However, because of the ministry of the baptized community articulated in the rite, one can argue that the rite implicitly calls for other roles of active service in the initiation process, such as hospitality and the catechumenate team.

The term ministry, the recognition of ministries, and the proper function of ministries is often a point of confusion and debate. Even in the early Christian community, we see evidence of differences in the understanding and functioning of ministries. In the Jerusalem community, we see ministries revolving around the role and function of the Twelve (i.e., those who walked with Jesus) and the elders of the community. Rooted in the experience of the synagogue, this model of ministry eventually expands—because the needs of the Hellenistic community were not being met—to include the seven (the deacons). At the same time, the church in Antioch, under the guidance of Paul, struggled under a different model of ministry as articulated in 1 Corinthians 12:27f. The controlling image was the body of Christ, with the variety and diversity of gifts—apostles, preachers, teachers, and the other expressions of service. There were two different understandings and perceptions of the function and order of ministries—ones that would cause some heated arguments between the two communities.

Eventually, the responsibility of ministry becomes associated with the offices of the episcopacy, presbyterate and diaconate. For most of us, this was our understanding of ministry until Vatican Council II. With the council, new questions about ministry led to new studies on the role and function of ministries. Of special interest was the call of the baptized to service and how this service is expressed.

EXPLICIT AND IMPLICIT MINISTRIES IN THE *RITE OF CHRISTIAN INITIATION OF ADULTS*

Within this context, the *Rite of Christian Initiation of Adults* promotes an important vision of ministry for initiation. While acknowledging the role of service of the more traditional ministries—bishop, priest, deacon—the *Rite of Christian Initiation of Adults* clearly states that the responsibility of initiation rests in the hands of the baptized community. Noting that the ritual text states this in various ways throughout the rite is important. However, the ritual text specifically states it in the Introduction under the title "Ministries and Offices": ". . . the people of God, as represented by the local Church, should understand and show by their concern that the initiation of adults is the responsibility of all the baptized" (*RCIA*, n. 9).

Ministry of the Parish Community (RCIA, n. 9)

The primary minister of initiation in the *Rite of Christian Initiation of Adults* is the parish community. The quality of their lives, the concern and interest they show, the manner of worship, the commitment to social action— all of this is the where and how of the *Rite of Christian Initiation of Adults*. People come to a particular community to become part of that community. It is the community's responsibility not only to welcome them, but to show the interested persons what makes the community distinctive, what makes it a Catholic Christian community. Ultimately, the community needs to ask: Why do we initiate? Into what do we initiate?

All of this suggests a level of awareness in the community. Shaped by authentic worship and good pastoral leadership, the community grows in its awareness of its own baptismal commitment: to serve the mission of the reign of God, to be leaven in the world. It is because of this living witness to the ministry of Jesus that the community is eager to welcome new members into its midst, to help in this service to the world community. The community is enlivened by its experience of the presence of the Risen One healing, reconciling, empowering them to lives of charity, justice, and compassion. It is in this spending of itself that the community discovers salvation in its midst.

Therefore, the involvement of the community in the initiation process is both primary and key. It is into this community that one is welcomed. Therefore, the community needs to know and meet the candidates and catechumens. The names of those who seek full initiation in the community should be familiar to all and should be a regular part of the community's prayer. The community needs to extend welcome, not only at parish gatherings, but also into the homes of members of the parish. The community actively participates in the ritual celebrations of initiation, extending its support in prayer and witnessing.

Ministry of Sponsors (RCIA, n. 10)

Sponsors are members of the local community who are chosen to accompany the candidates and catechumens through the initial periods of conversion. Sometimes the sponsor is a friend of the candidate—perhaps the person the candidate first went to talk to about the Catholic Church. Often the sponsor is someone from the parish who has volunteered to serve as this important and special companion. The sponsor needs to be a fully initiated member of the Church, and also an active member of the parish community. Besides being a direct support to the candidate or catechumen, the sponsor will help in the discernment process for the candidate, and also give testimony at the rite of acceptance into the order of catechumens.

The responsibility of the sponsor for a particular catechumen ends at the rite of election, when the godparent assumes the responsibility for the catechumen. The sponsor of someone expressing a desire to celebrate full communion in the Catholic Church continues with the candidate throughout the process.

Ministry of Godparents (RCIA, n. 11)

The godparent is the individual who accompanies the catechumen through the final periods of the *Rite of Christian Initiation of Adults* and continues as a companion with the individual throughout life. The godparent must be a fully initiated member of the Catholic Church; a person fully initiated in another Christian denomination may serve as a godparent if there is also a fully initiated Catholic as a godparent. The godparent, whom the catechumen chooses, formally begins his or her role at the rite of election. Election is the formal pronouncement of the catechumen's readiness for full sacramental initiation. Thus, the ongoing companion who will witness and affirm this commitment formally begins the journey with the catechumen. Realistically, the godparent needs to be part of the catechumen's journey already.

The godparent is chosen because of his or her witness to the Christian life, character, and level of friendship with the catechumen. Because the role of godparent is more than a ceremonial function—indeed it is a commitment of lifelong friendship in the Lord—we give the same level of consideration as sponsors regarding choice and formation to godparents. The popular practice of requesting people to serve as godparents for our children based on purely social or obligatory reasons has contributed to the functioning of godparents as purely ceremonial witnesses. Hopefully the ongoing relationship stressed in the *Rite of Christian Initiation of Adults* will inform the practice on the level of infant baptism. The same is true of sponsors for confirmation.

Godparents give testimony at the rite of election, witness the celebration of the Easter sacraments, and remain part of the catechumen's life as they together struggle and grow in faith. Sometimes a catechumen may ask his or her sponsor to serve as godparent. While this may be appropriate, the sponsor needs to recognize the ongoing nature of this responsibility. Candidates for full communion do not choose godparents for full sacramental initiation. They retain the relationship established with their godparents at baptism. However, it might be good to include their godparents in this process of initiation to help establish the connection with their own baptism and to express ecumenical sensitivity.

Ministry of the Bishop (RCIA, n. 12)

The diocesan bishop, as shepherd of the diocese, presides over the entire process of initiation (see *NS*, n. 11). It is his responsibility not only to regulate the implementation of the *Rite of Christian Initiation of Adults* in the diocese, but to promote the formation of candidates and catechumens. In the early Church, it was the bishop who welcomed the new members into the community. The bishop continues this role of guidance and support indirectly and directly. Indirectly, he does so through the competent leadership he appoints in parishes and diocesan offices that function to serve the implementation of the *Rite of Christian Initiation of Adults* (such as the diocesan Initiation Office, Office of Worship, and Office for Religious Education) and which provide adequate care and formation for catechumenate teams and for those enrolled in the initiation process. Directly, the bishop presides at the rite of election (see *NS*, n. 12) and the celebration of the sacraments of initiation (when possible), and also brings the neophytes (newly initiated) together during the Easter season to celebrate the eucharist together.

Ministry of Presbyter and the Parish Pastoral Ministry Team (RCIA, nos. 13-15)

The parish pastoral ministry team (pastor, associate pastors, deacons, pastoral ministers) is responsible at the local level for the care of the candidates and catechumens. The initiation process needs to hold priority for the staff or else it will not hold priority for the parish community. Specifically, this means the necessary investment in resources, time, talent, supervision, and direction to the various people involved in the process. The staff can regularly participate in the process as members of the initiation team. Their regular presence to the catechumens and candidates not only offers support, but helps to establish personal relationships with them. The parish pastoral ministry staff (or the person(s) they designate, such as the parish coordinator) are responsible for the decisions about carrying out the initiation process in the parish. Specifically, they are responsible for the approval of the choice of godparents, the appropriate adaptation of the rites, and the discernment throughout the process. It is advisable that at least once during the year (and preferably a number of times) the staff meet informally with each catechumen. This gives the catechumens a chance to become better acquainted with the pastoral leadership of the parish, and it opens an avenue to discuss personal issues, if needed.

Ministry of Catechists (RCIA, n. 16)

Besides sponsors, catechists have the greatest contact with the catechumens. They meet with them regularly to share faith, pray the scriptures, and share in the Catholic tradition. The catechists are to take an active part in the preparation and celebration of the rites. Their catechesis needs to be adapted to the liturgical year. As we will discuss in Chapter 7, the ministry of catechesis is an echoing of the gospel. One dimension of this is information. However, catechesis is more than information; it is formative. Thus, the skilled catechist will be sensitive to growth in faith, conversion, and appropriate expressions of prayer.

Each period of the *Rite of Christian Initiation of Adults* has a different focus. Having different catechetical teams to serve during each period would be appropriate: a precatechumenate team to help facilitate the early stirrings of faith and initial conversion; a catechumenate team to help pass on the essentials of the Catholic tradition within the context of the liturgical year, thus facilitating God's call to conversion; a team to serve during the period of purification and illumination that can facilitate the Lenten retreat for the elect (with an ongoing initiation process, there will probably be catechumens and elect at the same time and therefore the need for different catechetical teams); the postbaptismal (mystagogy) catechesis team responsible for reflection on the mysteries (sacraments), plus integration into the community through lives of service and charity.

Additionally, there are "informal" catechists—the men and women of the parish who often come to one or more catechetical gatherings to share their own experiences of marriage, prayer, or ministry.

Additional Roles of Service

The *Rite of Christian Initiation of Adults* clearly holds the vision that the primary responsibility of initiation rests in the hands of the community of the baptized. To facilitate this process, other roles of service have developed in parishes, flowing from the general ministry of the baptized. Some of these roles of service include:

The Initiation Coordinator. As a parish implements the *Rite of Christian Initiation of Adults,* it becomes clearer that the full implementation of the rite requires the coordination of a variety of ministries. One designated person can serve as coordinator—to do just that, coordinate. It would be this person's responsibility to see that all the ministries are well serviced and resourced, and also provide the overall choreography to the rite. In places that function at a high level of implementation, this role of service not only is essential, but will require a large commitment of time and dedication. This responsibility may initially fall into the hands of the parish director of religious education or one of the pastoral associates. It may evolve either into a full-time staff position, or within the care of a person responsible for sacramental catechesis in the parish. If anywhere in the rite one deems it necessary to have someone skilled and trained in theology and ministry, it would be in this role of service.

Hospitality. An initiating community is a community of welcome and hospitality. Throughout the initiation process, there are hospitality needs: celebrations, welcoming into parish functions, Sunday morning coffee and doughnuts. Parishioners can become involved in the *Rite of Christian Initiation of Adults* through the coordination and extension of hospitality.

Communications. The parish community, to welcome and serve, needs to know what is going on. Throughout the year, they need to hear about the various periods of formation, their role in the process, the people who are joining the community. The sponsors, godparents, and other team members need to stay informed as well. A group of people whose primary role is ongoing communication to the initiation team and parish community will heighten the involvement and ownership by all.

Prayer Partners. Besides the explicit sponsorship of candidates and catechumens, various members of the parish can be involved in the initiation process by serving as prayer partners. This would include parishioners or groups of parishioners actively remembering in prayer one of the catechumens throughout the process. This would be a wonderful way of involving the homebound in the initiation process and of recognizing their baptismal spirituality as well.

Liturgical Ministers. Besides the pastoral team, the *Rite of Christian Initiation of Adults* demands the active involvement of liturgical ministers— especially musicians—for full and rich celebrations of the rites. This requires a shift from liturgical planning to liturgical preparation that incorporates the experience of growth in faith and variety of conversions experienced by the catechumens. Along with the pastoral staff and initiation team, the liturgical ministers adopt and adapt liturgical rites of the *Rite of Christian Initiation of Adults* authentically to express the experience of the catechumens within this community. This would require a "listening in" to the movement of the Spirit in the catechumenate and in the parish community.

Spiritual Directors. Sometimes a catechumen will desire to seek additional companionship while naming and owning his or her conversion. The parish needs to make available men and women gifted in the art of spiritual direction or accompaniment.

Outreach. One sign of the interiorization of conversion is the outward expression in service. Catechumens will experience the call and desire to give away the gift they are receiving in the initiation process through concrete expressions of charity and service. Sometimes it is helpful to provide someone who can help them in discerning how they can best serve the larger community, as well as which explicit avenues of service are available to them (such as soup kitchens, shelters for the homeless, visiting the sick, helping in child care, or other expressions of charity).

The initiating community will continue to discover additional expressions of ministry flowing from the initiation experience. Implementing the rite seems to have a ripple effect—we risk bringing a variety of people together to help with the formation process, the *Rite of Christian Initiation of Adults* moves closer to the center of the parish's worship, more people will want to become involved, the variety of ministries that can develop become more extensive, the parish community becomes more involved and deepens the level of renewal that can happen in the community, the parish community expresses this renewal in forms of charity and justice resulting in more people wanting to affiliate with this community...and the ongoing cycle of formation and initiation of both individuals and the community continues.

FORMING AN INITIATION TEAM

The process and ministries we use to implement the *Rite of Christian Initiation of Adults* make an important statement about how we view initiation and the role of the community. If we are committed to a vision of Church that calls forth the gifts of all the baptized for service, then we are working toward a collaborative model of ministry. Collaboration requires the differentiation of ministries while respecting the fundamental responsibility of all the baptized. It is from a collaborative model for ministry that the notion of an initiation team can emerge.

Usually one person is designated to be responsible for the *Rite of Christian Initiation of Adults* in a parish—the initiation coordinator. The coordinator could choose to do most of the implementation alone. The results would be a definite vision of church, ministry, initiation—all of which would probably suggest a very privatized experience of Church—and one burnt-out person. Of its very nature, the *Rite of Christian Initiation of Adults* is communal and its implementation is communal.

The initiation coordinator will need to surround himself or herself with two teams of ministers. The first team comprises all the individuals who are sharing gifts in the initiation process—catechists, hospitality, environment, communications, sponsors, and so on. The second team is a smaller group of individuals who represent the various ministries in the initiation process and work with the coordinator to oversee the general development and implementation of the rite. This second team—commonly called the core team—could be as small as three to four or as large as twelve to fourteen. Whatever the size, the core team needs to represent all the various ministries in the *Rite of Christian Initiation of Adults.*

The Initiation Team

How do people become involved as team members in the *Rite of Christian Initiation of Adults?* Usually it is through word of mouth. The best publicity is the feedback from friends and neighbors. So begin small and provide wonderful care and support. The message will quickly get around.

Another way to get team members is to begin to ask around. Who are the people in the parish who are good care givers, willing to share faith, friendly, prayerful—basic active members of the community? The basic active members need not be the "faithful fifty" we always call upon to do things. Rather, they are the ordinary Jane and Joe in the community who need to be asked, who are waiting to be invited to help serve the parish.

The bulletin can be a helpful communicator in the parish. However, avoid blank ads such as "We need catechists for the *Rite of Christian Initiation of Adults*" or "We need sponsors for the *Rite of Christian Initiation of Adults.*" This limits the ability to help discern with the individuals their own gifts for service. A more general announcement will still attract people, and will give the initiation team the opportunity to help place them where they can be of best service—though nothing replaces face-to-face invitations.

Some parishes offer an "Initiation Gathering." The gathering is an evening of reflection about baptismal spirituality and the *Rite of Christian Initiation of Adults.* Its purpose is to expose people to the *Rite of Christian Initiation of Adults* and its ministries to the needs in the parish. While the gathering needs to be open to everyone in the parish—and be advertised as such— we may give certain individuals a special invitation to attend because they are prospective team members. The format of the evening can vary, but some basic elements would include a short overview of the *Rite of Christian Initiation of Adults,* prayer time, and reflection on ministry. We coerce or force no one to make a commitment. Rather, we invite people to explore their own baptismal spirituality. At the end of the gathering, we can provide an opportunity for joining one of the teams.

What are the qualities of people who serve on the initiation teams? Basically, they need to be men and women from the community who honestly struggle to live the gospel in the ordinary ways of life. As people of prayer, they have come to trust their experience of God in the Catholic community and desire to share that experience with others. Because they are each unique, the team members will bring different gifts and talents—leadership skills, hospitality, humor, critical sense, intuition—and different perspectives of living as church—single, progressive, divorced, married, traditional, and so on.

We need to remember that team members are volunteers. People volunteer to help for a variety of reasons. However, beneath all the reasons are two basic ones—one external and one internal. The external reason usually deals with contributing to this particular group, and hoping to gain some sense of affiliation, support, and a sense of accomplishment and worthwhileness—that my contribution counts. The internal reason usually deals with some inner need or desire that the individual hopes to have fulfilled by participating with this group, such as a deepening of my hunger for God, or coming to a new awareness of my relationship with God. Whatever the reasons, the initiation coordinator will need to help the team members name their needs, and then help them feel some satisfaction and fulfillment of those needs. If we are not caring for them, the volunteers will go somewhere else to have those needs satisfied. Thus, good resourcing and support for the initiation team is essential.

Minimally, this means providing ongoing gatherings for the team for support and personal enrichment. Some topics that need to be discussed with the team throughout the year are:

◆ An overview of the *Rite of Christian Initiation of Adults*—process, history, theology. Each team member should have either his or her own copy of the rite or easy access to a copy.

◆ Conversion and Faith Development. The team needs to be sensitive to the dynamics of conversion and faith in their own lives to be attentive to them in the catechumens' lives.

◆ Storytelling and Faith Sharing. The team will need to begin to develop a basic level of naming and telling their experience of God to share the faith of the community and help the catechumens enter this same process of naming God's activity.

◆ Basic Communication Skills. The team will need to practice basic skills for effective communication: active listening, feedback, appropriate confrontation and challenge, affirmation and support, and so on.

◆ Basic Catechetical Skills. Those involved in catechesis will need to spend some time exploring methodological options to provide the finest opportunities possible for the catechumens.

◆ Burnout in Ministry. The *Rite of Christian Initiation of Adults* tends to engender enthusiasm and high levels of commitment from team members. However, if the team does not reflect on realistic expectations and develop skills for stress, the result could be burnout.

◆ Time to talk about their needs, concerns, and so on. Besides these training modules (and any other needs of the team), the team members need time together simply to talk about their experiences with the initiation process, to inform and be formed together in support and care.

The Core Team

The second team the initiation coordinator may work with is the core team. This smaller team would be responsible for the general implementation of the *Rite of Christian Initiation of Adults*. The members of the core team, who come from the initiation team mentioned above, meet more regularly to discuss the needs and direction of the initiation process. Depending on the size of the basic team, the core team could be composed of:

◆ Initiation coordinator.

◆ Member from the pastoral staff. It is advisable that if the initiation coordinator is not a part of the pastoral staff, one member of the staff joins the core team to represent the needs and concerns of the pastor and staff.

◆ Liturgy coordinator. This person serves as liaison with the liturgy team and liturgical musicians, bringing them in when necessary as the team prepares for any celebrations.

◆ Hospitality coordinator. This person represents those who provide formal (receptions) and informal (coffee breaks, greeters) hospitality in the initiation process.

◆ Catechist coordinator. This person serves the needs of the catechists in the *Rite of Christian Initiation of Adults*. If the parish differentiates the catechetical team into four subgroups—one for each period of the rite—it might be helpful to include one representative from each group.

◆ Sponsor and godparent coordinator. This person keeps in touch with the sponsors and godparents, communicating any of their needs to the team.

◆ Communications coordinator. This person is responsible for keeping the parish community aware of the initiation process and the various rites when celebrated.

The core team will vary depending on the needs of each individual parish. What is important is that a team of people involved in the *Rite of Christian Initiation of Adults* gather to help discern how they can best be of service to both the parish community and the catechumens in this process of initiation.

SPONSOR AND GODPARENT FORMATION

Perhaps one of the most important ministries in the *Rite of Christian Initiation of Adults*—second only to the role of the local community—is the support and care given by sponsors and godparents. Catechumens and sponsors meet regularly to discuss the basic concerns, hopes, and fears that develop as the catechumen listens to God's call in his or her life.

Sponsorship is an important service, and therefore the team needs to be cautious about who sponsors. Idealistically, the Church calls everyone in the community to be a sponsor. However, given the limits that surround us, we want to provide the best possible experience for the catechumen as he or she journeys in faith with this community. A sponsor sensitive to the needs of the catechumen will be of great assistance in this journey.

We need to inform sponsors up front that their ministry will involve a large commitment of time: regular gatherings with the catechumen, witnessing for the community, and catechetical sessions.

The formation of sponsors (and godparents, whenever possible) is similar to the formation of the initiation team, with stronger emphasis on faith-sharing skills, shared prayer, reflection on the scriptures, discernment, conversion theories, and communication skills. Sponsors need to be sensitive to the fact that choosing to affiliate with a community is both a joyful and a painful process. There is a death to an old way of life, and the catechumen will often experience something akin to grieving. (A helpful resource is my *Walking Together in Faith: A Workbook for Sponsors in Christian Initiation,* published by Paulist Press.)

Regular gatherings for sponsors will help them talk about what is going on in the initiation process, as well as keep them informed of any developments. The following guide for sponsors helps outline some responsibilities and expectations of sponsors. These would also be helpful for godparents, with appropriate adjustments.

GUIDE FOR SPONSORS

The following offers a summary of the role of sponsor. It can be adapted to include the responsibilities of the godparent. Permission is given to copy this section on the "Guide for Sponsors" for use with sponsors.

◆ The role of sponsor is one of spiritual friend, of support and care. You represent the parish community in a special way. You also provide the one-on-one support the person needs during this period of growth and development. Your role is a privilege and a responsibility in the parish.

◆ Catechumens and sponsors need to meet on a regular basis. The definition of regular basis differs, of course, depending on individual needs. However, the following can serve as a guideline: that catechumen and sponsor meet to talk about the catechumen's faith development and concerns *at least* once every week. The gatherings are informal sharings—to be supportive and to help clarify some issues for the catechumen. If a particular week passes and you cannot be available (or vice versa), then call the catechumen at least to touch base. Ongoing communication is essential here.

◆ What do you do when you meet? Share faith together. You become the resource person for the catechumen, for all those questions he or she has, for those concerns he or she may feel uncomfortable bringing up in the inquiry/catechumenate gatherings. But what is more important, you serve as a support and a friend. Here are some conversation starters: How has your week been? What happened at last Sunday's session? Did you understand what we talked about? You will find the catechumen has many questions. Feel free to share with him or her your experience of being Catholic, and of being part of this parish. A helpful resource (when reflecting on the Sunday scriptures with catechumens) is *A Catechumen's Lectionary,* edited by Robert M. Hamma (Paulist Press). Besides providing the scripture texts for each week of all three liturgical years, it includes reflection and discussion questions.

◆ Another vital role of the sponsor is to help the catechumen feel welcome in the parish community. Here are some suggestions about how you can do this:

    — Alert the catechumen to upcoming parish events (lectures, socials) and suggest that perhaps you go together.

    — If you are involved in a parish organization, invite the catechumen to one of your meetings.

    — Introduce the catechumen to some friends. While you do not want to overwhelm, you do want to welcome them into the parish family. The only way they will feel welcome is if you introduce them to parishioners.

◆ Be creative, be innovative, be daring. Some sponsors have invited catechumens over for dinner on occasion. Others have met at the local diner for a cup of coffee and a chance to chat. What is important is that you find quality time to welcome this person, to make him or her feel important and special to this parish through you.

◆ Your catechumen will raise questions, concerns will come up, and you may feel inadequate in handling them. That is fine. Let the catechumen know, "I don't know…" and then find out. Call up one of the team members or check it out in the *New Catholic Encyclopedia* or any other resource text in the parish library. This can become a good learning experience for both of you. The catechumen will learn that the Catholic experience is one that is always new and growing. And you will have the chance to clarify some important questions and concerns you may have with the community.

◆ During the inquiry period, we will make opportunities for the candidates to meet weekly. Stay informed of the day and place of these gatherings. Hopefully, you can join with the inquiry team and the candidates each week. This will be a good opportunity to get to know your candidate, as well as to set up a time for you to meet privately.

◆ If the candidate you are sponsoring chooses to become a member of the Catholic community, he or she will celebrate the rite of acceptance into the order of catechumens. The catechumenate team will meet with you to discuss the importance of this transition for the candidate. During those last days before the celebration, your discussions with the candidate will need to focus on why he or she is joining the community, and what he or she will need from both the community and from God. Your witness at the rite of acceptance will be valuable.

◆ During the period of the catechumenate, the catechumens will be gathering weekly to pray, reflect on the word of God, and explore the issues of Catholic faith—and how all of this impacts on their daily lives. The catechumenate team will let you know when the catechumens will be gathering. The presence and participation of the sponsors in these catechetical gatherings are important. These gatherings can also serve as a starting point for your weekly gathering with the catechumen.

◆ When your catechumen is ready to celebrate the Easter sacraments, he or she will celebrate the rite of election on the First Sunday of Lent. Your witness to the growth and development of the catechumen at this celebration will be valuable. If you are sponsoring a candidate for full communion in the Catholic Church, he or she will celebrate a similar rite of recognition.

◆ During the final days of preparation, the catechumen (or elect) will be spending more time with his or her godparent who will continue to be a companion with the catechumen during the years ahead. You are encouraged to continue your relationship with the catechumen. However your responsibility as a sponsor finishes at this time. Of course, you are welcome to join with the catechumens and their godparents and families at the Easter Vigil. If you are sponsoring a candidate for full communion, however, you will continue in your role as sponsor with him or her throughout the remainder of this formation process.

◆ Throughout the year there will be a number of gatherings that will be of service to you as a sponsor. The catechumenate team will give you the dates for these gatherings. These will be times of prayer, include discussion of the concerns and issues of the catechumenate process, and provide support and direction for all the sponsors.

◆ We thank you for your service. Please feel free to let any of us on the initiation team know how we can support you in this important ministry.

Part Two

Implementing the Rite

5

Period of Evangelization and Precatechumenate

INTRODUCTION

The period of evangelization and precatechumenate is a time of inquiry when an individual begins to respond to some stirrings within to seek out life with Christ in this community of Catholic Christians. The reasons vary and are as many as there are individuals. The parish provides an opportunity for the individual to step back and explore this call as well as what the Church offers to respond to this call for life. This is a period of searching, asking questions,

	Period of Evangelization and Precatechumenate				
	UNBAPTIZED ADULT	CHILDREN OF CATECHETICAL AGE	BAPTIZED, UNCATECHIZED CATHOLIC	BAPTIZED, UNCATECHIZED CHRISTIAN	BAPTIZED, CATECHIZED CHRISTIAN
Reference	*RCIA*, nos. 36–40	*RCIA*, nos. 36–40	*No directives given*	*No directives given*	*No directives given*
Required	Should not be omitted	Should not be omitted	Limited time might be helpful	Limited time might be helpful	Limited time might be helpful (NB: *RCIA*, n. 473)
Focus	evangelization	evangelization	awareness of conversion and initial affiliation	awareness of conversion and initial affiliation	awareness of conversion and initial affiliation
Goal	faith and initial conversion	faith and initial conversion (according to age and ability)	awareness of conversion and initial affiliation	awareness of conversion and initial affiliation	awareness of conversion and initial affiliation
Name	inquirers	inquirers	—	—	—
Time	unlimited duration	unlimited duration	limited time, if at all	limited time, if at all	limited time, if at all
Rites	none (cf. *NS*, n. 1)	none	none	none	none

81

and the initial stirrings of faith before making a public commitment to follow Christ in this community of faith.

WHAT DOES THE RITE SAY?

Again, we return to the introductory notes in the *Rite of Christian Initiation of Adults* for the period of the precatechumenate to discover its underlying vision and meaning.

Read RCIA, *n. 36.*

This section provides a general description of the concerns of the period of the precatechumenate. The rite describes two key concepts here: evangelization and the process of conversion. About evangelization, we read how the rite is using this broad term: "faithfully and constantly the living God is proclaimed . . ." Because of this evangelization, one enters the process of conversion that is the work of the Holy Spirit. Note that conversion is to the Lord and not to the Church (see *NS*, n. 2).

Read RCIA, *n. 37.*

This section defines the goal of this period of formation: the evangelization (noted in *RCIA*, n. 36) that leads to faith and initial conversion. This is important because the rest of the rite presumes such a firm foundation. At *RCIA*, n. 42, the text notes that the recognition of this first faith and initial conversion is key to the discernment to celebrate the rite of acceptance.

Read RCIA, *n. 38.*

The agenda of this period of formation is set out for us here. As with the rest of the ritual text, the text broadly defines the catechesis without specific methods or details. It is left to the local community to interpret these guidelines within their current situation. Hence, the agenda of the precatechumenate is threefold: suitable explanation of the gospel, spiritual support, and explicit connection with the community. The insights on faith formation and liturgical catechesis in chapter 2 will help us in exploring how this can be done.

Read RCIA, *n. 39.*

This section refers to the possibility of a public ritual for receiving candidates into the period of the precatechumenate. *National Statutes,* n. 1 clarifies the policy for implementation in the United States. Clearly, the directives want to avoid confusing any ritual with the rite of acceptance.

Read RCIA, *n. 40.*

Not only should the pastoral leadership take an active role in the initiation process right from the beginning, but initial formation into liturgical prayer (simple blessings and the like) is appropriate for this period of formation.

WHAT IS NOT SAID

A quick review of the ritual text is interesting, especially for what it does not say. It does not say anything about starting this only in September. In fact, if one takes the directives about evangelization and conversion seriously (*RCIA,* n. 36 and 37), one can presume that the work of the Holy Spirit will be ongoing and frequent, outside the normal academic calendar.

The ritual text also does not speak of many practical dimensions of this period of formation: interviews, the "how" of this catechesis, the specific content of the catechesis (beyond a suitable explanation of the gospel), and the like. Many practices have emerged in many parishes to attend to the directives on the period of the precatechumenate. We need to be sure that our initiation practice, though, is consistent with the vision explicated here in *RCIA,* nos. 36-40.

GETTING SOME DIRECTION: LITURGICAL CATECHESIS

Often, when discussing the period of precatechumenate, someone will say something along these lines: "Telling stories—is that all there is to do?" The question betrays the confusion and concern about what is appropriate for precatechumenate. The lack of specifics intensifies this concern in the ritual text regarding the period. What do we do?

Some people gather with the inquirers and "just tell stories" about their lives, about what has been happening—whatever the inquirers want to talk about. For them the sense of hospitality, belonging and welcome is important. Others gather the inquirers and give teachings about the Catholic Church. For them, having the inquirers know the basics about the Catholic Church before entering the catechumenate is key.

Both extremes are inadequate for this period of formation. If the goal of initiation were merely membership in the Church, then information sharing would be appropriate. Yet the goal of initiation is not membership—it is discipleship for mission. And hence, formation for mission is more than passing on the information. It is immersion into a way of life. Stories and storytelling can be one way to help illustrate this way of life. But "simply telling stories" is not the storytelling of the precatechumenate.

Telling Stories

Why tell stories at all, much less during the precatechumenate? Because our lives are filled with stories, and it is in the exchange of these stories that we can come to know and be known by another. But we just do not ramble on with stories merely for the sake of telling stories. Stories during the period of the precatechumenate have a particular focus as noted earlier: *RCIA,* n. 36.

The stories are a part of the process of evangelization and conversion.

Thus, the stories of inquirers need to be met with the stories of our tradition—stories from the Hebrew and Christian scriptures, as well as stories from the community of believers over the ages. Which stories do we tell? We can't possibly tell all of them.

Here is where we are reminded that the period of the precatechumenate is a part of the larger ritual structure called the *Rite of Christian Initiation of Adults;* we must refrain from trying to see it in isolation, but rather as part of the whole initiation process. Hence, it is squarely situated within the context of liturgy. And it is within this context that we can find our answer to the questions about catechesis during this period.

Recall that liturgical catechesis situates the liturgical event itself as the center for the catechesis that both precedes and follows the liturgical celebration. It would be helpful to review the section in Chapter 2 of this resource on liturgical catechesis before continuing in this chapter.

The Rite of Acceptance into the Order of Catechumens

If we want guidance regarding the shape of formation during the period of the precatechumenate, we turn to the ritual that serves as the transition rite from the period of the precatechumenate into the period of the catechumenate: the celebration of the rite of acceptance into the order of catechumens.

Whereas *RCIA,* n. 42 provides guidance for discerning when to celebrate the rite, the ritual text itself provides guidance for the catechesis that precedes and follows the celebration of the rite. Our concern here will be with the catechesis *for* the celebration, which happens during the period of the precatechumenate.

Those responsible for the precatechumenate need to review each of the ritual actions, texts and symbols of the rite of acceptance. We will limit ourselves to the primary ones for this discussion: opening dialogue, first acceptance of the gospel, signing of the candidates, and lectionary citations for the liturgy of the word.

Opening Dialogue

After the community has welcomed the candidates—an important gesture in which the community takes the lead—the candidates are engaged in a preliminary conversation focused on fundamental desires: what the candidates ask of God's Church. The ritual text suggests that the answers ("faith" which offers "eternal life") give direction for the intention of the candidates.

What must happen during the precatechumenate to enable candidates to discover their heart's desire as rooted in relationship with God? How do we help them articulate such a desire?

First Acceptance of the Gospel

All three ritual texts for the first acceptance of the gospel (*RCIA,* n. 52) highlight the importance of coming to know God through Christ. Thus, the gospel is set before the candidates as the way of life for the disciple. Having made public their desire to live in relationship with God through Christ, the Church now invites them to make a significant promise: to accept the teachings and way of life of the gospel. This promise serves as the centerpiece of this rite: It is only because of this public promise that the remainder of the ritual makes any sense.

What must happen during the precatechumenate for candidates to make such a promise with integrity? How do we help them discover this gospel way of life?

Signing of the Candidates

The signing of the bodies of the candidates with the cross is a significant gesture. The candidates have made public their desire and promise regarding the Christian community, and we meet that with the cross, a symbol of death and hope. We do not promise them an easy life; we promise them the paschal mystery, even the possibility of death. And we make this perfectly and profoundly clear by marking and claiming their bodies with the cross of Jesus Christ.

What must happen during the precatechumenate for candidates to recognize the paschal mystery? How do we help them find life through death?

Celebration of the Word of God

The readings cited for the rite of acceptance (*RCIA,* n. 62; *LM,* n. 743) provide important direction for the precatechumenate. There we discover stories of promise and trust, of searching and finding.

What must happen during the precatechumenate for candidates to be immersed in the great stories of promise, trust, searching and finding? How do we help them discover their own life stories within the great stories?

Liturgical Catechesis

What does all of this have to say to us about catechesis during the period of the precatechumenate? While not exhausting all the possibilities, it tells us a great deal about the shape and direction of the storytelling.

During the precatechumenate, we need to expose the candidates to the great stories of promise and trust (creation, the flood, Abraham and Sarah, the Exodus, Jesus and the Twelve, Paul), of life and death (the cross), of conversion and commitment (the disciples and other men and women of the tradition, such as Francis of Assisi, Teresa of Avila, Thomas Merton and Dorothy Day), of the Christian way of life (the Beatitudes). The candidates do not need to earn theology degrees in these areas; they need to be touched by these key parts of Christian living.

And that is where the storytelling comes in, because people are touched in their real, lived experiences (recall the sections on revelation and human experience in Chapter 2 of this resource). The task of this period of formation is to listen attentively to the lives of the inquirers and meet their lives with the life of the Christian tradition via the stories mentioned here, as well as many, many more. In that "meeting of stories," there is the potential for awakening, change, renewal, questioning. There is the potential for evangelization and initial conversion.

The formation appropriate for the period of the precatechumenate is, indeed, more than "just telling stories." It is allowing the telling of saving and healing stories to help people discover an invitation to new life in the gospel of Jesus Christ. It is about learning to live the great story of freedom.

STRATEGIES FOR IMPLEMENTING THE PERIOD OF THE PRECATECHUMENATE

As mentioned earlier, the ritual text gives little direction for the catechesis appropriate for this period of formation. Following are some general strategies and ideas for implementing this period in a pastoral setting. Appropriate adaptation will need to be made to suit the particular pastoral setting (e.g., rural setting, urban setting, various ethnic cultures, etc.).

Development of Relationships and Experiences of Trust
The precatechumenate is a time for people to begin to feel at home— with the community, with specific individuals in the community, and with themselves. It is only in an environment of genuine care and concern that people begin to entrust themselves and others with their questions, their concerns, their story.

People come seeking entrance into the Church for various reasons. Whatever the reasons why they come, the reason they stay is due to the quality of the relationships that are established.

Since the precatechumenate is a period of welcoming and at-homeness, the logical place for these gatherings is in parishioners' homes. Households throughout the parish can be used for gatherings at which inquirers can ask questions about Christian life. As the initiation process develops in a parish, there may be several households that have gatherings on different evenings to accommodate the various needs and demands of the inquirers.

The motivation for developing relationships of trust and centers of welcome is to create a space where the individual inquirer can experience a basic respect for his or her life journey. The focus is on the inquirer, not on membership. When our focus shifts, and it can in subtle ways, we are bordering on manipulation. It is then that we create false environments that are not authentic.

The Value of Questions and Storytelling

The precatechumenate is about questions and about stories. Usually, inquirers come with more questions than stories, until they realize they have permission to tell their story. Then the stories come.

Stories are our basic mode of communication with each other. When we want to share something of our self, when we want to understand someone, when we want to include others, we begin to tell and listen to stories. Storytelling is a language of self-disclosure.

Real storytelling happens best when there is a caring and trusting environment, when people do not have to fear being judged or evaluated because of their story. Then they can tell stories—simple ones, significant ones, transformative ones, funny ones. When people begin to tell stories about their lives, they also begin to discover questions about their lives.

Most of the questions that inquirers come with are either profound life-questions (e.g., Why is there suffering?) or questions of interest (e.g., Why do Catholics light candles in front of statues of saints? Isn't that idolatry?). During the experience of storytelling, new types of questions often emerge: personal questions (What do I really want?), questions of truth (How do I really discover who I am?), questions of value (What is really important in my life?), questions of responsibility (What am I choosing to do with my life?). Storytelling becomes one way of helping people to ask better questions about themselves and others and their relationships.

In dialogue with the stories the inquirers bring, the period of the precatechumenate is also filled with the stories of the community: the stories told by team members and sponsors, the stories of the parish community, the stories of Jesus and his followers, other stories from the Hebrew and Christian scriptures, the stories of men and women in the Catholic community who led inspiring lives (saints) . . . and more stories. When we begin to tell stories, others begin to tell stories. When we begin to move to another level of storytelling that raises questions of meaning, others join us in the search.

Naming the Experiences

The precatechumenate, though, is more than a discussion club. We raise stories, we ask and answer questions so that we can begin to name them, so we can begin to look at all of them from a new perspective, from a new vantage. The precatechumenate is the beginning of helping inquirers experience that in their life stories—the ordinary and extraordinary, the painful and the joyful, the calm and the stormy—are those places where we can come to meet and know God. It is the beginning of recognizing the stirrings of God within our human lives and relationships.

Initial Faith in Christ and Initial Conversion

And not only do we begin to name God in our experience, but we begin to name a call from God within our experience. We give inquirers the opportunity to explore their life within a new frame of reference: the story of Jesus. And from this, they may feel drawn, compelled, invited. Questions may be answered, but usually a deeper longing begins to become more apparent. "I came here because I wanted to become Catholic to marry my fiancée. But something has happened. I can't explain it. There is something more in all of this. I want to find out what it means for me."

The precatechumenate helps the inquirers establish and name a relationship with God— and not just any relationship with any God, but a loving relationship with the God revealed most fully in Jesus and proclaimed within the Catholic Christian community.

Some inquirers will be ready to tell stories. Others will have good questions. Others will have an established love relationship with God. All of them, in different ways, will need to come to a point where they can say, "Being in the Catholic community does make a difference in my life." Not that they can articulate the difference at this time. Rather, it's an inkling, a stirring, a dim light. But it is nonetheless a conviction.

And being in the Catholic community means being in relationship with God as revealed in Jesus. Again, the meaning of this may be very simple. But it is real. And it is worth committing oneself to. It is worth saying yes to the gospel of Jesus proclaimed in the Catholic community.

The period of precatechumenate—a period of evangelization—is about facilitating the possibility of this initial conversion. It is helping people name their current reality (the story of their lives), their possibility (God's desire for them), and the movement to allow all of this to emerge (responsibility).

During the precatechumenate, we are helping the inquirers to begin to develop a heightened sensitivity to the depth dimension of human experience by enabling them to create a space in which they can trust that experience, name that experience, tell that experience, and then dialogue that experience with our Catholic Christian tradition. The period of the precatechumenate takes storytelling very seriously.

Pastoral Assessment

As we mentioned earlier, people come to our community for a variety of reasons and due to a variety of influences: a Catholic spouse or future spouse, the influence of other Catholic people, a search for community and relationships, a feeling of emptiness, a desire to start a new life, the response to evangelization, a death in the family, a feeling of guilt for past deeds, and so on. More often than not, however, the reasons for staying change radically as the individuals begin to allow the healing hand of God to emerge for them within this community.

Each person's needs and concerns will be different. And each will come with a very different background. Hence, the process of formation, while respecting the basic steps and periods of the *Rite of Christian Initiation of Adults,* will still be structured in such a way as to respect those differences. Someone who has had very little exposure to the Catholic community and is unbaptized will probably enter a more extensive process than someone from another Christian denomination who can name explicit calls from God for deepened conversion.

One way to assess the needs of the inquirer, as well as helping the catechetical teams best serve the inquirers, is through pastoral assessment. Pastoral assessments are an important dimension of the pastoral formation in the initiation process. Not only do they help everyone involved to get a better picture of the inquirer's particular situation and needs, but they also force us (i.e., those of us responsible for initiation) to create newer and better models of initiation formation to respond to those various needs. One set program just will not do.

What is pastoral assessment? It is an early step in the discernment process. As the term "assessment" implies, it is a review of one's experience and particular needs in order best to respond to them. It is not a test, nor a prerequisite list of qualities that are acceptable before entering into the initiation process.

The other side of the coin is the pastoral side, i.e., how the community can best respond to those needs in a way that fosters an awareness of God's abiding presence. Pastoral assessment is an exploration of one's life within the context of God's saving love and of the ways a community of faith can best repond to the individual.

The shape of such a pastoral assessment will differ in each situation. However, the basic model is one of conversation—we invite someone to explore the basic terrain of his or her life, and the pastoral care giver is there to help highlight and raise to awareness the fingerprint of God. The task of the care giver is not to "tell" someone what he or she is experiencing or needs. Rather, this is a shared conversation that is intent on discovering together those needs. Such a model presumes a great deal of respect for the individual.

While pastoral assessment needs to be continuing throughout the initiation process, a significant time for such conversation is during the initial meetings with the new inquirers. The initial conversation often sets the tone for the inquirer for quite some time. If the individual felt welcomed and cared for during the conversation, he or she will be more willing to invest time seeking this community.

The *Rite of Christian Initiation of Adults* does not provide any guidance for the initial conversations before a person becomes part of the precatechumenate. Instead, we need to know the direction of the entire rite to assess an inquirer's background and needs regarding initiation.

Some people find it helpful to have a form to record all the information. If that is the case, fine—but do not give the form to the inquirer to fill out. And, preferably, do not have the form during any of the conversations with the inquirer. Instead, consider keeping the form in the office and make some notes during the conversation. Then transfer the information later. Completing forms gives people the image of an application process—far removed from evangelization and hospitality.

What are the issues that need to be explored during the initial conversations? The following items would help the inquirer and the pastoral care giver assess the initiation needs of the inquirer:

Personal information
• Legal name and address
• Daytime and evening phone
• Current employment
• Interests and hobbies

Family information
• Current family situation
• Any previous marriages
• Any need for annulments

Religious background
• Understanding and images of God
• Religious experiences
• Sacred places, objects, events in his or her life
• Prayer

Religious affiliation background
• Baptism in any Christian community?
• If baptized, by water in the name of the Trinity?
• Religious rituals or ceremonies in any religious group?
• Experience of the Christian community, if any.
• Experience of the Catholic community, if any.
• Experience of this parish community, if any.
• Any affiliations with religious organizations or groups

Current situation
• What brings the person to your community now?
• Does the person know anyone from the community?
• What is the person looking for from this community?
• What is the person looking for in life?
• What are any specific concerns the person has at this time?

Multiple Conversations

The listing above is suggestive, not exhaustive. Nor is it meant to be used to grill the inquirer. Rather, the pastoral minister keeps these questions and concerns in mind as a backdrop for the conversations with the prospective inquirer. Then, as the conversation emerges, the pastoral minister can guide and direct it around these issues. Obviously, all these issues will not emerge in the first conversation, nor should they.

Probably the first conversation will establish an initial rapport between the inquirer and the pastoral care giver and reveal some basic information. Building on that rapport, several subsequent conversations will probably help both the inquirer and the pastoral care giver get a clearer picture of the inquirer's situation and needs. This should happen before inviting the inquirer to the precatechumenate.

Responding to the Inquirer

Besides responding to the inquirer's actual requests for information, these initial conversations provide a good opportunity for the pastoral care giver to explain the initiation process that the parish can provide for the inquirer.

Because each inquirer's needs will be different, there must be some flexibility to the initiation process that still respects the foundations of initiation (e.g., we fully initiate at the Easter Vigil). If someone from the Episcopal Church seeks to join the Catholic Church, the direction and form of that person's formation will differ from that of someone who has no religious affiliation at all.

The specifics of the initiation process will emerge during the next months with the inquirer. But now is a good time to explain the various periods and steps and the reasons we move through them as a community. Providing some resources for the inquirer at this point might be helpful.

Liturgy Training Publications (1800 North Hermitage Avenue, Chicago, IL 60622-1101) has published a handy pamphlet with an overview of the initiation process which can be given to inquirers. Paulist Press (997 Macarthur Boulevard, Mahwah, NJ 07430) has released a video, *Invitation to New Life: The RCIA Described,* that gives a visual overview of the initiation process in non-technical language. Perhaps the pastoral minister and inquirer can watch the video together and then discuss the various periods and stages.

First of Many Conversations

Pastoral assessment will continue throughout the initiation process. At various times, the candidate or catechumen and sponsor—along with someone from the initiation team—will need to step out of the experience and ask questions about what is happening and in what direction they need to go. This becomes especially critical in the discernment process for the various rites.

The initial conversations with inquirers can set an atmosphere and expectation that the future will be filled with such conversations. This will send an important message that initiation is not forms, applications or programs. Rather, Christian initiation is concerned with helping each individual to be faithful to God's call. And it takes time talking together to allow that call to emerge in discernible ways.

At the end of the conversation (or series of conversations), the inquirer can be invited to attend the next precatechumenate gathering. Arrangements can be made to meet the candidate so she or he does not have to come to this new home alone. Sensitivity to the needs of the inquirer in this new environment is important.

FORMING THE PRECATECHUMENATE GROUP

The precatechumenate gatherings seem to work best when they take place in the homes of people from the parish. The team and pastoral staff will need to know the location, day, and time of gatherings. The size and style of the group will change as people move in and out of the precatechumenate. However, it is advisable that the group not get too large or else it will be difficult to foster an environment for sharing and discussion. If there are several inquirers, a parish may choose to have many precatechumenate groups meeting at different times to accommodate the needs of the inquirers. The various small groups could come together periodically to touch base with each other. Another format could be to rotate the location of the gatherings every few weeks. Except in the situation when there are only one or two inquirers, it is not a good idea to separate the inquirers into individual households (one-on-one). The sense of community, however basic and primitive at this point, established in the homes helps the inquirers to develop a sense of trust and affiliation.

If we are meeting with prospective inquirers regularly, and we provide an ongoing precatechumenate, then doesn't this simply get out of hand? It doesn't have to. A principle about group dynamics is that the group changes whenever anyone enters or leaves the group. A second principle is that the group returns to square one and starts to rebuild itself. A third principle is that a healthy group can assimilate new members effectively and move to a level of interaction comparable with the group's status before the change; an unhealthy group will either alienate the new persons or focus exclusively on them to the neglect of the others. These few principles need to be kept in mind when working with the precatechumenate because of its fluid nature.

Here is one possible strategy to respond to this situation. Whenever someone comes to the community for initiation, invite him or her to the initial conversation (or multiple conversations). Designate one date a month (presuming the precatechumenate meets weekly) to integrate new members into the precatechumenate. Continue to meet one-on-one with the inquirer until he or she is ready to move to the inquiry group (and the date has come) and then arrange to bring this person to the inquiry group; don't simply send the person. The group leader welcomes the new inquirer and a brief set of introductions takes place, followed by a non-threatening activity to start the integration process. The group leader is sensitive to when the discussion leaves the new person out of the loop (e.g., something discussed last week) and invites some-one else from the group to help bring the person on board through an explana-tion or in some other manner. Because of the open-ended nature of the precatechumenate, there is no need to return to earlier sessions. Rather, keep attentive to the needs of the group and its direction. Eventually issues already discussed will reemerge—but by then many of the inquirers will have moved to the catechumenate, while others will remain.

CATECHESIS DURING THE PRECATECHUMENATE

The informal catechesis of the period of the precatechumenate is informed by what was said earlier: the directive of *RCIA,* n. 36 and the expec-tations for celebrating the rite of acceptance. Following are some tools that have been used effectively in precatechumenate gatherings to attend to these catechetical issues.

Biography Sharing: Encourage all present to share something about themselves and their lives. As new people join the group, it helps for all briefly to go around again and introduce themselves. Usually, each time the group tells something about themselves, new and unique dimensions emerge.

Journaling: Early on, the inquirers can be given a journal or notebook and encouraged to begin a journaling process that could include reflections gleaned from the gatherings, new questions, their history, their hopes, and so on. Journal keeping is different from diary writing. The latter is usually a record of events. Journaling attempts to move to a level of meaning and inter-pretation of experiences. Basic journaling skills and techniques could be given to the inquirers.

Life Map: In order to help inquirers situate their present search within the larger context of their life, one journaling technique is the life map. We ask the inquirers to think of major transition points in their life (perhaps ten or twelve), beginning with their birth and ending with the present moment. These marker events can be drawn as if they were a road, indicating the highs and lows of the events and the periods between them. These serve as possibilities for discussion. Throughout the initiation process, they can be encouraged to fill in the details of this map.

Church Tour: Art, architecture, and sacred space have always served the community in a variety of capacities. One service has been catechetical. We can discuss the life of both the local community and the larger Church during a church tour. Spending time with the pictures, statues, windows, carvings, and so on, are all ways of basic instruction. Bring the inquirers to the sacristy, show them vestments and vessels. Open the reconciliation room. Bring them into the sanctuary and show them the altar. Help them feel at home.

Parish History: Parishes preserve their history in a variety of ways: photos, anniversary journals, booklets. Spend time discussing the life and growth of the parish, indicating some unique features of this particular parish community.

Parishioners: Invite members of the community to visit with the inquirers. Have a cross-section of people: old, young, involved in organizations, and so on. Ask them to spend a few minutes sharing who they are and why they are part of this parish. Allow the inquirers to ask questions about life in the parish.

Liturgical Year: There are some beautiful liturgical calendars published that are relatively inexpensive. Have one available to show the inquirers the various seasons and movements in the life of the community as indicated on the liturgical calendar: feasts, Ordinary Time, Advent, Lent. Talking about these seasons and the various colors of the liturgical year is a good way of telling some of the stories of our faith.

Symbol-Making: Provide opportunities to help inquirers name and discuss basic life symbols as well as personal symbols. Perhaps those who would rather not write in their journal could draw or describe a symbol that captures the day's experience for them. These symbols, followed in sequence, can begin to tell the story of the inquirer during this period of life.

Open-Ended Sentences: These are usually good for discussion. Provide a sheet with a series of opening phrases of a sentence, and allow the inquirers to have time to respond to them. The sentences could be constructed in response to the issues raised in the previous gathering.

Some examples:

My greatest hope…
I'm here because…
When I think of death…
What I really want…
To love…

Photo Stories: Whenever people show family photos, immediately they begin to tell stories. Encourage people to bring in a few photos—perhaps of different periods of their life. This is also a good opportunity to show photos of people and places in the Catholic tradition.

Storytelling: Of course, this is going on all the time throughout the precatechumenate gatherings. As people begin to tell their stories, the team can also begin to tell the stories of the Catholic community.

Telling the Jesus Story: Throughout the precatechumenate, it will be important to tell the story of Jesus, stories of the Hebrew and early Christian communities, and the story of the Catholic Christian community again and again. This will be most effective when coordinated with the questions and concerns of the inquirers.

Current Events: An important part of the journey of faith is to be able to recognize the movement of God in the ordinariness of life. Encourage inquirers to bring in news clippings to discuss with the group: What's happening? How am I affected by this? How is God present in this? How can I respond? How do we respond? The team may also want to keep abreast of news that would have a particular interest for the inquirers—things they have talked about, newsworthy events in the Catholic community, items or concerns that call us to prayer.

Scripture: Inquirers need to see the Bible—to recognize its basic structure, how it is broken down into a variety of books, and so on. This can be done very informally. Include a story or passage from the scriptures at each gathering and let them know where it came from. Some of the inquirers from other Christian denominations will have questions about the so-called Catholic books of the Bible.

Written Questions: At the end of each gathering, the inquirers can be encouraged to spend a few moments, and each can write at least one specific question he or she has about what they discussed, or Catholic life. The team can review the questions and use them to help prepare for the next gathering.

Prayer: Regularly the inquirers need to be invited into experiences of prayer. Variety of prayer forms can be used to accommodate the needs and differences of the inquirers. This is a good time to use simple and spontaneous prayer with them, leading them into an awareness of prayer of petition and thanksgiving.

These are only a few examples of the variety of tools the team can use to help facilitate an initial awareness of God's ongoing conversion in the inquirer's life. At the end of each gathering, the catechists meet to review the issues raised during the gathering. Based on this reflection, the catechists begin to plan the next gathering.

HOSPITALITY

Throughout the Judeo-Christian tradition, hospitality has always been a central and key virtue. It is welcoming the guest in the name of God. For the Jew and Christian, all men and women are God's children and are due the respect and dignity of such an ennobled people. In recent times, we have seen the diminishment of this important dimension of community life. The precatechumenate provides a good opportunity for a parish community to begin to grow in its awareness of the responsibility of hospitality.

People will choose to respond to God's call to fuller life in the Catholic Christian life when they encounter members of the community who welcome them and willingly share with them the good word of God's presence in the community. Hospitality becomes the first word of welcome for the inquirer.

Various parish organizations can help with hospitality throughout the catechumenate process. With some coordination, a different parish group or organization can provide refreshments for the various gatherings. Someone from the parish could provide child care during sessions. Transportation can be made available. Invitations to various parish functions, as well as to parishioners' homes, can be extended. The possibilities are endless. The effect is powerful.

Focusing catechesis on the needs and questions of the inquirers is another expression of hospitality. The message becomes clear: We are here to care and support you, to welcome you, to answer your questions (rather than this is what we want from you).

SPONSORS

As the inquirers continue to gather in the precatechumenate households, the coordinator of sponsors—in dialogue with the team—can begin to discern how best the inquirer can experience sponsorship. Each inquirer will have different needs. Spending time listening informally at gatherings will help to select a sponsor for the inquirer who can be a helpful companion. Sponsors can begin to gather occasionally at precatechumenate gatherings. Or perhaps having a social with all the inquirers and sponsors on a periodic basis will give people a chance to meet and get an initial sense of each other. Try to avoid having sponsor and inquirer meet for the first time when they are matched for the remainder of the process. With a minimum of effort, the sponsors can become known to the inquirers before decisions are made.

The sponsor's role at this period of formation is very informal. As the decision for a deepened commitment to the process approaches, the sponsor begins to take a more active role in the life of the inquirer. By the time the inquirer celebrates the rite of acceptance into the order of catechumens, the inquirer and sponsor should have had ample time to know each other and to have the beginnings of a trusting relationship.

TIME LINE

This period of the *Rite of Christian Initiation of Adults* is of unlimited duration. This is the time to look around and see what Catholic life is all about.

But it is also the time to stop and listen to what God is asking of the inquirer. Some people will be ready to move to a new level of involvement and commitment. Others will want to gaze and explore for a longer period of time. There is no need to rush, there is no hurry. As long as someone is interested and has basic questions, then the members of the precatechumenate team make themselves available and offer gracious hospitality. Sometimes a person may discern that this particular parish community—or this particular Christian denomination—is not the right place for them. Our response is one of continued support and blessing, encouraging them that they will find their heart's desire. Others will determine that this is the place they can come to know God more deeply. They will ask to join us, to seek their true hope and joy within our community. To them, we also extend our support and blessing. We welcome them into our family—the family of our parish and of the Catholic community.

DISCERNING READINESS FOR THE RITE OF ACCEPTANCE

There is a popular axiom to describe the initiation process, and it applies especially to the period of the precatechumenate: "How long does it take? As long as it takes!" When do we know when "as long as it takes" has happened? In other words, how do we know when it is appropriate to celebrate the rite of acceptance?

The decision to celebrate the rite of acceptance is a mutual decision between the inquirer and the community. This is another opportunity for pastoral assessment and discernment that includes not only the inquirer but pastoral leadership, the team and sponsors. Ultimately, the decision to choose to commit oneself to the gospel within this Catholic community is made by the inquirer. This decision, however, needs to be supported by the community. That is why it is a two-sided discernment.

The discernment to celebrate the rite needs to happen weeks before the scheduled celebration (presuming model three and multiple celebrations of the rite of acceptance). The team and sponsors aid in this discernment process by reflecting back to the inquirer his or her growth in consciousness and change in lifestyle because of the initial exposure to the gospel within the Catholic tradition. The rite suggests some of the "indicators" that help us in this discernment of initial conversion (*RCIA*, n. 42):

Evidence of first faith: Does the individual have a desire to be in relationship with God? Does he or she want to discover more to life?

Initial conversion: Has the individual begun to recognize that his or her life will change because of God? Have there been any preliminary changes and adjustments in the individual's life, attitudes, or actions because of what he or she has experienced to date?

Intent to change one's life: Does the individual desire to leave behind all that is inauthentic? Does he or she desire to live life fully, whatever the cost?

Intent to enter into relationship with God in Christ: Does the individual desire to follow the way of Christ in the gospel? Is he or she able to embrace the demands of the gospel willingly, at least as much as he or she knows of them now?

First stirrings of repentance: Does the individual recognize that there are areas of his or her life that are wounded and broken? Has he or she begun to accept responsibility for areas of failings in his or her own life?

Beginnings of the practice of prayer: Has the individual begun to pray outside of the gatherings? Does he or she recognize that prayer is an essential dimension of Christian life?

Sense of Church: Has the individual had the opportunity to discuss basic issues of the Catholic Church? Does he or she have a basic awareness of the distinctiveness of the Catholic Church?

Some experience of the community: Has the individual expressed an interest in getting to know more about the parish, especially through participation in parish activities? Has he or she had the opportunity to meet and spend time with members of the parish?

What happens if we don't agree at the end of the discernment? Then the discernment is not over. One of the fruits of discernment is either congruence (i.e., we come to a similar response that is in keeping with the values of the reign of God) or peace in a decision (i.e., one may not totally agree with the decision, but it is clear that a good process has been entered into and therefore can accept the decision without feeling violated). It might be helpful to review the discernment process (see Chapter 13 of this resource). And perhaps we need to review if we are being reasonable with our expectations or if we are placing demands on the inquirer that are inappropriate. Entering this discernment in community helps eliminate such unreasonable expectations.

If the parish has an ongoing precatechumenate, celebrates the rite of acceptance more than once a year, and provides an environment of pastoral care to assist inquirers discover God's call to new life—then this will not be much of a problem because the inquirer has come to trust the community and is willing to extend his or her time in the precatechumenate because of the care provided.

ADAPTATION WITH CHILDREN OF CATECHETICAL AGE

Part II, chapter 1 does not address the precatechumenate, so we can presume the normative vision of part I for children of catechetical age. All of what was said in this chapter applies to children, simply accommodated to the age and needs of children.

Consider adjusting the precatechumenate to be family-based rather than child-based. Include the family in the pastoral assessments. Avoid predetermining the length of the precatechumenate based on a pre-conceived idea of the initiation calendar (e.g., some parishes require a one-year precatechumenate for all children, which does not have support from the rite) but allow children to develop and grow in their own time and respond accordingly.

It is important to note again the importance the rite gives to the companions and parents (family) of the children (see *RCIA,* n. 254). Both need to be involved in the initiation process right from the very beginning.

ADAPTATION WITH BAPTIZED CANDIDATES

Part II of the ritual text does not explicitly suggest immersion in the period of the precatechumenate for baptized candidates. Presumably, they have already responded to the call of God (evangelization) and entered the way of faith (conversion). Pastoral experience, of course, recognizes that the extent of such a response varies from person to person.

Gathering with the inquirers during the precatechumenate may be helpful for the baptized candidates as long as it is clear to them and everyone else their status as baptized persons. Some may need an extended time in the precatechumenate because of various factors: little exposure to the Christian message, little exposure to Christian community and the like. Others will need a short time—if any—due to their religious life; they are ready to celebrate the rite of welcome. Here, as with the unbaptized, entering into pastoral assessment early on to help determine how best the community can support the journey of faith of the individual is critical. And here, as throughout the initiation process, we need to be careful to accommodate appropriately lest we send the wrong message to the individual and the community (e.g., Everyone has to do the same thing; This is not important, so we'll just move you through). The rite of welcoming candidates (part II, chapter 4A) provides the context for understanding if and when one enters the precatechumenate and for how long (similar to the method of discernment in the precatechumenate with the unbaptized using the rite of acceptance).

6

First Step: Rite of Acceptance into the Order of Catechumens

INTRODUCTION

We always celebrate important moments in life. That is why the entire ritual process of Christian initiation prescribes a series of ritual celebrations to mark the conversion journey of catechumens. These ritual celebrations are at the heart of the whole initiation process. We need to care for these rites and celebrate them well if they are to nourish the catechumens and the whole assembly.

The first of the public rituals celebrated in the *Rite of Christian Initiation of Adults* is the rite of acceptance into the order of catechumens. After an

Rite of Acceptance into the Order of Catechumens					
	UNBAPTIZED ADULT	CHILDREN OF CATECHETICAL AGE	BAPTIZED, UNCATECHIZED CATHOLIC	BAPTIZED, UNCATECHIZED CHRISTIAN	BAPTIZED, CATECHIZED CHRISTIAN
Reference	*RCIA*, nos. 42–74	*RCIA*, nos. 260–276	*RCIA*, nos. 405, 407–408; 411–433	*RCIA*, nos. 407–408; 411–433	*RCIA*, nos. 478, 411–433; (NB: *RCIA*, n. 473)
Rite	Rite of Acceptance into the Order of Catechumens	Rite of Acceptance into the Order of Catechumens	Rite of Welcoming the Candidates	Rite of Welcoming the Candidates	Rite of Welcoming the Candidates (adapted)
Combined Rite	Celebration of the Rite of Acceptance into the Order of Catechumens and of the Rite of Welcoming Baptized but Previously Uncatechized Adults Who Are Preparing for Confirmation and/or Eucharist or Reception into the Full Communion of the Catholic Church				
Required	Yes	Yes	Recommended	Recommended	If helpful, recommended
Time	2 or 3 times a year (*RCIA*, n. 18)	2 or 3 times a year (*RCIA*, n. 18)	2 or 3 times a year or as needed (*RCIA*, n. 414)	2 or 3 times a year or as needed (*RCIA*, n. 414)	If helpful, as needed

appropriate period of inquiry during the precatechumenate, the inquirers now publicly declare their intention to continue their journey of faith toward full initiation in the Catholic Church. The entire community, represented by the sponsors and the assembly, offers its support and witness to these women and men.

WHAT DOES THE RITE SAY?

Read RCIA, *n. 41.*

The rite of acceptance into the order of catechumens is the first of the public rites celebrated in the *Rite of Christian Initiation of Adults.* During this important ritual, the inquirers publicly declare their intention to continue their journey toward full initiation in the Catholic Church, and the community accepts them, offering its support and witness during the journey.

Read RCIA, *n. 42.*

In rather vague and broad language (presumably to be adapted for various circumstances), the ritual text defines what is required for an inquirer to make this first step: the beginnings of the spiritual life and the fundamentals of Christian teaching have taken root. The formation of the period of the precatechumenate, as discussed in Chapter 5 of this resource, should provide for this. This section then lists the various indicators that would suggest that the earlier directive has been accomplished. Recall that this resource recommended these indicators for the discernment for readiness to celebrate the rite of acceptance.

The closing sentence notes the appropriate instruction to the candidates for the rite. The long-term preparation for the rite has already happened throughout the precatechumenate. We will discuss strategies below for the immediate preparation and the reflection back on the experience that honors the insights of liturgical catechesis noted in Chapter 2 of this resource.

Read RCIA, *n. 43.*

This section affirms the importance of communal discernment for the celebration of this rite. Furthermore, it notes the importance of not repeating baptism (something that will need to be determined before the celebration of this rite, usually during the initial pastoral assessment conversation).

Read RCIA, *n. 44.*

We celebrate the rite at various times during the year depending on need and local conditions. One of the significant "local conditions" is the liturgical year as celebrated in the community. In Chapter 2 in this resource we discussed reasons why we celebrate this rite outside the major liturgical seasons of the Church calendar. The text also references *RCIA*, n. 18 and the guidelines provided for celebrating the rite of acceptance:

(1) celebrate only after we have discerned the demands of *RCIA*, n. 42;

(2) celebrate when there are enough people to make it feasible (by

inference, though, we do not skip the rite because there is only one person; in that case—with no one else expected for a while—we celebrate the rite);

(3) determine 2 or 3 dates ahead of time for the usual celebration of the rite.

This section also notes some options that may be incorporated into the rite, depending on the decision of the conference of bishops. Recall that in *RCIA*, nos. 33.2, 33.4, and 33.5, the U.S. bishops decided:

(1) inclusion of a first exorcism and renunciation of false worship only at the discretion of the local bishop, not a national practice (*RCIA*, n. 33.2);

(2) no new name is to be given as a national practice, while leaving it to the discretion of the local bishop (*RCIA*, n. 33.4);

(3) inclusion of an optional presentation of a cross as a national practice, while leaving any other practices to the discretion of the local bishop (*RCIA*, n. 33.5).

Read RCIA, *n. 45.*

This section highlights the importance of the baptized community in the celebration of this rite, and the various ministries appropriate to its celebration. Presumably, considering this and everything else said about the central role of the liturgical assembly, we celebrate this rite at the Sunday eucharist.

Read RCIA, *n. 46.*

The ritual text reminds pastoral leadership to include the names of the new catechumens and their sponsors, along with the information about the rite (date, presiding minister) in the registry of the catechumens, as directed in canon 788§1 of the *Code of Canon Law*. This book should be kept in a secure place, along with other registries such as the baptismal registry.

Read RCIA, *n. 47.*

This section reminds us that catechumens are now members of the Church, although not fully initiated members (see *CIC*, canon 206). Therefore, they should be actively involved in the liturgical prayer of the Church (as will be outlined in Chapter 7 of this resource). If a catechumen marries before full initiation, the appropriate rites from the order of celebrating Christian marriage are used (see *NS*, n. 10). Similarly, if a catechumen dies, he or she is to be considered a member of the Christian faithful (see *CIC*, canon 1183; *NS*, nos. 8-9).

IMMEDIATE PREPARATION FOR CELEBRATING THE RITE OF ACCEPTANCE

In Chapter 5, we discussed the appropriate discernment for celebrating this rite. As the day draws closer to the actual celebration, there will need to be various forms of immediate preparation for the celebration.

Day of Prayer

It seems appropriate that part of the immediate preparation for celebrating the rite of acceptance include a day of prayer and reflection for the candidates and their sponsors (with anyone else from the parish community who wants to join with them).

Once the decision has been made to enter the period of the catechumenate, let the inquirers and sponsors know the date and time of the reflection gathering. The Saturday morning before the celebration of the rite is a good time. Following the period of reflection, there can be a review of the ritual with the sponsors. If it is Saturday morning, the initiation team can ask members of the hospitality team to prepare a breakfast for those gathered.

There can be a variety of components to the reflection gathering. Following are a few suggestions of elements that one can include in such a gathering:

Periods of Private and Communal Prayer: We can so construct the gathering as to include communal prayer experiences (such as an adaptation of the Liturgy of the Hours, or a guided meditation in common) and private prayer time (a significant period of quiet time needs to be part of the time together).

Proclamation of Scripture: Texts can be chosen that highlight the importance of the rite of acceptance and God's call. The texts prescribed for the rite itself (*RCIA,* n. 62) are especially good. Since most people celebrate the rite on Sunday, and the Sunday lectionary texts are therefore used, the candidates will not hear these texts during the rite itself. Their use here can be a helpful preparation for them.

Inquirer and Sponsor Time: We may invite the inquirers and sponsors to pair off and spend time together. We can give reflection questions based on the scripture texts and the rite to them at this time, such as:

— Do you recognize that you need other people to become a full human person?
— Do you recognize a need for Jesus Christ in your life?
— Why do you want to become a member of this parish?
— How have you experienced God in this parish?
— How is your life beginning to change?
— Are you willing to follow the way of life of Jesus?
— Are you willing to accept the challenge of the cross in your life?
— How can you welcome the word of God in your life?
— What is it that you ask of God at this time of your life?
— What do you ask of us as a church?
— What do you need to help you in your journey of faith?

Shared Reflection: Besides the opportunities for sharing with one's sponsor, the inquirers can come together with the rest of the participants for a period of faith sharing. This will help to encourage a sense of community and provide support during this transition period.

Preliminary Preparation for Rite: Before ending the reflection period, the leader of prayer can ask the inquirers if the community can do anything to help them prepare for the rite. There is no need to "walk through" the rite with them—that will only add more to their stress and anxiety levels as they try to remember everything. Rather, let them know about the dynamics (not the specifics) of the rite: this is a ritual of commitment. Let them know that the sponsors will gently lead them through the rite. If they have been meeting with their sponsors for a while, this should not be a problem. If they are just meeting their sponsor for the first time, this will be a problem—and the solution is to incorporate sponsors much earlier in the precatechumenate.

Thank the inquirers for their commitment, and then send them home to prepare for the celebration.

Overview of Rite with Sponsors: After the inquirers have left, the team reviews the rite with the sponsors. A possible model can be:

— Discuss the experience of the reflection day with the sponsors.
— Review the importance of the rite of acceptance.
— Review the role of sponsor during the catechumenate.
— Review the rite, perhaps using a guide sheet for the sponsors.
— "Walk through" the rite with the sponsors in the worship space.

CELEBRATING THE RITE OF ACCEPTANCE

Once the "what" of this celebration is clear, we need to ask: How will we celebrate this rite so it will speak what it wants to communicate? Now it is time to return to the ritual text and begin to prepare the ritual celebration for the parish community.

Often the rites contained in the *Rite of Christian Initiation of Adults* will be celebrated by both unbaptized and baptized candidates, as noted in Chapter 3 of this resource. We will base the following reflections on celebration exclusively on part I of the ritual text (for the unbaptized). Later in the chapter, we will address adaptations with children of catechetical age and baptized candidates.

Receiving the Candidates

The rite says in *RCIA,* n. 48 that the opening of this rite takes place outside the church (or at least inside at the entrance). This is important because this is a transition ritual: people who are not yet members of the community are passing over the threshold (literally) into the community. Once within the community, they will be set apart for a time of formation and preparation.

Thus, it is very important clearly to create this movement of passing over into a new relationship without having to explain it to people.

The directives further say that we have gathered members of the faithful outside with the candidates and their sponsors. It leaves unclear if the remainder of the community stays in the church when the presider goes to meet the candidates. It does note that the assembly of the faithful would sing an appropriate processional piece.

This is why knowing what the rite celebrates is important. As a rite of transition, inclusion and public promise making—by the candidates, sponsors and the assembly of the faithful—it seems more than appropriate (read: necessary) that the assembly of the faithful also gather outside for these introductory movements of this rite.

What might that look like? First, determine the place for the outside part of this rite, a place large enough to accommodate the entire assembly. Some newer churches have included large gathering spaces as foyers that could easily accommodate this. Other parishes will need to go outside to the front entrance or a side walkway. Or even part of the parking lot may have to be cornered off. Second, the parish staff will need to have an outdoor speaker system set up so everyone can hear the dialogue that will happen. Don't trust that people will speak loudly, because they won't.

Then the celebration itself could be something like this: We gather the candidates and sponsors at this gathering place, along with some members of the community (*RCIA*, n. 48). The sponsors provide support to the candidates (it is normal for there to be some anxiety at this time, especially because the candidates are set apart from the community). The sponsors can also inform the candidates that the presider will be asking some basic questions in a few minutes. This will give the candidates a few moments to collect their thoughts. It seems pastorally sensitive to wait to let them know about the questions until just before the celebration. If the candidates know about this questioning process before the celebration, they may focus on this part of the rite instead of on the overall importance of this day.

Meanwhile, the assembly of the faithful has gathered in the church. They would need to be informed of the upcoming ritual (presumably, this is not the first time they are hearing about this celebration) and their important role in this ritual of acceptance. Then we can invite the entire community to go in procession to meet and welcome these inquirers (*RCIA*, n. 48).

Once outside, ministers of hospitality could direct the community to gather around the inquirers, perhaps in a semicircle or even totally surrounding them (a wonderful womb-like image). It is important not to create a "them and us" image but a "them within us" image by where everyone stands. Then entering the prescribed dialogue with some integrity will be possible.

"Wait a minute. They'll never go outside in my parish." Yes, this might be new for many communities. And yes, we can fashion more excuses why they would not go outside than there are people in our parishes. But are these our excuses and not the community's? There will be some people who will not want to go outside, just as there are people who will not go outside for the lighting of the new fire at Easter.

But if we take care to give a context for the rite at the initial gathering of the assembly and the importance of the welcome we will offer, many of the people will be willing to go outside. It takes a simple invitation to join in the welcome.

Greeting

The presider greets the candidates and sponsors (*RCIA,* n. 49). The rite says that the presider recalls for all gathered the particular experience and religious response of the candidates. It seems more appropriate, however, for the presider to invite each sponsor to introduce the candidate she or he is sponsoring and share something about the religious journey that has brought the candidate to this community on this day. This brief testimony by the sponsor helps make explicit—in a ritual setting—the sponsor's role as companion and guide. One by one, the sponsors present the candidates to the community.

It is important that provisions be made so these introductions (and the following conversations) can be heard by the gathered assembly. Use a good, portable sound system. Having this conversation is not helpful if the community cannot hear anything. To do so would ritually minimize the importance and role of the community.

Opening Dialogue

After being introduced in some manner, the presider now invites the candidates to express their desire or intentions. The ritual text is helpful in providing direction for this dialogue (*RCIA,* n. 50). Some parishes choose to adapt the text at this time. Knowing the reason for this dialogue in order to construct an alternative is helpful. The rubrics for *RCIA,* n. 50 say that the purpose of this dialogue is to disclose the catechumens' intentions. Furthermore, it notes that the catechumens may answer in their own words.

Thus a question such as "Marilyn, what is it that you seek at this time of your life?" or "George, what does your heart desire from God?" or similar words can get at the intention/desire issue that, of course, has been the agenda of the precatechumenate. Candidates are not to have rehearsed this dialogue. Candidates know the answers because of the long weeks of inquiry that have led to this celebration. Perhaps the initiation team can focus the conversation between candidates and sponsors during the day of prayer around these ritual questions.

We could then follow the first question by a second, more focused question such as, "And how can this community help you?" or "What do you seek from this community on your journey?"

First Acceptance of the Gospel

Now that the community clearly knows their intentions, the rite moves to a pivotal moment. The presider asks each candidate if he or she is willing to accept the gospel way of life. The affirmations by the candidates complete and clarify their intentions: everything they said in the initial dialogue is now focused through the lens of the gospel way of life.

It is important that we uphold the solemnity of this public promise. Perhaps we could address the opening words of *RCIA,* n. 52 to the group of candidates. Then, one by one, the presider can ask each individual candidate to respond to this question: "Are you ready to accept the gospel way of life?" The community needs to hear the promises being made by the candidates (again, the importance of a good sound system). Perhaps the community can respond in the best way it knows how in ritual settings: through an acclamation of praise.

"Where's the second acceptance of the gospel?" The answer is simple: the celebration of the sacraments of initiation.

Affirmation by Sponsors and the Assembly

The promise-making in this rite is not one-sided. The assembly and sponsors then make explicit their intention to support these candidates in the formation process over the next months and years. Since the community is gathered, the presider could ask the question in *RCIA,* n. 53 twice (appropriately adapted): once to the sponsors who will serve as companion-guides, and then again to the larger assembly who will witness to the gospel way of life for the candidates. Again we could sing an acclamation of praise after the promise-making. Now the entire assembly is responsible for the candidates.

This promise-making is completed with a prayer of thanksgiving for the gift of these candidates. Again, the community responds in an acclamation of praise. Now the community is different. Something new has happened. A new set of relationships has been established. It is important that the space, gestures, movements, and sounds (and the ability to hear and see all of the above) clearly indicate a shift in relationship. This shift in relationship is the reason it is crucial for the assembly to "shift," go to and gather around the candidates and hear their story.

It is at this point that many parishes adapt the rite. The first choice is usually to move the rite into the church. This will allow a more expansive signing of the senses. This adaptation affords the assembly with a greater role in the rite.

Another possible choice is to continue with the Liturgy of the Word at this point and resume with signing of the senses after the homily. Supporters of this adaptation emphasize the importance of ritual action and response flowing from the proclamation of the Word. As with any of the adaptations, it is very important to know the why of the adaptation.

To assist with a pastoral implementation of the rite, we will choose the adaptation of proceeding into the body of the church for the continuation of this part of the rite, leaving the Liturgy of the Word to its prescribed place in the ritual text.

Procession into the Church

Using the instruction and text of *RCIA,* n. 60, the presider invites the catechumens to the celebration of the Word. The presider might adapt the text to say something such as, "We have heard your desire to follow the way of the Lord Jesus, and you have heard our promise to support you in that journey. Come, join with us now at the table of God's Word where together we will be formed as disciples of the Lord Jesus."

In song and procession, led by the cross, the entire assembly moves from outside to the inside—a movement that is not lost on the newly welcomed catechumens. The catechumens take their seats within the assembly alongside their sponsors.

Signing of the Candidates with the Cross

After the procession, the presider can invite the assembly into the next part of the rite with one of the introductions (or adaptation) found in *RCIA,* n. 55A or B. If the assembly has made the move into the church, the sponsors can then lead the catechumens to the place of this rite. This is a good time to use the entire worship space and not limit the signing of the senses to the sanctuary area. Space the catechumens and sponsors throughout the church—down the aisles and across the front. Not only will this help the assembly to see the ritual action, it will also give them a chance to get more involved.

Sponsors face the catechumens and continue to offer signs of physical support such as holding their hands or arms. The presider continues with the first invocation, "Receive the cross on your forehead..." During this proclamation, the sponsor slowly and reverently marks the forehead of the catechumen with the cross.

The sponsor needs to use full gestures: with an open hand, the sponsor marks the forehead using the palm of the hand in a large and deliberate fashion. Remind sponsors that while it may feel a bit awkward to use such large gestures, it allows the assembly to see the gestures and allows the catechumen truly to feel the gestures. Help sponsors fight the urge to make the signings with their thumbs. After the presider makes the invocation, the community can sing an antiphon as recommended in the ritual text.

Signing of the Other Senses

The rite continues with the option of signing the other senses of the body. If we are trying to impress on the catechumens (and the assembly) the importance of the cross as a sign of this way of life, then we need to be lavish with our use of the cross. Furthermore, the extension of the signings to the other senses sends an important message about the sacredness of the full person, the whole body, and the proclamation that Christ makes a claim on the full person. Catholics celebrate the sacredness of the body by marking it in this ritual fashion with the cross. This is just one of the reasons why it is important that the sponsors and the catechumens have developed relationships over the period of the precatechumenate. Otherwise, they can experience this ritual gesture as invasive.

The presider continues with the invocations listed in *RCIA,* n. 56, pacing the invocations to give sponsors time slowly and deliberately to mark the part of the body named, followed by the community's response in acclamation. Following the last signing—the signing of the feet (and sponsors need to get down on the floor and sign the feet)—the presider then prays a summary invocation: "I sign you with the sign of eternal life..." During this summary the sponsor can stand back and sign the full body of the catechumen.

Some communities present the catechumens with a cross at the end of this part of the rite. Wooden crosses on leather cords are popular choices for this option. The ritual text does mention this possibility (see *RCIA,* n. 64) and ritual planners need carefully to consider this adaptation. The power here is in the actual signing of the body with the cross, not in giving a cross to someone. This part of the rite concludes with the prayer (or its adaptation) found in *RCIA,* n. 57.

As with all the rites of the initiation process, care needs to be taken to include the assembly in active ways throughout the rite. This can be done in several ways during this part of the rite. We have already mentioned the positioning of the catechumens and sponsors within the assembly and the repeated acclamations during the signing of the senses. Some other possibilities to consider: inviting people from within the assembly also to sign the catechumens during the signings or inviting the assembly to extend hands in prayer during the concluding prayer. Again, ritual planners will need to ask why they are making these adaptations and what they are communicating to the assembly. We should not include token gestures. Nor should we clutter the ritual with numerous auxiliary gestures. Plan and choose wisely to allow the ritual action to speak on its own.

Liturgy of the Word

Instruction

The rite prescribes a short exhortation by the presider to the catechumens on the dignity of the Word of God, especially as proclaimed and heard in the liturgical assembly (*RCIA*, n. 61). The manner and content of this exhortation needs to embody the very dignity to which it is pointing. In other words, casual comments about the Word of God seem inconsistent in this highly charged liturgical experience. Prepare the text beforehand to avoid the appearance of this exhortation as a casual after-thought in the ritual. The text can be as simple as: "My friends, now that you have gathered with us as a community, we desire to break open with you the rich fare of God's Word. In the proclamation and reception of this sacred Word, we experience the true and real presence of Christ in our midst. We invite you to this feast." If the presider gives a similar exhortation weekly to the catechumens, the catechumens will indeed know Christ present in Word in this community.

The rite continues with the suggestion that the lectionary or a Bible be carried in procession and placed at the ambo. This directive makes sense only if the entire assembly started this rite outside and have now just gathered at the table of the Word. Most probably, the community gathered before meeting the candidates outside—and at that time, the lectionary was carried in procession and enthroned. The specifics of the celebration will determine when the lectionary is enthroned. The key here is that the book be given some prominence.

Readings

Normally, we celebrate the rite of acceptance on Sunday with the community gathered. Whenever we celebrate it on Sunday, we use the readings from the lectionary of the current liturgical season or cycle assigned for that Sunday rather than the lectionary texts assigned for the rite (*RCIA*, n. 62). The texts noted in *RCIA*, n. 62, however, provide both a foundation and a vision for preparing for the rite with the catechumens.

As mentioned earlier, it is crucial that the celebration of the Liturgy of the Word be done with grace and dignity. Lectors should truly proclaim the texts (as should be the custom every week). It is imperative that the parish community provide whatever resources are needed for lectors to proclaim the scriptures with integrity and with a style that befits the importance of the event.

Homily

Authentic preaching then enriches such fulsome proclamation of the scriptures as directed in *RCIA*, n. 63.

Presentation of a Bible

In a bracketed section (indicating that this is an optional part of the rite), the rite provides for the possibility of presenting catechumens with a book of the gospels and/or a cross (*RCIA*, n. 64). The cross option was discussed earlier in relation to *RCIA*, nos. 56-57 (and, if one is to be given, it seems appropriate to give the cross then).

The practice around the presentation of the book of the gospels varies. The key point to remember is that it is optional. This is key because the rite places priority on the reception of the Word of God within the context of the celebration of the Liturgy of the Word. A physical, tangible collection of scripture readings is a useful and important gift. But it is secondary to the actual experience of the Word in the community. The same is true for the marking with the cross. Some parishes present the catechumens with an opened Bible that the catechumens can keep. This can be confusing if the scriptures have already been a part of their formation (which presumably it has in the period of the precatechumenate). Others present the lectionary since this is the primary book for their formation in the period of the catechumenate. However celebrated, the rite encourages a short proclamation when giving the gift. Another option might be a sung acclamation.

Intercession for the Catechumens

The presider then invites the assembly to pray for the catechumens. The rite gives a formulary of intercession in *RCIA,* n. 65, though the rite also gives the freedom to construct new intercessions. The directives additionally provide for the possibility of including general intercessions for the Church and the world if we will omit the general intercessions for the faithful later (to be discussed below).

We should invite catechumens into a posture appropriate for this prayer. As with the signing of the senses, the catechumens should be in the midst of the assembly. At the very least, they should be facing the assembly, with the sponsors by their sides. Some communities sing the intercessions in a chant style to heighten the solemnity of the celebration.

Prayer Over the Catechumens

After the intercessions, the presider prays one of the prayers prescribed in *RCIA,* n. 66 of the ritual text. The presider may invite the entire assembly to extend their hands in prayer over the catechumens as the presider prays in the name of the assembly for the catechumens.

Dismissal of the Catechumens

The rite provides four formularies for dismissal of the catechumens in various circumstances (*RCIA,* n. 67). *RCIA,* n. 67A and B are intended for use when the community will remain for the celebration of the liturgy of the eucharist. *RCIA,* n. 67C is for the extraordinary circumstance when the catechumens would not be dismissed and would remain while the baptized community celebrated the liturgy of the eucharist. *RCIA,* n. 67D is used when everyone is being dismissed (therefore, with no celebration of the eucharist).

Let us look at the exceptions first. *RCIA,* n. 67D is rarely if ever used. The normative time of celebration is the Sunday assembly, and hence the eucharist would follow. *RCIA,* n. 67C also is rarely if ever used. The text indicates that this option is used only for serious reasons. Thus, the presumption is that we will dismiss the catechumens.

The ritual dismissal needs to have the same reverence and dignity as the rest of the rite. The catechumens are reminded of the great joy of this celebration, and then sent to share their experience with the help of some members of the faithful (presumably a catechist or someone else from the initiation team). In some instances, the presider gives the lectionary to the catechist with a ritual blessing and exhortation to break open this Word with the catechumens. Then all leave in a ritual procession. An antiphon or song of blessing can accompany their procession from the community.

The Liturgy of the Eucharist

The liturgy of the eucharist then continues for the order of the faithful. *RCIA,* n. 68 notes that, for pastoral reasons, we may omit the general intercessions and profession of faith. Although there have been intercessions prayed in *RCIA,* n. 65, they were directed specifically to the catechumens. It would further confuse the focus of that prayer to include general intercessions. Although a great amount of time has been spent in the celebration of the rite of acceptance, it is difficult to imagine a Christian community gathered for worship who neglects its priestly responsibility to pray for the needs of the world (general intercessions) and situates itself within its baptismal covenant (profession of faith).

Since the rite of acceptance is a celebration of initial affiliation and welcome, there should be some small reception following the community's eucharist. Perhaps the catechumens can be present at the rear of the church to greet and be greeted by members of the community.

Optional Rites

The rite continues in *RCIA,* nos. 69-74 with optional rites: exorcism and renunciation of false worship, giving of a new name, and presentation of a cross (cf. *NS,* n. 5). The United States National Conference of Catholic Bishops has decided that we may include the presentation of a cross (*RCIA,* n. 74) in this rite. Keep in mind the cautions noted earlier about giving this cross.

The remaining options are left to the discretion of the local ordinary. In most cases, we would not celebrate these rites and, therefore, we will not discuss them (see *RCIA,* nos. 33.2, 33.4, and 69).

CATECHESIS FOLLOWING THE RITE

Following the principle that we experience liturgy first, and then reflect on the experience to discover new meanings, the major movements and experiences of the rite become the content of the ensuing catechesis.

There will be many feelings present for the catechumens. Give them an opportunity to talk about the experience, and their hopes and desires. Some ideas for this reflection include:

- What was it like to be left outside the church?
- What did it feel like when the community came to greet you?
- Did you feel welcomed by the community throughout the service?
- How significant was your promise to follow the gospel way of life? (Reminder: this is the pivotal moment of the rite—the formal pronouncement of their intention and the reception and affirmation of that intention by the community.)
- What was it like to be signed by the cross, the way of life you committed yourself to?
- How did you feel about being dismissed from the community? Was there any longing to stay? Why do they stay?

ADAPTATION WITH CHILDREN OF CATECHETICAL AGE

The ritual adaptation for children of catechetical age has some problems. When reviewing *RCIA,* nos. 260 and 261, it is difficult to align these directives with the vision found in part I of the ritual text. Instead of placing children within the community, the text suggests not celebrating with the Sunday assembly, perhaps even in a place other than the church, and not at the Sunday eucharist. The rite gives no reasons for these recommendations. One can only presume that the authors hoped to be accommodating to the needs of children, but they actually send a different message about the place of children in the Christian assembly. Thus, opting for the directives found in part I for the when and where of this celebration seems prudent. Furthermore, if both children and adults are ready to celebrate the rite, it seems reasonable to celebrate together rather than having separate liturgies.

Regarding the ritual structure, again we can presume the adaptations are intended to respond to the needs of children. However, there are some curious omissions in this adaptation: no calling the children by name and no formal proclamation of the first promise to accept the gospel (the text includes it in the last rubric of *RCIA,* n. 264). Also the language is sometimes awkward or problematic (see *RCIA,* n. 275: "You have filled these children with the desire to become *perfect* Christians"—italics added).

If we celebrate the rite only with children of catechetical age as inquirers (as opposed to a joint celebration as noted above), then it is important carefully to review the language, and reinsert key dimensions of the rite as outlined earlier in this chapter. Reviewing the *Directory of Masses for Children* for ideas on celebration with children will also be helpful, including the possibility of someone other than the presider preaching.

ADAPTATION WITH BAPTIZED CHILDREN

Part II, chapter 4 and chapter 5 note that candidates (both uncatechized and catechized) may benefit from the celebration of liturgical rites (similar to those celebrated by the catechumens) with appropriate adaptations. For the uncatechized candidate, it is most probable that the parish would celebrate the Rite of Welcome. For the catechized candidate, the decision to celebrate the rite will depend on many factors (review part II, chapter 5 of the ritual text).

Rite of Welcome
The rite of welcoming the candidates (*RCIA*, n. 411f.) is provided in part II, chapter 4 of the ritual text for the baptized candidate. The significant difference from the rite of acceptance is the recognition that these candidates are, indeed, baptized and nothing is to be done to suggest otherwise (*RCIA*, n. 412). With different text and different intention, the ritual structure is similar to the rite of acceptance with some changes: we replace the first acceptance of the gospel with the candidate's declaration of intent (*RCIA*, n. 419) and the text provides no ritual dismissal for the candidates (*RCIA*, n. 413 presumes the candidates will remain with the Sunday assembly for the eucharist).

Combined Rite of Acceptance and Welcome
If the rite of welcoming is to be celebrated at the same time as the rite of acceptance into the order of catechumens, then the rite gives the directive in *RCIA*, n. 415 to use the combined rite found in Appendix I of the ritual text (*RCIA*, n. 505f.) which is particular to the church in the United States.

The ritual structure of the combined rite attempts to integrate the two aforementioned rites while maintaining the important distinction between the catechumens and the baptized candidates (see *RCIA*, n. 506). The primary way this is done is by first addressing the catechumens and then, when there is a parallel moment in the rite, addressing the candidates. At times, this becomes cumbersome (see for example the signing of the senses, *RCIA*, nos. 514-519). Careful planing with the ritual text can maintain the important distinction while tightening up the ritual structure. So, for example, at the signing of the senses, both groups of people could be placed in the body of the church—catechumens together, baptized candidates together—and the presider could first turn to the catechumens and proclaim *RCIA*, n. 515. Then the presider could physically turn to the baptized candidates and proclaim the *RCIA*, n. 518. This could be followed by a joint proclamation of the signing of the other senses (especially since the text is the same for both).

A FIRM FOUNDATION

The rite of acceptance and the rite of welcome are the formal entry points into the period of the catechumenate. During this prolonged period of formation, the catechumens and candidates will have the opportunity to be opened to the mystery of God's presence in their lives and in the Christian community. Through catechetical, liturgical, spiritual, and apostolic formation, the candidates and catechumens, along with their sponsors, team, and the community as a whole, journey in faith, discerning God's call to authentic life and discipleship. This first ritual step will provide a firm foundation upon which we can build this formation process.

PREPARATION REMINDERS

❏ The community needs to be informed beforehand about the celebration. This can be done through pulpit and bulletin announcements, as well as by informing all the various parish groups.

❏ The sponsors need to walk through the entire ritual with the initiation coordinator and presider. The sponsors will need to focus their gatherings with the candidates to raise the questions and issues reflected in the rite.

❏ The hospitality people need to be informed of their responsibilities: greeting the assembly as they enter, facilitating the movement of the assembly to the place where we gather the candidates, facilitating the movement back to the place of worship, and any reception that may follow the celebration.

❏ The environment people will need to make sure that the worship space speaks the festive nature of the celebration and that the space where we sign the candidates is uncluttered.

❏ The final ritual text, with adaptations, etc., needs to be placed in a ritual book for the presider.

❏ A speaker system needs to be set up for the initial dialogue with the candidates, especially if this is outside the church building.

❏ If the candidates will receive a Bible, be sure enough are available. If part of the plan is to have them receive the lectionary, be sure the lectionary is nearby.

❏ If the candidates will receive a cross to wear, be sure they are available.

7

Period of the Catechumenate

INTRODUCTION

Tertullian, a theologian of the second century, said it best: "Christians are made, not born." One does not become a Christian simply by saying he or she wants to be a Christian (though that is an important step) any more than one becomes a doctor by enrolling in medical school. Both decisions are life-shaping decisions. One is formed into the life chosen.

For the doctor-to-be, this includes years of study in the science of medicine and its cognates, followed by an internship under the watchful and skilled eyes of mentors. Not only does one learn medicine but, if the gift is truly there, one becomes a doctor. Being a doctor becomes a way of life for the individual.

The same is true of the Christian. It just does not happen (that would be magic). Rather, slowly and gradually one is opened to the good work of God in his or her life and God's call to share life together. This process of becoming Christian—a lifelong process—is called conversion: falling in love with God in a radical way ("radical" meaning down to the roots). The dynamics of this way of life are explored, taught, shared and given by members of the Christian community to the new member, as in any apprenticeship. Not only does one learn about the Christian way of life but one becomes a Christian, a disciple.

The good news is that we cannot make people into disciples. That is God's work. Only God can literally turn someone around and redirect him or her into a way of life rooted in the values of the reign of God. The hard news, however, is that we the baptized have a responsibility to create an environment within which one can be open to the possibility of God's call to renewed life. Again, we do not create the call. Instead, we create the place where one can possibly hear the call

This "creating the environment" happens in many ways, and the *Rite of Christian Initiation of Adults* outlines for us in this section on the period of the catechumenate a model for forming Christians. In doing so, it insinuates an underlying presumption: the process of formation reflects the normative life of the Catholic Christian.

116

Period of the Catechumenate					
	UNBAPTIZED ADULT	CHILDREN OF CATECHETICAL AGE	BAPTIZED, UNCATECHIZED CATHOLIC	BAPTIZED, UNCATECHIZED CHRISTIAN	BAPTIZED, CATECHIZED CHRISTIAN
Reference	*RCIA*, nos. 75–117	*RCIA*, nos. 75–117	*RCIA*, nos. 402, 406–408, 75–89; 95–96; 104–105; 434–445	*RCIA*, nos. 402, 406–408, 75–89; 95–96; 104–105; 434–445	*RCIA*, nos. 477–478, 402, 406–408, 75–89; 95–96; 104–105 (NB: *RCIA*, n. 473)
Required	Yes	Yes	Yes, adapted	Yes, adapted	Yes, adapted and modified
Focus	*RCIA*, n. 75 * Catechesis * Way of life * Liturgy * Apostolic service	*RCIA*, n. 75 * Catechesis * Way of life * Liturgy * Apostolic service	*RCIA*, n. 75 * Catechesis * Way of life * Liturgy * Apostolic service	*RCIA*, n. 75 * Catechesis * Way of life * Liturgy * Apostolic service	*RCIA*, n. 75 * Catechesis * Way of life * Liturgy * Apostolic service
Goal	Training in Christian life; maturity of faith	Training in Christian life; maturity of faith (according to age and ability)	Training in Christian life; allow baptismal faith to grow and take deep root	Training in Christian life; allow baptismal faith to grow and take deep root	Doctrinal and spiritual preparation
Name	catechumen (cf. *NS*, n. 2)	catechumen (cf. *NS*, n. 2)	candidate (cf. *NS*, nos. 2–3)	candidate (cf. *NS*, nos. 2–3)	candidate (cf. *NS*, nos. 2–3)
Time	minimum up to one year	minimum up to one year	usually up to one year	usually up to one year	relatively short time depending on need
Celebration of the Word of God	*RCIA*, nos. 81–89	*RCIA*, nos. 81–89	*RCIA*, nos. 81–89	*RCIA*, nos. 81–89	*RCIA*, nos. 81–89
Minor Exorcisms	*RCIA*, nos. 90–94	*RCIA*, nos. 90–94	—	—	—
Blessings	*RCIA*, nos. 95–97	*RCIA*, nos. 95–97	*RCIA*, nos. 95–97	*RCIA*, nos. 95–97	*RCIA*, nos. 95–97
Anointing of the Catechumens	*RCIA*, nos. 98–102	*RCIA*, nos. 98–102	—	—	—
Presentations [anticipated]	*RCIA*, nos. 104–105	*RCIA*, nos. 104–105	*RCIA*, nos. 104–105	*RCIA*, nos. 104–105	—
Rite of Sending	Sending of the Catechumens for Election (*RCIA*, nos. 106–117)	Sending of the Catechumens for Election (*RCIA*, nos. 106–117)	Rite of Sending the Candidates for Recognition by the Bishop and for the Call to Continuing Conversion, (*RCIA*, nos. 434–445)	Rite of Sending the Candidates for Recognition by the Bishop and for the Call to Continuing Conversion, (*RCIA*, nos. 434–445)	If helpful (*RCIA*, n. 478); Rite of Sending the Candidates for Recognition by the Bishop and for the Call to Continuing Conversion, (*RCIA*, nos. 434–445)

WHAT DOES THE RITE SAY?

Similar to the period of the precatechumenate, the ritual text provides only a few sections to describe the formation for the period of the catechumenate. Yet, as we will see, those few sections include a wealth of material for reflection.

Read RCIA, *n. 75.*

The opening paragraph describes the period of the catechumenate as a time of formation to bring to maturity the faith and conversion celebrated in the rite of acceptance into the order of catechumens. The text uses the image of training in the Christian life (the reader is encouraged to read the footnoted reference to the *Decree on the Church's Missionary Activity,* n. 14 for a fuller understanding of this training in the Christian way of life) to describe this process of formation. Wisely, the text also notes that the time frame is long: it is an extended period. There is no reason to rush through this mentoring in the Christian life.

The ritual text then explicates how we accomplish this maturity of faith: catechesis, the Christian way of life, liturgical rites, and apostolic witness.

RCIA, n. 75.1 describes the catechesis appropriate to the period of the catechumenate. It is complete ("thoroughly comprehensive," see *NS,* n. 7), accommodated to the liturgical year, and supported by celebrations of the word. Why? Because part of being mentored in the Christian life includes exposure to the foundational truths of the community. The "syllabus" of the community, therefore, is the agenda for initiation. We find that syllabus in the liturgical prayer of the community; there is no contradiction between immersion in the teaching of the community and the liturgical life of the community. Rather, the liturgical life (i.e., the liturgical year) sets the direction.

Further along in that section, we read that the goal of this catechesis is twofold. First is the appropriate acquaintance with dogma and precepts—an awareness of the breadth of Christian teaching, especially as it is expressed in the Creed (proclaimed in the liturgy). More important, though, is the second: a "profound sense of the mystery of salvation..." This is not a catechesis of information. This is a catechesis that truly "echoes God's word," allowing it to make a claim on people's lives. How do we help lead people to this mystery of salvation? In our community, it is through word and sacrament. Scripture and symbol will be foundational for any catechesis.

RCIA, n. 75.2 describes the second part of this formation: immersion in the Christian way of life. One becomes a Christian by living with Christians. Furthermore, knowledge of people in the community provides a basis for life with the community after initiation (see *NS,* n. 4). We are not initiating them into our catechumenate: we are initiating them into the Body of Christ.

As the catechumens become more and more exposed to the Christian way of life (community), they will then be more attentive to the spiritual life within, and also to the manifestation of the spiritual life in their relationships to others.

RCIA, n. 75.3 describes the third dimension of this formation: the support of liturgical rites that assist and strengthen the catechumens, and also tutors them for their eventual participation in the eucharistic assembly. As we will see, the ritual text prescribes a variety of liturgical rites to accomplish this: celebrations of the word, blessings, exorcisms, anointings. This section further discusses the appropriate rite of dismissal for catechumens.

RCIA, n. 75.4 briefly describes the fourth aspect: apostolic witness. Not only are the liturgy and the life with Christians a "school" for catechumens, but service in the name of Christ is also a way by which the Christian is formed. It is not a question of waiting to serve after initiation. Rather it is serving the authentic needs of the world in witness to God right from the very beginning.

Read RCIA, *n. 76.*

This section raises the question: How long? The response is simple: Nothing can be determined beforehand. In fact, because of the expectations for this period, it may take years for the "conversion and faith to become strong." What is important here is the refusal of the rite to lockstep everyone into a particular time frame, especially an academic calendar, while at the same time highlighting the need to be attentive to several variables: the grace of God and various circumstances.

The pastoral wisdom of the church is that this mentoring in the Christian life will take at least a year (see *NS,* n. 6). Besides signaling us that there is no need to rush, perhaps this is also reaffirming the connection to the liturgical year where "through the yearly cycle the church unfolds the entire mystery of Christ" (*GNLYC,* n. 1).

Read RCIA, *n. 77.*

This section notes again the importance of the bishop to oversee initiation in his diocese, and the conference of bishops to establish norms appropriate for their region. This section also references the abbreviated catechemunate (noted in Chapter 3 of this resource) that requires the permission of the bishop.

Read RCIA, *n. 78.*

This section clarifies *RCIA,* n. 75 regarding the instruction appropriate for this period. Notice the language: enlightens faith, directs the heart toward God, etc. This is not merely informing people of the Christian faith. Rather, it is helping them in their journey of faith. Some have suggested we could use this section to help define who is a catechized adult (when discerning part II, chapters 4 & 5).

Read RCIA, *n. 79.*

This section reminds us of the importance of the liturgical rites, especially celebrations of the word. One can infer from this that these celebrations, along with the other liturgical rites, should be a frequent and regular part of the formation.

Read RCIA, *n. 80.*

This section reminds us of the various persons involved in the initiation process and the need to include them, especially in the liturgical rites.

CATECHESIS

Catechesis is an echoing of the gospel. It is a ministry of the word that proclaims the good Word of God in Jesus. It is a full and robust proclamation that invites the full person to a response in faith, a response embodied in charity and justice. Catechesis calls and challenges the full person.

Catechesis during the period of the catechumenate is concerned with helping the catechumen name the experience of God within his or her own life and respond to that experience of salvation. Additionally, the catechumen needs to come to know the story of the community named Catholic and how, throughout the centuries, we have come to name the experience of God in our midst.

Catechesis is not about passing information. It is about enlivening faith. How can we incorporate the great symbols of our community—including the rich word symbols of doctrine—to empower and enliven the faith of the catechumens? This exciting challenge is the challenge of catechesis: making the Word of God—in scripture and as articulated in the faith of the community— credible and meaningful. This is not a watering down of the Word of God, but rather a raising up of that Word so that it has a bearing on ordinary life.

There are various catechetical models that one can use during the period of the catechumenate. Whatever model one adopts, the model needs to respect and integrate the insights of adult learning. That means that we respect the individuals as adults with valid questions and concerns. They are there not to get information but to raise up their life questions for exploration and reflection. Therefore, the place to begin is with their questions, their concerns, their experience. Also adults are able to sift and find what is necessary and important for them. There is no coercion or proselytizing with adults. Instead, there is a genuine trust that what needs to be received will be received. Since adult learning is a co-learning experience, the catechist will also need to have a posture of hospitality to accept whatever gift the catechist receives from the adult in terms of insights and experiences. No one comes to the catechetical gathering finished. Everyone comes as a learner. What are essential are respect and trust. Adults can make their own choices and live with the consequences of these choices. Catechesis helps inform the decision-making process; it does not replace the fundamental freedom of a person to respond to life. Therefore, we do not manipulate adults with our agenda. Rather, we offer them the truth as we experience and know it and allow them to receive it in the manner appropriate for them.

Another issue that needs to be addressed is the when of catechesis. The rite is clear that there is some reflection on the Word after the dismissal (see for example *RCIA,* n. 67B). Presumably, the initiation catechesis would be part of this reflection following the dismissal. This would mean that the catechumens continue to gather after the assembly has completed the celebration of the eucharist. Then, the sponsors and spouses can join the catechumens for the continuation of the catechesis. For such a gathering, one would need to plan to meet for at least another 1 1/2 hours after the community's dismissal. The hospitality people can arrange refreshments, as well as babysitting.

Sometimes the extended catechesis cannot happen following the dismissal. Don't dismiss the dismissal. Meet for the allotted time (usually until the community's dismissal) and then regather later during the week. The difficulty with this model, though, is that if we are bringing the catechumens out for another night of catechesis, when will they have time for other experiences of immersion in the community or apostolic witness?

In some parts of the country, parishes are working together on the catechumenate. If this is the case, dismissal can happen at the individual parishes on Sunday with some reflection on the word, followed by the joint session later in the week.

Catechesis also needs to be holistic. There needs to be variety in presentation that energizes and challenges the catechumens' minds, hearts and wills. Sometimes there will be cause for guided reflections, other times for journaling. Sometimes a presentation will be necessary, and other times some discussion. Perhaps a short reading will get the point across, or else a case study. Music or video will sometimes help. What is important is the diversity of styles that both respects people's learning preferences and also challenges areas that need growth and development—variety not for the sake of variety, but to touch and gently till the rich soil of human life, with all its variety and complexity.

Foundations for Catechesis Accommodated to the Liturgical Year

A catechesis accommodated to the liturgical year is one correlated with and flowing from the liturgical prayer of the Church. Besides the primary experience of praying with the liturgical assembly, key resources for such a catechesis are: the liturgical calendar itself with its celebration of feasts and seasons, the sacramentary and the lectionary, and the primary liturgical symbols of the community.

Chapter 2 of this resource already addressed the importance of the liturgical calendar and its place in initiation. Later in this section we will look at catechesis rooted in the primary liturgical symbols. The following foundations will look at the whole experience of initiation catechesis based on the Liturgy of the Word, with a special focus on the use of the lectionary for such catechesis. However one crafts the actual catechetical session, it is important that these building blocks be included each week.

Textual Interpretation

The catechist must explore the interpretation of the lectionary texts in at least two forms. In addition to the necessary scriptural exegesis, there must to be a liturgical exegesis, that is, an understanding of a particular scripture text within the context of the liturgical celebration and the liturgical year. Not only must we understand the texts within their scriptural contexts (how they fit within the picture the particular writer is creating), but we also must understand the texts within the Church's cycle of prayer.

Celebration of the Word

The assembly's rite of gathering and the proclamation of the Word at the Sunday Liturgy of the Word are essential for initiation catechesis. The preaching is a particularly significant piece of this catechesis. The dismissal rite—a liturgical action—happens within this ritual context. If for some reason the catechumens are not gathering with and dismissed from the Sunday assembly, then when they gather, the celebration of the Word (patterned on the Liturgy of the Word from the previous Sunday) is to be the heart of the gathering. Insights from the Sunday assembly (for example, what was highlighted in the preaching) would be incorporated into this celebration.

Faith Sharing

The experience of the Word proclaimed makes demands on each of us. Therefore, allowing catechumens to talk about their personal encounter with the Word is necessary both to build and to encourage faith. What must be clear, however, is that personal interpretation of the Word, however valid in one's experience, is incomplete. The Word stands within the midst of the praying community. Thus, personal sharing of faith must be expanded and, perhaps, challenged by the community's experience of the Word. Otherwise, we risk religious narcissism.

Life Experience

It is the task of the catechist to discover how the Word is making a claim on the life of the community and on the individual in the community. Such a claim will have an impact on ordinary human experience. In the dialogue between lived experience and the Word, the transforming power of grace is at work.

Catholic Tradition

The lectionary is not intended to be a catechetical book. In fact, it would be a gross distortion of the liturgical prayer of the Church to imprison it in educational models. However, the liturgical year does provide for us—through the proclamation of the Word and the prayer of the community—an unfolding of "the whole mystery of Christ, from his incarnation and birth until his ascension, the day of Pentecost and the expectation of blessed hope and of the Lord's return" (*SC*, n. 102). Thus "through the yearly cycle the church unfolds the entire mystery of Christ" (*GNLYC*, n. 1). By the rhythm and life of the liturgical year, the Church fashions the faithful repeatedly in the mystery of Christ. In the same way, catechists can foster and reinforce an awareness of Catholic Tradition—teaching, way of life, primary symbols—that emerges from the praying of these texts rather than impose some other order for teaching the tradition.

A brief description of the essentials of Catholic teaching as explained in *National Catechetical Directory: Sharing the Light of Faith,* Chapter 5 will help us to remove the mystique over what Catholic doctrine needs to be covered (cf. *NS*, n. 7). These topics are developed in more detail in the *Catechism of the Catholic Church,* which serves as an essential resource for catechists during this period of formation.

Mystery of the One God (NCD, nos. 83-84): Personal presence of God in the history of salvation; the Trinity; revelation in Jesus Christ; covenant relationships with God; worship of God in liturgy, communal prayer, and personal prayer; God's will; the desire for God.

Creation (NCD, nos. 85-86): Creative work of God; relationship of creation and salvation; the human person as climax of God's creation; the ongoing presence of God in and through creation.

Jesus Christ (NCD, nos. 87-91): Salvation and reconciliation in Jesus Christ; continuing mission of Jesus; Jesus, truly divine and truly human; proclamation of the reign of God; life, death and resurrection of Jesus; the meaning and destiny of life most fully revealed in Jesus Christ.

The Holy Spirit (NCD, n. 92): Presence of the Holy Spirit in the world and in the Church; ministry.

The Church (NCD, nos. 93-96): Origins and foundations; the new people of God; servant; prophetic and priestly roles; hierarchical structure; role of pope and bishops; infallibility and inerrancy; on-going renewal of the Church; community of people; universal call to holiness; vocation; unity in the Church; ecumenical respect; mission of the Church to bring the message of salvation; call to serve the world community.

The Sacraments (NCD, n. 97): Christ, the sacrament of God; the Church, the sacrament of Christ; sacraments as actions of Christ; purpose of sacraments for sanctifying humanity, building up the Body of Christ, and giving worship to God.

The Life of Grace (NCD, nos. 98-100): Sin; original sin; personal sin; effects of sin; grace as God's generous and free gift of self, a sharing in God's life; Christ's offer of grace is universal and everlasting; sacraments as sources of grace; on-going conversion; role of penance in conversion; discipleship; fulfillment in Christ; beatitudes as way of life; living the reign of God.

The Moral Life (NCD, nos. 101-105): Call to holiness; concrete expression of love; fidelity to moral norms and values; genuine human freedom; value of the truly good; true morality as accepting humanity restored in Christ; natural moral law; judgments of conscience; moral decision-making; informed conscience; discernment; guidance of the Church in moral questions; specifics of moral life in light of the ten commandments, sermon on the mount, and the last supper discourse; duties toward God, others, and self.

Mary and the Saints (NCD, nos. 106-107): Mary, model of faith and charity; Mary, mother of God and mother of the church; the immaculate conception; the assumption; the communion of saints.

Death, Judgment and Eternity (NCD, nos. 108-110): Christian understanding of death; personal and final judgment; hope; final union with God; the return of Christ in glory.

Hopefully, one can recognize, based on good experiences of preaching, that we raise all these essentials continually throughout the year at the Sunday liturgy. An effective catechesis that flows from the lectionary, and is informed by the preaching on the texts, will be able to address these issues throughout the liturgical year.

The goal of catechesis in the period of the catechumenate is to facilitate conversion. Concretely, this does include a basic awareness and understanding of Catholic life and teaching. The key emphasis here, though, is basic. We are working to provide an environment for the response of faith to grow to a new level of commitment. Included in this commitment is a lifelong process of growing in awareness of Catholic Christian doctrine.

Ritual and Prayer

The catechetical gathering is not meant to be a cognitive experience. Rather, it is a faith-forming experience centered in prayer. This understanding must shape the style and format of the gathering. In addition to the orations from the Sunday Mass found in the sacramentary, the *Rite of Christian Initiation of Adults* provides blessings, anointings, exorcisms and the presentations of the Creed and the Lord's Prayer to deepen the experience.

Servanthood

Catechists help awaken a sense of mission based on the experience of the Word in the scriptures and the community. Apprenticeship in discipleship calls for one to be fashioned into the life of the authentic servant for the mission of the reign of God.

Spiritual and Communal Formation

We must integrate the catechumens also into the living, praying and serving community. Not only do we need people to gather with the catechumens during the initiation catechesis (we should always invite the whole parish to be part of this), but catechists need to know what is happening in the life of the community that week and help make explicit links between what is discussed during the catechetical session with the real life of the community.

Planning the Catechetical Session: One Model

A helpful image to understand initiation catechesis is conversation. Together we enter into conversation around the Word of God and the best of our Catholic Christian Tradition. This does not mean that the catechist can simply "go with the flow" without any preparation. No, in fact, the opposite is true. Truly to engage in a worthwhile conversation around these issues of Christian living, the catechist and other members of the initiation team will need to prepare thoroughly so that they can lead the conversation with confidence.

Catechist Preparation for Initiation Catechesis

What kind of preparation is most needed? Here are some suggestions for catechists preparing for initiation catechesis based on the Liturgy of the Word. Whenever a group of catechists can work together—from the same team, from neighboring parishes, from other groups in the parish, such as religious education—there are the added benefits of shared resources and shared experiences.

◆ *Start with an overview of the scriptures of the liturgical year.*

Because in the current structure of the lectionary, the gospel text provides the direction for the first reading, begin with background work on the gospel. With the help of introductory materials, get a good sense of the direction of the particular gospel of the year. The scriptures are more than religious texts. For the Christian, they are the revealed Word of God. Hence, one approaches the scriptures, whether for study or meditation, in a spirit of prayer and anticipation. Prayerful presence to the scriptures becomes an important and necessary posture to allow them to speak to us personally and to our life situation.

◆ *Follow this up with work on the particular liturgical season (even if the preparation is for only one or two weeks within that season).*

This will allow us to have a larger picture of the season and get a sense where the particular week(s) falls into the picture. Having a group of people work on this is especially helpful, each taking a particular week of the season and doing an initial overview for the group. Then the various pieces—like gems on a mosaic—are put together and we see the picture the liturgical year is crafting for us at this time.

◆ *Be very aware of the liturgical calendar.*

Not only do we want to review the scriptures within their own context (e.g., how this text fits into the larger picture of Mark's gospel), but also how the Church is using these texts within the liturgical context (e.g., how this text fits into the larger picture of Advent).

◆ *With the larger picture before us, now it is time to work on the particular Sunday.*

Remember, we are preparing for an engaging and insightful conversation, not a lecture. Hence, our preparation and materials will need to reflect this. The best way to prepare for such a conversation is to have a personal conversation with the texts themselves.

◆ *Start a conversation with the scripture texts based on our experience.*

Recognizing any attitudes one brings to the text is important: one's understanding of the scriptures in general (e.g., Do I take the scriptures "literally?") as well as any previous encounters with the particular text. Sometimes we think we have exhausted the meaning of a text because we have heard it so many times. Yet every text has the power and possibility for new meaning. The first step toward such an encounter is our acknowledgment of any pre-understandings we have concerning the text. For example, in the familiar parable of the prodigal son, many people focus on the story of the son who runs away, returns home, and is forgiven by the generous and kind father. With that focus again and again, the message of forgiveness can become stale for some. Recognizing this may allow new insights to emerge, such as the significance of the elder brother and his claim on justice.

After situating oneself in reference to the text and bringing to awareness one's pre-understanding of the text, one can then become open to the text and ask the simple question: What is new? These guidelines for interpretation are similar to any encounter. If we presume the result already, the encounter is barren. However, if we can stand in expectation before the painting, or the piano piece, or our friend, something new can come to us.

Coming to an awareness of one's pre-understanding of a text presumes a preliminary reading of the text. One needs to return to the text and read it again, slowly, expectantly. The text has its own authority, its own life. It has something meaningful to say each time we encounter it. Simply be *present* to the text. There are a variety of ways of reading the text at this point. Read it aloud. Image the text. Converse with the text. Sing the text. The important aspect to keep alive is that the text is ever new.

After reading the text, it is appropriate to ask, "What does this mean to me? How does it make me feel? What images emerge for me? What do I think God is saying in this text? What impact does this have on my life?" Although the personal interpretation of the text may not completely reflect the sense of the text, such an interpretation is nonetheless valuable at this point. We must allow ourselves to be drawn into conversation with the text. It is important to write down those feelings, images, insights, prayers, and reflections that occur as we meet the text. It is also important to recognize that the meaningfulness of the text needs time and scholarship to allow it to emerge. Therefore, one does not stop at the private interpretation of the text.

◆ *After sufficient time in this initial conversation, begin the work of inviting others into the conversation.*

Widen the circle with those more trained than ourselves in understanding some of the images and background information of the texts. Thinking that our personal interpretation of the texts is sufficient and accurate would be naive and foolish. As mentioned earlier, it is valid and valued, but incomplete. Now is the time to gain the insights from the many other conversations (i.e., the commentaries) that have been held with this text.

The text has a history of interpretation already. Scholars have done extensive research and study with the text. Now is the time to become familiar with that material (and not before the personal dramatic reading of the text). These scholars, using the tools of critical literary research such as form criticism and redaction criticism, provide for us a context and background for the text. They help us identify the literary genre of the text (e.g., mythic literature is very different from biographical accounts), as well as discover the meaning of particular words and phrases within the culture and time of the writer. We can learn the particular audience the text was intended for (e.g., Palestinian Christians or Hellenistic Christians), its use in the community (e.g., hymn, letter, moral principle), its theological significance within the larger piece of writing (e.g., why Jesus journeys to Jerusalem when he does), and the historicity of the event (e.g., what really happened). All of this is valuable information for us. Luckily, there are many commentaries available to us that serve a wide range of audiences.

It is important to note, though, that the work of interpretation of a text cannot rest solely on one's personal encounter with the text as described above, nor on the official commentaries. Rather, there must be a coming together of the two with the text. When a person has respected the text by taking it seriously, by recognizing the agenda he or she brings with him or her to the text, and by informing himself or herself of current scholarship, one can then allow the text to emerge with new meaning, with new possibilities, with new insights. There is a new coming together of the text with the individual. The encounter has changed both the person and the text: the person, by the values that emerge from the experience of the text that informs his or her life, and the text, by the individual's particular experience of interpretation. This process takes time. One cannot force the text. Rather, one allows oneself to mull over the text, befriend the text, take it to one's interior home.

◆ *Now it is time to ask an important question: So what?*

What difference does this scripture make in my life and, more important, in the lives of people today? What do these texts tell me about living life as a disciple of Jesus today? It is important that we answer these questions in concrete ways rather than in elusive statements.

One of the values of allowing oneself to encounter a text (whether that text is verbal, visual, literary, or personal) is that the encounter changes the individual in some way and the person must now assimilate this newness in concrete, categorical terms. We need to apply the meaning that has emerged to everyday life. The process of *exegesis* allows for the truth of the text to emerge and speak. This process is very different from the experience of someone attempting to impose a meaning on the text (proof-texting) to support the individual's claim—a case of manipulating the text to serve one's purpose rather than serving the truth of the text. Once the truth emerges from the text, there is the invitation to live out this truth. One needs to recognize the current needs and concerns of life, and prayerfully explore how this text speaks to these issues.

◆ *Having spent time reflecting on the impact of the scriptures on our world today (and not just our personal lives but for the larger community), we can then ask: How does the Church respond? What is the dimension of the Catholic Christian Tradition that addresses the concerns or issues raised in these readings?*

Be careful not to limit the Tradition to only the teaching dimensions of Christian life. The Tradition also includes our forms of prayer, our moral life, and our acts of justice, to name a few. Try not to impose something on the scripture texts. Instead, ask, "What has emerged from the previous conversations that can be further expanded upon by exploring the best of the Catholic Tradition?"

◆ *Most probably, many "Catholic responses" will emerge from our reflection.*

Again, this is most helpful when done with other people to avoid focusing on our own agenda. List all of the responses and then ask if they truly are responses to the conversation with these scripture texts. Mark the ones that are clearly part of the conversation.

◆ *Now it is time to step back from our conversation with the scriptures and the Tradition and think of the catechumens and candidates with whom we will be in conversation.*

The Catholic issue we will choose to prepare will be influenced by the needs of the catechumenal community we serve. Which of the issues listed are fundamental and foundational? Given the previous conversations on the Catholic Tradition, which issue do we need to explore together? (Refer back to the earlier listing from the *National Catechetical Directory.*)

◆ *Having chosen one or two Catholic responses, it is time to enter into a similar process of conversation with the Catholic Tradition.*

This, unfortunately, is where many get trapped into the lecture mind set. Many of us seem comfortable engaging in a disciplined conversation with the scriptures. However, when it comes to the Catholic Tradition (including our teachings), we sometimes seem to become frozen in place. Such a posture can lead to a fundamentalistic approach to Catholic teaching and way of life. Instead, we want to invite people into intelligent and critical conversation with the Catholic Tradition so that it may be appropriated (like the scriptures), not merely absorbed.

◆ *The process for entering into this conversation is similar to the one used with the scriptures: What do we understand and know about this Catholic issue or teaching?*

Jot that down. What does the Catholic community say itself about this issue? Read a lot. What difference does that make for living as a disciple of Jesus in today's world? Pray about it. This is a helpful place to use the *Catechism of the Catholic Church* as a resource. But do not stop there. Just as investing in good commentaries for the scriptures is necessary, investing in good resources for the Catholic Tradition will also be necessary: documents of Vatican Council II, the post-conciliar documents (especially the liturgical documents), along with recent theological resource books that provide concise summaries of major theological themes.

◆ *Planning the Gathering*

With this preparation behind us, we are ready to plan the gathering for initiation catechesis. It might be helpful to list the various movements, key questions, and other activities that we will propose during the actual gathering.

What is central in the pastoral presentation and application of the scripture texts and the Tradition is that it is meaningful for the particular audience. Hence, the experience of the minister in coming to meet the text provides the backdrop but not necessarily the lesson. One does not bring to the gathering all the research, insights, and reflections from his or her process of interpreting the text. Rather, with all of that as one's foundation, the catechist approaches the text for its message and meaning for the catechumens with which he or she is working. The key here is not forcing a meaning from the text on the catechumens, but rather using good catechetical and group skills to effectively (and accurately) convey the text, presenting it in its best form, and allowing the catechumens to meet the text in their own encounter. The catechist serves as a guide, a curator, and a companion.

The scriptures offer the Christian community a powerful and unique experience of God. Through the power of the Word proclaimed, we can come to encounter reconciliation and salvation from our God. However this revelation of God can be distorted, and at best hampered, by private interpretations, poor scholarship or the refusal authentically to encounter and interpret the scripture text. The heralds of this message of goodness bear an important responsibility in the community. Part of that responsibility includes taking the time necessary to grapple with that Word for the community today, and then authentically proclaiming that message through preaching, catechesis, and sponsorship. It is this Word proclaimed that will continue to shape and form us as the people of God.

The Catechetical Session

◆ *Catechumens gather with the community for the Sunday celebration of Mass.*

In many communities, the catechumens (and candidates) sit with sponsors and other family members in designated places. Other parishes encourage the catechumens to sit anywhere they choose (with their sponsors) in the body of the community so that they are truly in the midst of the assembly.

◆ *The whole assembly experiences the Liturgy of the Word with the proclamation of the Word of God and the subsequent preaching.*

An invitation follows this to the catechumens (and, in many parishes, the candidates) for the dismissal rite (see *Rite of Christian Initiation of Adults,* n. 67 for some examples).

◆ *We dismiss the catechumens to a time of deeper reflection and prayer on the scriptures and their meaning for discipleship.*

Therefore, the dismissal rite needs to be done with dignity. It often includes a procession to the place where the catechumens will continue this reflection. Including the whole assembly in the dismissal rite will enhance it. We can invite them to extend hands in prayer over the catechumens, or join in singing a short acclamation during the procession.

◆ *The environment of the place where the catechumens will gather is very important.*

Because this gathering is an extension of the liturgical experience with the whole assembly, the space needs to model that in some way. It is really a matter of out with the classroom and in with liturgical space. Even if we use one of the classrooms of the school building, we will still need to reconstruct it to model the liturgical environment: cross, candles, ambo, liturgical hangings, etc. If the parish has a small daily Mass chapel, consider using that space. What is important is the message being sent by the space: It should be warm, welcoming, and explicitly linked with the liturgical assembly. Remember that initiation is not about information-sharing; it is about immersion into the liturgical community as it witnesses to discipleship.

◆ *Once gathered, invite the catechumens into an initial conversation with the Word of God, a conversation very similar to what was experienced in preparation.*

What did they hear? What message was disturbing? Hopeful? Confusing? How did the preaching tie the readings into their lives? The catechist will need to prepare a series of probing questions (not questions that can be answered with a yes or no) to engage the catechumens in conversation. The catechist will need to be very careful to respect the insights of each person in the conversation. This is not the time to be impressing the catechumens with all the newly-learned insights on the scriptures (in fact, there will be no such time). Rather, it is a time of listening to their inquiry and engaging them in conversation. This conversation usually lasts until the end of Mass.

◆ *Once Mass is ended, there are two options.*

Either the catechesis will continue and include the sponsors and other interested folk from the parish (such as spouses and friends) or this period of gathering will end and resume later in the week. Whichever option is chosen (and there are many factors that go into making this decision), it is important to remember that the ensuing gathering is still an extension of the liturgical assembly. We do not move into "classroom" mode at this time (or anytime during these gatherings).

◆ *Whenever the gathering continues, welcome the new participants in the conversation and bring them on board.*

Invite the catechumens to offer a summary of their experience of the Word, and briefly invite the new participants to offer their own insights into the readings. Note: If the gathering resumes later in the week, create a similar environment (use of space, prayerful atmosphere, etc.), and begin with a celebration of the Word, using the lectionary readings from the Sunday celebration.

◆ *With this larger group, proclaiming the scriptures again would be appropriate.*

We will all hear them differently now, based on the shared conversation that was just completed. Give ample time for quiet and reflection.

◆ *How to proceed at this point will depend on personal style.*

Some people work better with a clear plan—step by step. Others are more comfortable moving in and out of the material in response to the conversation. So rather than dictate what the next period of time will look like, the following are elements that need to be part of it.

◆ *The conversation needs to be continued and to include (and explore) some of the critical background and understanding of the scriptures (based on the preparations).*

Remember that this is not the time to take out the charts and lecture for twenty minutes on a topic of biblical archaeology. Rather, again through conversation, invite the participants to explore areas of the texts and expand their understanding by the few comments the catechist makes. Make links back to what was shared earlier to expand an insight ("Earlier, Jan mentioned how the story about the blind man was a bit confusing to her. Did you know that in Jesus' time blind people were outcasts because people thought the blindness was due to someone's sin?"). Move back and forth in conversation. If the catechist has used up all the material based on the preparation, then there is too much material.

◆ *Additionally, the conversation needs to include the issue of Catholic life that was prepared.*

Some people prefer to ask the catechumens to raise the issues of Catholic life that need to be addressed. However, preparing the material before the gathering is quite appropriate. Most catechists do not feel comfortable responding to issues of this nature on the spot. Also, part of the task of the period of the catechumenate is to provide an overview of Catholic Christian teaching. Thus, it seems quite reasonable for the catechist to take the lead on this.

◆ *We can integrate the "Catholic agenda" into the conversation without making it appear as a separate section.*

In the give and take of conversation, the skilled catechist—having done the preparation—will be able to direct the conversation (and respond, when necessary) with issues of Catholic life and teaching.

◆ *Ultimately, all of this comes together with the major "So what?"*

Given all of the time spent in conversation, the final task is to move all of us forward to seeing the concrete implications in our real, lived worlds of work and home. We need to be stretched—however uncomfortable that may be—to respond in new ways because of today's experience of God in scripture and Tradition. The catechist needs to be prepared to offer such challenges and provide concrete examples of living the gospel with lives of justice and mercy.

◆ *Integrated throughout all of this—and serving as the context—are opportunities for liturgical prayer as prescribed in the ritual text.*

Avoid the "start and end" prayer times. Rather, when the conversation is leading us into painful turf, perhaps it is time to pray an exorcism. When we are seeking and find ourselves in need of God's presence, perhaps it is time to pray a blessing. Or perhaps it is time to step back and ritually proclaim the scripture texts so they can, again, make a claim on us. Or maybe it is time to sing the responsorial psalm again. The prepared catechist will become more comfortable with filling out the whole experience with rich experiences of prayer.

◆ *At all times remember this:*

Our chief goal is, as St. Augustine reminds us, to help the catechumens come to know that they are loved by God. All else seems to pale after that.

Liturgical Symbols Shape Who We Are

Earlier, this resource noted how catechumens are formed into the Christian way of life by word and sacrament, and how the word of God proclaimed in the Sunday assembly plays a crucial role in this process. The lectionary serves as a resource for this dimension of formation.

Along with the word of God, the primary liturgical symbols of our community also shape and inform our Catholic Christian identity. Thus, catechumens need to enter into conversation with these symbols along with the word of God (i.e., symbolic discourse). Those primary liturgical symbols are brought together for us in the premier gathering of the community—the Easter Vigil. Among these primary symbols are the assembly, cross, fire (light), water, oil, touch (laying on of hands), exchange of peace, bread and wine, and new garment.

All the liturgical symbols are profound expressions of primary truths in our Catholic Christian lives: they are foundational expressions of our identity and our mission. When we experience the symbols—the play, as it were—we discover and learn to integrate the essential way of life as Catholic Christians. Only after we have experienced the liturgical symbols do we begin to make the meanings explicit through teaching and practice. In effect, the liturgical symbols—and their interaction together in worship—both sum up our experience and thrust us into the future. Each of the liturgical symbols has a past, present, and a future, both individually and collectively.

Symbols are not static; they are not things. Thus, we are not talking about the "objects" of bread and wine, water, oil, and so on, but the interaction with these elements that is transformative. Each of the liturgical symbols is expressed through an action: the gathering of the assembly, the marking with the cross, the passing of the fire (light), the immersion into the water, the smearing with oil, the laying on of hands, the sharing of the exchange of peace, the breaking of the bread and sharing of the wine, and the putting on of the new garment.

Dimensions of Liturgical Symbols

There are five dimensions to the experience of liturgical symbols: the human experience, the biblical experience, the Church's experience (ecclesial), the liturgical experience, and the future meaning or discipleship experience. Here are some thoughts on what each of these dimensions means for the parish's approach to initiation.

Human Experience

Symbols are evocative because they bring together a variety of basic human experiences (and meanings) in the experience of the one symbol. It is important to tease out some of those meanings in daily life to experience the challenge of the symbols for Christian living. Those meanings are both personal (personal stories and memories) and cultural. What are my experiences of water: on a hot summer afternoon? during the cold of winter? to cleanse? to nourish a plant? What does the culture say about water and how does it use it?

Biblical Experience

The biblical experience of the symbols begins to shape the experience of the symbol within a particular perspective: the Christian experience of God as revealed in and through the Hebrew people and, most especially, in the Christ.

Thus, both testaments of scripture are used to provide a context and foundation. What are some key stories of people being gathered? Of people being anointed? Of meals shared?

Ecclesial Experience

The Church's experience of the symbol deals with its missionary mandate. Liturgical actions need to embody and express the Church's mission. Thus, we look into the transformed way of living. Where does the Christian community gather together people to enable them to discover themselves as God's very own? Where does the Christian community break the bread with the poor and needy to feed them? Where does the Christian community clothe the naked with garments of cloth as well as garments of dignity?

Liturgical Experience

The liturgical experience of the symbols, then, captures all of those experiences and becomes the present living and experience of the symbols. The liturgical expression of the symbols makes present (really present) all of the meanings behind the experience of the symbol. We discover this in the actual event of the symbol. Thus, while the symbols are the same again and again (ritual action is purposefully repetitive), the encounter is always new and the meaning emerging is always new if we allow ourselves to enter into the experience of the symbols.

Future Meaning or Discipleship Experience

The future meaning of the symbol is shaped by our encounter with the symbol and the future it opens up to us because of the encounter: One's identity is shaped and reformed by the symbol. How can I be bread for others in their hunger, both physical and emotional? How do I "put on Christ" and cloak others with such garments to protect them? How do I gather people to discover their dignity, touch others with healing? How am I the fragrant oil of anointing in people's lives so they discover themselves as truly blessed?

The future meaning is also communal: How do we feed the poor? How do we clothe the naked? How do we welcome the stranger? How do we raise up human dignity? Both personally and communally, we discover new gifts from God (charism) to embody this future. We become the Body of Christ in the world.

Integrating Word and Symbol in Formation

How far do we go with symbol formation? It seems reasonable that all the primary liturgical symbols are explored before the celebration of the sacraments of initiation at the Easter Vigil. To do this, the first three movements (human, biblical and ecclesial) are developed in catechetical gatherings over the course of the year. We experience the fourth movement (liturgical) in the very praying at the Easter Vigil. The fifth movement (discipleship) becomes the agenda of mystagogy.

Some of the lectionary texts will lend themselves naturally to incorporate one of the liturgical symbols noted above. In those times, we can adjust the catechetical session to include some formation in symbolic consciousness. Some supplemental gatherings need to be scheduled to immerse the catechumens in the other symbols. Perhaps this could be done more effectively during a retreat weekend or an evening of prayer.

IMMERSION IN THE CHRISTIAN WAY OF LIFE

Throughout the initiation process, we are helping the catechumens come to a deepened awareness of God's loving presence that brings life. This presence of God is clearly experienced in the midst of the community. Hence, the period of the catechumenate also concerns itself with the immersion of the catechumen into the very life of the community (cf. *NS,* n. 4). As one enters more fully into the life and community of the parish, one begins to examine and (hopefully) embrace the moral values that inform a Catholic Christian way of life. All of this—community, moral values—becomes part of the process of spiritual formation. Spiritual is seen as more holistic and not isolated to an interior disposition. Rather, it is about living life most fully within the community.

The goal of the spiritual formation dimensions of the catechumenate is the fostering and development of relationships that help the catechumens respond to the call of conversion. They can only nurture and strengthen the response of faith that is demanded by a life of prayer.

Initiation into prayer happens best when people pray. The same is true for any love relationship. We can talk about friendship and the commitment of love, yet it is only in the actual living out of such friendship that one comes to a heightened appreciation and understanding of the concepts. We can talk about prayer and prayer forms during the catechumenate. But the catechumens will best understand and appreciate prayer through the experiences of prayer we offer to them.

Catechumens need to be invited to experience a variety of prayer forms: praying from scripture, using the imagination in prayer, *lectio divina* (holy reading) as a form of meditative prayer, the prayer of intercession, centering prayer, discursive prayer, prayer of praise, body prayer, and so on. These prayer experiences can be incorporated into the catechetical gatherings of the catechumens. Prayer between catechumens and sponsors needs also to be encouraged.

Private prayer needs to be nurtured and encouraged. Rather than merely presenting prayer formulas to memorize, we can highlight a balance between spontaneous prayer and some of the traditional prayer forms. Emphasis needs to be made on the importance of regularity in private prayer: perhaps encouraging the catechumens to designate a particular time of day for a specified period of time for prayer.

The issues and concerns of growth in the spiritual life will emerge naturally throughout the catechumenate process. Often we address them at catechetical gatherings, time with one's sponsor, or during opportunities to meet with team members. Days of recollection and retreat are excellent opportunities for catechumens, sponsors and team members to spend quality time reflecting on their experience of God.

Sometimes a catechumen will want additional support and guidance in the spiritual life. With the assistance of the team, the catechumen may discern the need for a spiritual companion or spiritual director. This may not be the case for everyone, and often the intense formation process of the catechumenate is sufficient support and direction for many catechumens. Opportunities for spiritual direction need to be made available for those who want additional support and direction. Later, in Chapter 13, we will explore the art of spiritual direction in Christian life.

LITURGICAL RITES

The rite also provides ample opportunities for the catechumens to enter into the public prayer and worship of the community. This liturgical formation is intimately connected with the catechetical, spiritual and apostolic formation dimensions of the catechumenate period. They flow from each other.

Rite of Dismissal During the Catechumenate

We celebrate the dismissal rite after the proclamation of the scriptures and homily and before the intercessory prayers of the faithful. Since the catechumens do not yet share in the priestly ministry of baptism, they do not participate in the priestly functions of the assembly: intercession and prayer of thanksgiving (see *RCIA*, 75.3). The norm for the dismissal rite is given in *RCIA*, 67.

Call

The presider invites the catechumens forward along with their discussion leader. Some communities have the catechumens sit together (along with their sponsors) in the front of the assembly to serve as witnesses to God's work in the community. Other communities prefer the catechumens to sit with their sponsors anywhere in the assembly since it is from this assembly and into this assembly that they are formed. Wherever we seat them, the catechumens come forward (without sponsors) to the designated place in front of the assembly.

Exhortation

The presider "urges them [the catechumens] to live according to the word of God they have just heard" (*RCIA*, 67). Options B and C give a model for the presider to make an explicit connection between the Word of God and the formation that will follow. Using these as a basis, the presider may wish to refer to the scripture texts of the day. There is no need, however, to give another homily here.

The presider may also encourage the discussion leader to assist the catechumens in deepening their understanding of the Word of God by the sharing of his or her own faith. At this point, many parishes have the practice of giving the lectionary to the discussion leader for use with the catechumens since the time to follow will be based on the scriptures proclaimed that day. If the lectionary is formally presented to the discussion leader, he or she holds the lectionary up as appropriate for the lectionary in any liturgical procession.

Good pastoral sense needs to dictate the "how" of the dismissal. This is not a major moment in the liturgical celebration, but it is an important one. It is inappropriate for the presider to make light of this ritual action and say something like, "Well, you gotta go now. We're throwing you out. Only kidding!" Unfortunately, such dismissals do exist in some parishes.

Some options to consider: Invite the entire assembly to extend hands in blessing during the dismissal formulary. Create dismissal texts that include acclamations for the assembly to proclaim or sing during the dismissal.

Dismissal Procession

The final words of the presider are words of dismissal. At this point, the discussion leader leads the catechumens in procession through the assembly to another place as clearly stated in the rite (*RCIA,* n. 67).

Some options to consider: Invite the community to sing a short refrain or acclamation—perhaps a seasonal piece or acclamation of blessing—during the dismissal procession. Have one or more acolytes accompany the procession with lit candles (especially if the lectionary is carried in procession) to the place of their continued gathering—and leave the candles with them.

Celebrations of the Word of God

Celebrations of the word are normative in Christian life and worship. Hence, it is appropriate that they serve as a centerpiece for catechumenal formation.

Read RCIA, *n. 81.*

Priority is given to celebrations of the Word during catechumenal formation. The ritual text suggests that these regular celebrations of the Word combine three important dimensions of formation: the liturgical cycle, the catechesis of catechumens, and the community. It further specifies three types of celebrations of the Word: special celebrations of the Word, the Sunday Liturgy of the Word, and celebrations during catechesis.

Read RCIA, *n. 82.*

This section outlines the purpose of special celebrations of the Word.

Notice how careful the rite is to establish the link between the Word and catechesis. Presumably, whenever the catechumens gather for special events (e.g., an evening set aside to explore further a topic of interest that was not covered sufficiently), we would center the gathering around the celebration of the Word.

Read RCIA, *n. 83.*

This section assumes that catechumens may be meeting separate from the Sunday Liturgy of the Word (and dismissal) until they are integrated into that experience. It seems to suggest that a pastoral model might be to first gather with catechumens at the special celebrations of the Word noted above until the catechumens are accustomed to the liturgical prayer form. Then they are integrated into the Sunday Liturgy of the Word (which presumably replaces the special celebrations of the Word).

Read RCIA, *n. 84.*

The third type of celebrations of the Word are those held in connection with catechesis. This is especially important if the extended catechesis happens at a time other than Sunday. Presumably, whenever the catechumens gather for catechesis (after the dismissal or on another evening), they do so within the context of this celebration. Usually, the celebration of the Word in connection with catechesis would proclaim the scriptures prayed at the recent Sunday Liturgy of the Word.

Read RCIA, *nos. 85-89.*

Here the text provides us a model for a celebration of the Word. Note both its simplicity and striking resemblance to the Sunday Liturgy of the Word. Recall *RCIA,* n. 83: we are forming them into people who pray the Sunday Liturgy of the Word.

Note the directive in *RCIA,* n. 87 that a baptized member of the community proclaims the scriptures. Also, note the inclusion of other liturgical rites noted in *RCIA,* n. 89.

It seems reasonable that one way of integrating the catechesis with this celebration of the Word would be to replace the homily with the extended catechesis (conversation with the Word and Tradition).

Minor Exorcisms

An exorcism is a prayer that acknowledges the darkness or void of sin, calling upon the very presence of God to breathe life where there is only death. Once properly explained, minor exorcisms can be especially effective following a catechetical gathering during which time we uncovered a great deal of pain and anguish.

Read RCIA, *n. 90.*

This section highlights the purpose of the minor exorcisms in catechumenal formation. Note the first line that specifies that we address the exorcism prayers to God (in contrast to earlier forms of exorcism addressed to the Evil

One) in the form of petitions (in contrast to declarative statements "I command you…"). Clearly, the exorcisms are not intended to frighten the catechumen (despite the word) but to be a source of strength and new power from God.

Read RCIA, *n. 91.*

This section notes who is qualified to preside at these minor exorcisms. In the United States, according to *Study Text 10: Christian Initiation* published by the United States Catholic Conference, appointed catechists are deputed to preside at minor exorcisms unless stated otherwise in diocesan policy.

Read RCIA, *n. 92.*

Normally, the minor exorcisms are integrated into a celebration of the Word and/or the catechetical session. When necessary, we can also celebrate them privately. Because of the nature of minor exorcisms, including other members of the community seems prudent always if we need a private celebration.

Read RCIA, *n. 93.*

The directive is given to allow the use of the minor exorcisms more than once during the catechumenate.

Prayers of Exorcism (RCIA, *n. 94*)

The rite provides eleven different exorcism prayers. Reviewing all eleven texts to be familiar with the content of each of them is helpful. There is a basic structure or movement to the exorcism prayer: invocation/address to God, petition(s) for freedom, petition(s) for God's strength and help.

Don't be deceived by the relative simplicity of the ritual. It is within this simple structure that the words take on focused meaning. The catechumens assume a posture of kneeling (or bow their heads). Although the text does not specify the role of sponsors, we can presume they are present and at the side of the catechumens offering support (symbolized by hands on their shoulder or similar gesture). The presider extends hands over all the catechumens and slowly prays the exorcism text, perhaps pausing between paragraphs. No other ritual gesture accompanies the exorcism prayer.

An option to consider: invite the baptized community to extend hands in prayer as they join in prayer.

Blessings of the Catechumens

To bless is to acknowledge God's presence. It is the recognition that in this person, this meal, this community, we come to know God. Blessing is a form of recognition and thanksgiving. The *Code of Canon Law* (cf. canon 1170) reminds us that we can give blessings to catechumens (see also *NS*, n. 8).

Read RCIA, *n. 95.*

This section describes blessings and their purpose in catechumenal formation.

Read RCIA, *n. 96.*

Normally, we give blessings at the end of the celebration of the Word, as well as when gathered for catechesis or, if the need warrants, privately. These blessings can be ample and frequent, heightening the awareness of the catechumens of the graciousness and abundance of God's loving presence. As with minor exorcisms, appointed catechists in the United States are deputed to preside at blessings.

> *Prayers of Blessing, n. 97*

The rite offers nine different blessings for use with the catechumens. The ritual structure is straightforward: call to prayer, celebrant extends hands over all the catechumens, invocation, followed by an optional laying on of hands.

An option to consider: invite the baptized community to extend hands in prayer as they join in prayer.

Anointing of the Catechumens

The anointing appropriate to the period of the catechumenate is one for strength: that the catechumens be confident in their relationship with God so that they can move forward in the journey of faith.

> *Read* RCIA, *n. 98.*

This section gives specific directives about anointing catechumens with the oil of catechumens. This first anointing (which may be repeated) is celebrated by a priest or deacon; the second anointing will be the chrismation at initiation.

Recall that *RCIA,* n. 33.7 (see also *NS,* n. 16) notes that in the United States, this anointing with the oil of catechumens is done during the period of the catechumenate (and the period of purification and enlightenment).

> *Read* RCIA, *n. 99.*

This section describes the purpose of the anointing. This is not to be confused with the anointing used in the pastoral care of the sick. That anointing is one of healing; in this case, this is an anointing of strengthening.

> *Read* RCIA, *n. 100.*

Here we read how to integrate the anointing into the celebration of the Word. The rite also gives permission to celebrate the anointing privately if necessary.

> *Read* RCIA, *n. 101.*

The oil of catechumens is blessed at the Chrism Mass each year by the bishop along with the oil for the sick and chrism. A ritual text is provided in *RCIA,* n. 102B in the event that more oil needs to be blessed.

> *Prayer of Exorcism or Blessing of Oil (RCIA, n. 102)*

As with all the other rituals appropriate for the period of the catechumenate, the ritual structure is rather simple for the anointing of the catechumens. The first part of the ritual is a prayer of exorcism (*RCIA,* n. 102A). The rite also provides a text for the blessing of oil, as noted above.

Anointing (RCIA, n. 103)

The presider then prays the text in *RCIA*, n. 103 to all the catechumens, followed by an individual anointing on the hands or breast. Note that the anointing of the head is reserved for the chrismation at the celebration of the initiation sacraments. The anointing needs to be full; not a little dab of oil. And there is no need to rush to wipe away the oil. After the anointing, the rite recommends a blessing for the catechumens.

An option to consider: Instead of praying the anointing text to all the catechumens, the presider could approach each individually, pray the text, and proceed immediately to anoint the catechumen.

If all the rituals discussed so far (except dismissal) were celebrated at one time, the probable order would be:

Song (*RCIA*, n. 86)

Readings and Responsorial Psalm (*RCIA*, n. 86)

Homily (*RCIA*, n. 88)

Concluding Rites (*RCIA*, n. 89)

• Minor Exorcism (*RCIA*, n. 94 or 102A)

• Anointing (*RCIA*, n. 103)

• Blessing (*RCIA*, n. 97)

Rites of Passage

Recall that *RCIA*, n. 33.6 left for the conference of bishops to decide about additional rites (termed rites of passage) for the period of the catechumenate. The U.S. bishops approved various rites of passage: anointing with the oil of catechumens (discussed above), early celebrations of the presentations, the ephphatha rite, and the catechumen's recitation of the Creed. Brief comments will be made to the use of these rites of passages. However, further exploration of them can be found in later sections of this resource (presentations in Chapter 9; ephphatha rite and recitation of the Creed, Chapter 10).

Presentations

Read RCIA, *nos. 104-105.*

The presentation of the Creed (*RCIA*, nos. 157-162) and the Lord's Prayer (*RCIA*, nos. 178-183) are celebrations designated during the period of purification and enlightenment; we normally celebrate the Ephphatha Rite as one of the preparation rites on Holy Saturday (*RCIA*, nos. 197-199). However, we may anticipate them during the period of the catechumenate, especially because the period of purification is already filled with the preparation, celebration and reflection on the scrutinies.

The presentations are the gifts of the community to the catechumens. The timing of the presentations will need to be the result of discerning the catechumen's readiness to welcome and receive these gifts of faith from the community.

Celebrating these presentations closer to the celebration of election seems reasonable.

If celebrating either the presentation of the Creed or the Lord's Prayer, the ritual structure would be as follows. Note this is not a combined rite for both presentations. However, since the ritual structure is very similar, the same pattern is given with differences noted in brackets. Also, the ritual text presumes this is celebrated with the larger assembly.

Liturgy of the Word: Readings (*RCIA*, n. 158 or 179)
[Gospel Reading for the Presentation of the Lord's Prayer
    (*RCIA*, n. 180)]
Homily (*RCIA*, n. 159 or 181)
[Presentation of the Creed (*RCIA*, n. 160)]
Prayer over the Catechumens (*RCIA*, n. 161 or 182)
[Ephphatha Rite (*RCIA*, n. 199)—not used if the recitation of the Creed
    will also be a rite of passage; otherwise, used with the presentation]
Dismissal of the Catechumens (*RCIA*, n. 162 or 183)
Liturgy of the Eucharist for the Community (*RCIA*, n. 163 or 184)

Rite of Recitation of the Creed

If celebrating the rite of recitation of the Creed, the ritual structure is as follows. Of course, the rite of recitation of the Creed *presumes* that the presentation of the Creed has already happened. As with the two presentations, one would not celebrate a combined presentation of the Creed with the rite of recitation of the Creed.

Liturgy of the Word: Readings (*RCIA*, n. 194)
Homily (*RCIA*, n. 194)
Ephphatha Rite (*RCIA*, n. 199)
Prayer before the Recitation (*RCIA*, n. 195)
Recitation of the Creed (*RCIA*, n. 196)
Dismissal of the Catechumens (*RCIA*, n. 162 or 183)
Liturgy of the Eucharist for the Community (*RCIA*, n. 163 or 184)

Sending of the Catechumens for Election

The rite of sending the catechumens for election (an optional rite) is the last of the rites appropriate for the period of the catechumenate. This ritual was crafted for use in the United States in response to the pastoral practice of celebrating the rite of election at the parish rather than at the cathedral. Once the rite of election at the cathedral became normative, many people expressed concern that the local church's testimony was missing (as experienced in the local rite of election). The rite of sending was developed to respond to this need.

The celebration of the rite of sending presumes that the appropriate discernment for election has happened. Later in this chapter, guidance for this discernment is given. Because of the close link of the rite of sending with the rite of election, we will discuss its celebration in Chapter 8 of this resource along with the rite of election.

APOSTOLIC WITNESS

The great mystics of our tradition have always reminded us that the fruits of the experience of God, especially that nurtured in prayer, are lives molded in charity and justice. There can be no authentic expression of faith that is not rooted in justice and charity for all men and women. To suggest otherwise is something private, but not the Christian gospel.

The American bishops had this to say in their February 1976 statement on *Political Responsibility* (no. 6):

> Christians believe that Jesus' commandment to love one's neighbor should extend beyond individual relationships to infuse and transform all human relationships from the family to the entire human community. Jesus came to "bring good news to the poor, to proclaim liberty to captives, new sight to the blind and set the downtrodden free" (Lk 4:18). He called us to feed the hungry, clothe the naked, care for the sick and afflicted, and to comfort the victims of injustice (Mt 25). His example and Words require individual acts of charity and concern from each of us. Yet they also require understanding and action upon the broader dimensions of poverty, hunger, and injustice which necessarily involve the institutions and structures of economy, society, and politics.

In many ways, the fourth dimension of catechumenal formation—apostolic service—stands as a corrective to the other three dimensions. There is the possibility of getting so wrapped up inside ourselves, whether it is personally or in the catechumenal group or even our parish, that we lose sight of the goal of initiation (initial and on-going): discipleship. Apostolic service gives flesh to the other dimensions of formation.

Initiation gatherings to share (or explain) the essentials of Catholic Christian life fall limp if they do not engender a true sense of mission and ministry in all those gathered (including the team). The *Rite of Christian Initiation of Adults* gives us some direction on this in *RCIA,* n. 75.4. This is disciple-making.

Apostolic service is how Christians care for the authentic needs of others and the world community. It is not primarily work inside the Church (though, at times, that is necessary). It is witness to the gospel message of the nearness of the reign of God by concrete actions that are symbols of reconciliation, mercy, justice and compassion. These "symbols" are the very actions on behalf of peace and justice that disclose and reveal the presence of the reign of God.

Apostles (from the Greek *apostelein*) are those sent forth by the Spirit, as was Jesus, to bring good news to the poor, liberty to captives, recovery of sight to the blind, freedom to the oppressed and announcement of God's salvation to all (see Luke 4:18f). Christian apostles are sent to their homes, neighborhoods, workplaces and the world community to serve in the name of Jesus and after the example of Jesus.

Where do we see this example? Throughout the gospels, the consistent theme of Jesus' lifestyle, preaching and teaching was clearly the reign of God. Whenever and wherever there is mercy, forgiveness, compassion, reconciliation and justice, there is the approaching reign of God. For Jesus, the approaching reign of God was not an abstraction. It was not something for later, but a reality to be lived now. The same is true for us.

It is interesting that, in the gospel of John, the eucharistic narrative is not focused on the bread and cup (as in the synoptic gospels) but on the washing of the feet. Spending oneself in service to the authentic needs of others is truly eucharistic. There is an intimate connection between liturgy/sacrament and mission/justice. We need both in a Catholic/Christian way of life. In our experience of liturgy and sacrament, we discover anew our identity—the Body of Christ—and our way of life—people on mission for the reign of God. Thus, it is essential in catechumenal formation that candidates and catechumens discover the close link between who they are and how they are to live.

A theologian once said that if we really want to know who we are, we should spend less time navel gazing and more time responding to the true needs of others. In the very act of giving ourselves away in service to another's needs, we find ourselves—one of the many paradoxes of the Christian life style.

Probably the worst way of forming people in apostolic service is to assign apostolic tasks to them (sometimes called "service projects"), as if the poor and needy were projects we needed to complete to get a passing grade. Rather, forming people in apostolic service is to expose them to the works of ministry and service, justice and peace.

• Always keep the mission of the reign of God as a centerpiece during the preparation of catechumenal gatherings. This does not mean explicitly saying "reign of God" as much as making clear connections between the values of the reign of God and daily life.

• Expose catechumens to the varieties of apostolic witness in the parish community and diocese. This is different from assigning "service projects." Rather, it is exposing them to the various forms of apostolic service, both traditional and new. To do this effectively, the catechumenate team needs to review the direction of prayer and catechesis over the next few months and integrate various opportunities for apostolic witness. Some examples include helping at a soup kitchen, helping with prayer and service at a nursing home, participating in the work of Catholic Charities in the inner city or participating in an AIDS walk to raise funds and awareness. And then spend some time together talking about the experience (mystagogy) and making explicit links between these works of mercy and justice and the sacramental life.

• Consistently include readings from the documents of the Church on justice and peace (including those from the bishops' conference, such as the pastoral letters on peace and on the economy) during each catechumenal gathering. We can integrate these into prayer times or use them as discussion starters.

DISCERNING READINESS FOR ELECTION

The catechumens have undergone an intense period of formation throughout the period of the catechumenate. Stirred by the Word of God and the life of the Catholic community, they have experienced the call to a new way of life again and again. At some point in the process, the catechumens, along with their sponsors and the team, discern their readiness to live faithfully the commitment of the sacraments they will celebrate with the Catholic community.

The discernment for election for catechumens takes place slowly during the weeks before the Lenten season. The rite suggests the criteria to judge and discern the readiness for the Easter sacraments (*RCIA,* n. 120). This needs to be complemented by the ritual explanation of the renunciation of sin and profession of faith at the celebration of the sacraments of initiation, with its emphasis on explicit faith in the paschal mystery (*RCIA,* n. 211).

Conversion in mind and in action: Has the catechumen come to know God in this community? Has he or she been open to receive the Word of God? Has he or she responded to the Word both in prayer and in a life of service? Does he or she struggle with the demands of the Word?

Sufficient acquaintance with Christian teaching: Does he or she welcome the insights of the Catholic community in its teaching about how to follow the gospel? Has he or she been exposed to the best in Catholic thought on the fundamentals of the Christian life?

Spirit of faith and charity: Does he or she seek God in prayer, with confidence and trust? Is there growth in the individual's capacity to give and receive love? Is there a personal relationship with God?

Acknowledged intention to receive the sacraments: Has the catechumen found this community to be a place of welcome and support? Does he or she desire to contribute to the growth and development of this particular community? Does he or she desire to receive the gift of freedom and salvation (and all its demands) from God in Christ through the Spirit. Or, if baptized already, does he or she desire to deepen the freedom God generously gives in Christ through the Spirit? Does he or she recognize himself or herself as a child of God?

The discernment for election and recognition is not a discernment for canonization and final perfection. Nor is this the "final exam," the test of religious knowledge. Rather, our posture needs to be of welcome, of waiting, of listening to the catechumen's willingness to embrace fully, with all his or her limits and gifts, the way of life of the gospel within the Catholic communion. We are inviting the catechumen to recognize God's stirrings and the response of faith. For some people, the time is not right. There is more growth, more challenge, more of a response needed before they can make the commitment to the sacraments. One needs honesty and courage to make any decision at this point. There is no right decision, just good decisions. The catechumen, sponsor, team and pastoral staff will suffer with (i.e., be compassionate toward) God's promptings.

The decision for election ultimately rests in the hands of the community, as represented by the pastor, to make their recommendation to the bishop. If the catechumenate process has been honest and willing to respect individual conversion, then the catechumen will most probably be able to respect whatever decision is made. Recommendation to celebrate sacraments (and the commitment that entails) or to continue in preparation demands a trust forged by respect and concern for the catechumens.

ADAPTATION WITH CHILDREN OF CATECHETICAL AGE

If we review part II, chapter 1 of the ritual text, we will find nothing written about the period of the catechumenate. Of course, this does not mean that we eliminate this period for children of catechetical age. No, instead we presume the vision and practice of part I. Hence, the pastoral notes for this chapter apply to children in all ways.

Hopefully, the peer companions and family are actively involved with the formation given the children at this time. Just like the adults, the formation continues for a minimum of a year. And, just like the adults, the formation does not happen in the classroom but in an environment modeled on the liturgical assembly.

We can more easily fall prey to the tendency for "academic" models when implementing with children than with adults. Part of that is due to our previous experience of sacramental formation with children: in the school environment. But, clearly, the *Rite of Christian Initiation of Adults* is calling for something more—and children have a right to the full formation the rite prescribes.

ADAPTATION WITH BAPTIZED CANDIDATES

If we take seriously the concerns raised in Chapter 3 of this resource (as well as in the ritual text itself in part II, chapters 4 and 5) regarding the appropriate distinctions that need to be made between the unbaptized and the baptized, we will need to grapple with the concern about the distinctions appropriate for their formation during this period. This, of course, presumes that the parish is not providing a separate process for baptized candidates. If it is, this is a moot point and we simply follow the directives of the rite in part II, chapters 4 and 5 accordingly. However, with a "combined" process, many questions arise: Do we include the baptized candidates in the catechumenate groups? Does their formation continue for a minimum of one year as it does with the catechumens? Do we dismiss candidates? Do we celebrate the rites from the period of the catechumenate with them also? Let's address each question.

To answer these questions adequately, we will need to make further distinctions about the baptized candidates: baptized and uncatechized (Roman Catholic or other Christian tradition as defined in *RCIA,* n. 400), and baptized catechized (other Christian tradition, see *RCIA,* nos. 473ff.; recall in Chapter 3 of this resource that we noted that the baptized, catechized Catholic is not involved in this process).

Do we include the baptized candidates in the catechumenate groups?

Baptized and Uncatechized
Acknowledging the appropriate distinctions that need to be made, *RCIA,* nos. 401-402 suggest that the baptized and uncatechized candidate enroll in a process of formation that corresponds to the one provided for catechumens. Hence, presuming their presence at the catechetical gatherings is reasonable, along with their sponsors.

Baptized and Catechized
Most baptized and catechized candidates will need a relatively short period of formation before celebrating reception into the full communion of the Catholic Church. These candidates might benefit from the atmosphere and dynamics of the catechumenal gathering, but more often than not there are specific issues or topics that need to be discussed with them based on their background and need. It is preferred, whenever it is possible, to align these candidates with other candidates in similar situations. Their catechesis will probably not be based on the liturgical year, though the other directive for catechesis (solidly supported by celebrations of the Word, etc.) would apply.

Does their formation continue for a minimum of one year as it does with the catechumens?

Baptized and Uncatechized

RCIA, n. 408 suggests that the catechesis for baptized and uncatechized adults be coordinated with the liturgical year, with the completion of the formation to coincide with Lent (as with the catechumens). The text does not prescribe one year; however, one can infer that there would need to be an extended period due to the lack of foundations in the Christian pattern of catechesis, way of life, liturgy and apostolic witness (*RCIA*, n. 75).

Baptized and Catechized

RCIA, nos. 473 and 477 give us direction here. The formation is to be such that the candidates receive the appropriate preparation needed for celebrating their reception into the full communion of the Catholic Church. However, "no greater burden than necessary" is to be added to their formation. Thus, a year immersion in catechesis is highly improbable for these candidates. In fact, they may be in this period of formation for a few weeks or months, depending on their need.

Do we dismiss candidates?

The rite does not say that candidates are to be dismissed. In fact, we can make an argument for their remaining with the assembly due to the specific dismissals of catechumens in the combined rites (Appendix I). Therefore, we need to make some pastoral decisions. The following points can assist us in making those decisions.

◆ *We never dismiss baptized Catholics who celebrate the eucharist.* This refers especially to sponsors of catechumens or Catholics preparing for confirmation (who have had little formation in faith but did celebrate the eucharist). For some reason, some parishes have gotten into the practice of dismissing these people who have a right and responsibility to be present for the eucharist. The only member of the faithful who leaves during the dismissal (and technically is not dismissed) is the presider over the subsequent gathering with the catechumens. He or she needs to arrange to celebrate the eucharist at a different time.

◆ *Baptized Christians* (i.e., people baptized Catholic but who do not celebrate eucharist yet and those baptized in other Christian communities who do not celebrate eucharist yet with the Roman Catholic community) have a right to participate in the priestly prayer of the eucharist by virtue of their baptism. Initiation leaders need to review the Ecumenical Directory for guidance regarding the participation of baptized candidates (who are not Catholic) in the community's worship.

◆ *Participation in the eucharist is broader than participation in the eucharistic prayer only.* Such participation in the eucharistic prayer reaches its climax in the assembly's communion rite and the subsequent dismissal for mission of all the faithful.

Should people in formation who have a right to participate in the eucharistic prayer but who do not presently participate in the assembly's communion rite remain for the eucharistic prayer? Or should they gather with other people in formation to continue to participate in the reflection on the real presence of Christ in Word and community? (Note: the distinction is made between people in formation and those gathered with the assembly who, for whatever reason, are not participating in the eucharistic feast.) Some consider it an act of hospitality to invite such individuals to participate in the dismissal rite of the catechumens and the subsequent reflection because they are unable to share in the eucharistic feast.

What we cannot overlook, however, is the baptized person's right to pray the eucharistic prayer with the community (a priestly role) because of his or her baptism. Hence, if a parish wishes to dismiss candidates, it can only do so with the permission of the candidates.

Pastoral teams need to reflect critically on the values at stake on both sides of the issues in dismissing candidates before the eucharistic prayer.

Do we celebrate the rites from the period of the catechumenate with them also?

Baptized and Uncatechized

The ritual text prescribes that baptized and uncatechized candidates would benefit during this period from celebrations of the Word (*RCIA,* n. 406), certain rites of passage: presentations of the Creed and the Lord's Prayer (*RCIA,* n. 407), and a presentation of the book of the gospels (*RCIA,* n. 407), unless this was already done at the rite of welcoming the candidates. The *Code of Canon Law* in canon 1170 reminds us that we can give blessings to Catholics and non-Catholics as well. If using the ritual texts for these rites, the wording needs to be changed.

Because of their nature as preparations for baptism, we do not celebrate the minor exorcisms and the anointings with candidates.

Baptized and Catechized

Similarly to the pastoral directives for the baptized and uncatechized candidates, the rite prescribes in *RCIA,* n. 478 that many of these rituals may be of benefit to the baptized and catechized candidate. Specifically, including celebrations of the Word of God and blessings would be appropriate.

8

Second Step: Rite of Election or Enrollment of Names

God our Father,
you always work to save us,
and now we rejoice in the great love
you give to your chosen people.
Protect all who are about to become your children,
and continue to bless those who are already baptized.
—*Opening Prayer, Ritual Mass:"Christian Initiation:*
Election or Enrollment of Names"

INTRODUCTION

The rite of election is a significant moment in the initiation process. After extended discernment, the community can give witness to God's election of the catechumens. This election is not about the catechumens choosing the sacraments of initiation. Rather, as in the great scriptural tradition of election, it is about God's choice of the catechumens to embrace the mission of Jesus, the mission of the reign of God. We ritually celebrate this commitment in the sacraments of initiation. Here, especially, the gift and responsibility of initiation confront us: it is truly God's choice and one responds freely (intention) and embraces the responsibilities (discipleship).

WHAT DOES THE RITE SAY?

Read RCIA, *n. 118.*
Bringing together two ancient traditions—election and enrollment of names—this section highlights this rite as a turning point in the initiation process: from the extended formation of the period of the catechumenate to the immediate preparation during the Lenten retreat. The formal preparation (as outlined in *RCIA,* n. 75) is completed.
Read RCIA, *n. 119.*
At the heart of this liturgical celebration is the election by God. Nothing in the rite (or the discernment for the celebration) can obscure this theological

Rite of Election or Enrollment of Names					
	UNBAPTIZED ADULT	CHILDREN OF CATECHETICAL AGE	BAPTIZED, UNCATECHIZED CATHOLIC	BAPTIZED, UNCATECHIZED CHRISTIAN	BAPTIZED, CATECHIZED CHRISTIAN
Reference	*RCIA*, nos. 118–137	*RCIA*, nos. 277–290; 118–137	*RCIA*, nos. 446–449	*RCIA*, nos. 446–449	*RCIA*, nos. 478; 446–449
Preparatory Rite	Sending of the Catechumens for Election (*RCIA*, nos. 106–117)	Sending of the Catechumens for Election (*RCIA*, nos. 106–117)	Rite of Sending the Candidates for Recognition by the Bishop and for the Call to Continuing Conversion (*RCIA*, nos. 434–445)	Rite of Sending the Candidates for Recognition by the Bishop and for the Call to Continuing Conversion (*RCIA*, nos. 434–445)	If helpful (*RCIA*, n. 478); Rite of Sending the Candidates for Recognition by the Bishop and for the Call to Continuing Conversion (*RCIA*, nos. 434–445)
Combined Rite	Parish Celebration for Sending Catechumens for Election and Candidates for Recognition by the Bishop				
Rite	Rite of Election or Enrollment of Names	Rite of Election or Enrollment of Names	Rite of Calling the Candidates to Continuing Conversion	Rite of Calling the Candidates to Continuing Conversion	If helpful (*RCIA*, n. 478); Rite of Calling the Candidates to Continuing Conversion
Combined Rite	Celebration of the Rite of Election of Catechumens and of the Call to Continuing Conversion of Candidates Who Are Preparing for Confirmation and/or Eucharist or Reception into the Full Communion of the Catholic Church				
Required	Yes	Yes	Recommended	Recommended	If helpful, recommended
Time	Normally First Sunday of Lent	Normally First Sunday of Lent	Normally First Sunday of Lent	Normally First Sunday of Lent	Normally First Sunday of Lent

foundation: God chooses for service of the mission of the reign of God. In light of this, godparents are entrusted with the responsibility to give testimony for the catechumens, and the Church, acting in God's name, chooses the catechumens for the celebration of the initiation sacraments that mark their immersion in the paschal mystery and, therefore, the mission of the reign of God.

This section also highlights the second dimension of the rite: the enrollment of names. This ritual inscription in the Book of the Elect is a public gesture to attest to the seriousness of the commitment of the elect.

Read RCIA, *n. 120.*

In broad strokes, the ritual text outlines the expectations of those continuing to the rite of election. This provides a foundation for the discernment before the celebration of the rite. Along with this text, initiation teams can find support from *RCIA,* nos. 131 and 211, and canon 865 of the *Code of Canon Law* for direction as to the content of the discernment.

Read RCIA, *n. 121.*

The bishop, who is responsible for initiation, presides at the ritual celebration. The rite of election is not a mere formality in the initiation process. It is pivotal because the catechumens, having undergone an extensive formation, give witness to their willingness to respond positively to God's call. Thus, the ritual text is clear that all those responsible for the initiation process engage in careful and prayerful assessment of the state of the catechumen in his or her formation.

Read RCIA, *n. 122.*

The deliberation called for here is intended to support the directive in *RCIA,* n. 120. This is not decision-making; it is discernment that takes seriously God's action in the lives of the catechumens. Clearly, God's choice of service for the reign of God takes shape in a person as he or she responds to this choice by God. This finds further manifestations in one's way of life. Hence, *RCIA,* nos. 131 and 211, and canon 865 of the *Code of Canon Law* provide signs of election.

Read RCIA, *n. 123.*

The text notes the important role of godparents here. Given what is said earlier about the public testimony of godparents, it is safe to presume their early and active involvement in the initiation process, and also their participation in the discernment to celebrate election.

Read RCIA, *n. 124.*

This section notes the various names used in the tradition to speak of the elect: *competentes* and *illuminandi.* The use of these terms highlights the richness of the theological foundations for this rite and the subsequent period of purification and enlightenment.

Read RCIA, *n. 125.*

This section gives direction for the role of the bishop in the rite of election. In particular, the bishop needs to be very careful in his preaching (and throughout the rite) to keep the focus on God's election of the catechumens and the meaning of this election within our Catholic Christian tradition. Thus, the declaration of election and other ritual moments should not be presented in any other manner than what they are: ritual expressions of God's election.

Read RCIA, *n. 126.*

The ritual text notes the normative time of celebrating the rite of election: the First Sunday of Lent. "Urgent" pastoral reasons can cause the anticipation or delay by a week—but it seems, given the character of the rite and its association with Lent, it is difficult to ascertain what those urgent pastoral reasons would be that bear more weight than the liturgical celebrations of the Lenten retreat.

Furthermore, if a community celebrates the initiation sacraments at an unusual time, they still celebrate the rite of election about six weeks before the celebration of sacraments. This is another place where the rite highlights the importance and pivotal nature of this rite both in the initiation process and in the life of the Church.

Read RCIA, *n. 127.*

This section highlights the location of the rite of election. Since normally the diocesan bishop is the presider, we celebrate the rite at the cathedral church. Other locations (depending on who is presiding, as well as other concerns) are also noted as alternatives.

Read RCIA, *n. 128.*

The ritual text notes that the usual time for celebrating the rite of election is after the homily during the Mass of the First Sunday of Lent. The practice in most dioceses is to celebrate the rite of election later in the day within a celebration of the Word. The lectionary texts for the rite of election should still be used when celebrated outside of Mass.

THE ROLE OF GODPARENTS AND SPONSORS

Godparents are companions for the Christian life for the catechumen. Unlike sponsors whose role it is to better acquaint the catechumen with the community and offer initial support and care, the godparents serve the catechumens by helping them integrate into the Catholic community by offering ongoing support, care, and the sharing of faith.

Godparents assume their public role in the *Rite of Christian Initiation of Adults* at the rite of election when the Church formally recognizes the catechumen as ready for the Easter sacraments (*RCIA,* n. 123). However, to assume this public role with any integrity, the godparents need to be actively involved in the life and formation of the catechumen well before the discernment for election.

The catechumen chooses the godparents. Usually they are friends or close acquaintances who honestly struggle to live the values of the gospel in the ordinariness of their daily lives. If there is one godparent, then he or she must be a fully initiated member of the Catholic Church. The godparent cannot be a parent; spouses are discouraged. A godparent from another Christian community may witness for the catechumen, but there still needs to be at least one Catholic godparent.

The initiation team needs to give some formation and support to godparents before the rite of election, and also during the period of enlightenment and purification. Many godparents will be unaware of the initiation process and what is expected of them in the life of the catechumen. Providing the necessary support will help alleviate any confusion for them.

With the rite of election, there is a shift in roles. The elect will now be accompanied by their godparents throughout the remainder of the initiation process; sponsors have completed their work (unless the sponsor is chosen for the role of godparent). While the rite is silent about the continued engagement between sponsor and elect, it would be insensitive simply to dismiss the sponsors at this time. Even if we did, the elect would probably still seek out their sponsors for support.

There is no reason not to include the sponsors during these next periods and steps of initiation formation. We need to be clear with them that they have completed their formal role of service (lest they try to usurp the responsibilities of the godparents); also, we want graciously to invite them to continue the journey with the elect. Given the importance of building relationship between elect and godparents, discourage the presence of the sponsor in any of the rituals (except, of course, as members of the assembly) unless there is no godparent readily available to help the elect at these times. Hopefully, as we move from godparents-at-a-distance to godparents-on-the-journey, the godparents will be actively engaged in the rites and other events from the rite of election forward.

DAY OF PRAYER

At some point before the celebration of the rite of election, gathering to prayerfully reflect on the significance of this transition would be beneficial for the catechumens. They have already struggled to come to a decision with their sponsors and the team regarding election. That had been done within the context of prayer. Now it is time to spend some initial reflection on the meaning of this call to the sacraments and a life of mission in service of the reign of God.

The format for this day of prayer can be very simple. It should be an opportunity for the catechumens, godparents, sponsors—actually anyone in the parish community—to spend time together in prayer and reflection. Following are suggestions of basic components that can be part of this period of reflection.

Private and Communal Prayer: The time together needs to be balanced between private, quiet time for personal prayer and reflection, and communal prayer experiences.

Proclamation of Scriptures: The period of reflection could be focused around the scripture texts that we will proclaim at the rite of election.

Initial Reflection Period: The first part of the day could be time alone, reflecting in various ways on the components that went into the discernment for election: conversion of mind and action, familiarity with Christian teaching, spirit of faith and charity, and the desire to celebrate the sacraments. This could be done through a guided imagery prayer experience on the call to discipleship, followed by a guided reflection on conversion during which we can give the invitation to reflect back to life before entering the initiation process and life now: How has it changed? How am I different? How would I describe myself then and now? The tensions of the various dimensions of conversion discussed earlier (moral, intellectual, affective, etc.) could be raised for further reflection.

We could also give the elect a reflection sheet for their use during the day. Following are some possible issues that could be raised.

— Spend some time in quiet and silence, asking God to help you be present to God's Spirit.

— Think back to when you first came to the parish seeking initiation. Try to describe how you felt about yourself, about God, about others. What words or symbols describe this time in your life?

— What were the turning points for you in the process? Who were the significant people along the way?

— Reflect about yourself now—your sense of self, your sense of God, your relationships with others, your relationship with the Church. What insights or images do you have to describe this period in your life?

— How are you different now? How have you changed? What is the cause of this change in your life?

— What has God done in your life?

— What do you need from God to grow more, to discover more the richness of your person and of this community?

If the elect have kept personal journals during the catechumenate process, they can be encouraged to bring them along for review, reflection and prayer.

Reflection on Election: Some time needs to be set aside for input and reflection on the meaning of election in the Catholic Christian tradition. Presumably, there is an implicit knowledge of election well before discernment for the rite. However, making some of that more explicit at this time is helpful. Later in the day, the catechumens could pair off with their godparents and sponsors and discuss this reflection on election. The questions for discernment outlined in the previous section might be helpful for discussion. This reflection period, as well as the numerous other times together, will help the godparents and sponsors to offer honest and authentic testimony at the rite of election.

Preparation for the Rite: Before ending the time together, briefly discuss the significance of the rite of election, i.e., it is a transition rite that brings them to a new period of preparation. There is no need to discuss the particularities of the rite beforehand. Arrangements need to be discussed regarding travel to the site of the rite of election.

Gathering with Godparents: After the catechumens have left, the god-parents will need to discuss the rite. This could be done within the context of discussing the day of reflection.

— How was your experience today with your catechumen?
— Did you learn anything new today about him/her?
— Did you learn anything new about yourself?
— Discuss the focus of the testimony given at the rite of sending or election with the sponsors (especially if using more than the ritual text).
— Review both rites, perhaps using a guide sheet for their reference.
— Together go to the worship space and "walk through" the rite of sending.
— Provide reflection time to write the testimony that will be used during the rite of sending.

A Word about this Testimony: The ritual text prescribes a ritual conversation for this testimony (*RCIA,* nos. 112, 131). Reviewing this testimony with the godparents would be very important for the initiation team, even if we follow the ritual text as written. Usually, at the rite of election, that will be the case due to the large number of catechumens. However, it is often the case in the parish rite of sending that godparents are free to give the testimony in their own words. In those cases, we should give a few guidelines to godparents to help them prepare their testimony:

• The testimony is not a toast. We are not gathering to celebrate the good things in the life of the catechumen, however worthwhile that might be. We are gathered to celebrate our discernment of God's election of these catechumens.

• Therefore, the focus of the testimony is on God's election of the catechumen, not how good the catechumen is or has become. The tendency is to want to talk about "Sally does this…" and "Harry does that… " with a "He or she is such a wonderful person." Instead, if one reviews the ritual text, the focus is on the clear signs of God's election: there is evidence (which we have discerned) that the catechumen is responding to God's choice of him or her to serve the mission of the reign of God.

• Since the testimony of the godparents will become the model for the remaining testimony (by the assembly), it is imperative that godparents carefully craft the testimonies so that it gets to the point of the testimony without going too long. It is advisable that the testimonies are written out and reviewed by the initiation coordinator beforehand. The godparent could rely on these notes during the rite of sending, if necessary.

• To support each other, it is advisable that the godparents review their testimony with each other (at the end of the godparent preparation period noted above). This will help clarify what people intend to say, steer people away from the "toast" model, and give direction to those who are having difficulty writing their testimony.

CELEBRATING THE RITE OF SENDING

Read RCIA, *n. 106.*
Sending of the catechumens for election is an optional, parish-based rite developed for use in the United States. In the earlier years of implementing the *Rite of Christian Initiation of Adults,* many dioceses did not celebrate the rite of election at the cathedral with the diocesan bishop as presider. They often celebrated the rite at the parish. With the publication of the 1988 translation of the *Rite of Christian Initiation of Adults,* this changed, placing the rite of election back in the cathedral church with the diocesan bishop as the presider.
Read RCIA, *n. 107.*
The rite of sending provides an opportunity for the local community to celebrate this pivotal moment in the initiation process ritually. Probably—for many reasons—most of the community will not gather at the cathedral church for the rite of election. However, the discernment for election occurred in the midst of the local community.
Read RCIA, *n. 108.*
Since the rite of election is normally celebrated on the First Sunday of Lent, the rite of sending will need to be celebrated at a time before the cathedral celebration. A recommended time would be the day of election, at an earlier Mass in the parish community.
Read RCIA, *n. 109.*
The rite of sending normally follows the homily, before the dismissal of the catechumens.
Read RCIA, *n. 110.*
We will discuss the combined rite for catechumens and candidates later in this chapter in the section "Adaptation with Baptized Candidates."

Sending of the Catechumens for Election

Liturgy of the Word
Presentation of Catechumens (RCIA, n. 111)
The initiation coordinator (or someone else responsible for the formation of the catechumens) speaks to the community concerning the readiness of the catechumens to celebrate the initiation sacraments. Having been part of the discernment process, the coordinator may choose to highlight some dimensions of conversion experienced by the catechumens while maintaining confidentiality.

The presider next invites the catechumens to come forward with their godparents. Each catechumen is then called individually.

Affirmation by the Godparents and Assembly (RCIA, n. 112)

The presider now requests some testimony from those responsible for the formation of the catechumens. The presider may also witness at this time if the presider had been part of the discernment process.

The godparents are the first to be invited to give testimony regarding the readiness of the catechumens. It is important that the godparents be heard by the community, so a portable microphone needs to be ready for their use. The godparents can complete their witness by recommending to the community that the catechumens be welcomed to the initiation sacraments.

Catechists are also encouraged to offer testimony. Hopefully, the catechumens have had a rich experience of the community. Therefore, the presider may invite anyone from the community to come forward to give testimony. In offering this invitation, the presider can briefly note the focus of the testimony (without making this a long statement) to guide the comments by the assembly. Again, to be effective, the community needs to hear these testimonies. Placing microphones throughout the worship space can facilitate this.

Public testimony is foreign for most Catholics. To start the process, the initiation team might consider asking members of the community beforehand to prepare a short testimony for the catechumens. After a few years—when the community is more familiar with the expectations placed on it—the testimony will come more spontaneously.

The presider, in the name of the community, summarizes the testimony given and notes that the catechumens receive the support of the community to celebrate the rite of election.

If the Book of the Elect is to be signed at the cathedral liturgy, the rite continues with the intercessions for the catechumens. However, because of the large numbers of catechumens, the signing of the Book of the Elect is happening frequently at the parish celebration. This would then be the appropriate time to invite the catechumens to sign the Book of the Elect. The godparent witnesses the signing of the book and may be asked to sign the book with the catechumen (*RCIA,* n. 113).

Care needs to be taken regarding the physical placement of the Book of the Elect during this part of the rite. Using the altar as a table for the inscription is inappropriate. Perhaps someone can carry the book to the individual to be signed while someone else (such as an acolyte) holds the book. Or perhaps the presider could hold the book and the catechumen can come forward to sign it. Or we can bring out a small stand for the inscription.

The signing in the Book of the Elect by the catechumens is a ritual gesture that demonstrates their clear intention to respond to God's election by celebrating the sacraments of initiation and all the responsibilities therein. The signing of the Book of the Elect by the godparents affirms their responsibility to accompany the catechumens in the life of the disciple.

The process of affirmation and enrollment may be done individually for each catechumen. While the catechumen signs the Book of the Elect, the community can sing an antiphon. The second possibility is that we give the affirmations for all the catechumens, followed by an individual signing of the Book of the Elect.

When the enrollment is completed, the Book of the Elect can be presented to the community for its witness. In some communities, they carry the Book of the Elect—still open to the page just signed—throughout the community as they sing an antiphon.

Intercessions for the Catechumens and Candidates (RCIA, n. 114)

The community prays for the catechumens. The liturgical ministry, especially the ministers of music, may want to adapt the text provided to meet the needs and circumstances of the catechumens and candidates. This will include some previous awareness of their journey, which can be discovered either through participation with the catechumens and candidates or through dialogue with the initiation team. If we will not pray the general intercessions at this Mass, intentions for the Church and the world are to be included in these intercessions.

Prayer over the Catechumens and Candidates (RCIA, n. 115)

The presider gathers all these prayers together in a prayer over the catechumens.

Dismissal (RCIA, n. 116)

We now dismiss the catechumens and candidates from the assembly to journey to the cathedral for the rite of election. It would be an appropriate sign for the presider to present the initiation coordinator with the signed Book of the Elect to be presented to the bishop at the rite of election.

CELEBRATING THE RITE OF ELECTION

Liturgy of the Word
Homily (RCIA, n. 129)

The proposed scriptures for the day are those for the First Sunday of Lent, Year A. Since most dioceses celebrate the rite of election during a celebration of the word rather than Mass, using the texts for this day is still normative. The homily follows, which should make a clear connection between the scripture texts and God's election.

Presentation of the Catechumens (RCIA, n. 130)

After the homily, the catechumens are presented to the bishop for election. If there are large numbers of catechumens from many parishes, one person may speak for all gathered. In some dioceses, each initiation coordinator comes forward and reads the names of the catechumens from his or her parish.

As the names are read, the catechumens and their godparents come forward. Presumably, they are seated throughout the cathedral. One option is to invite them to stand in place while the names are read for the particular parish, and then invite them to come forward. If the option is chosen not to read the names of the catechumens, it is important that this be done at the rite of sending beforehand. However, given the importance of naming in our culture, it makes good sense always to include the individual calling of names at this point of the rite.

Where the catechumens and godparents will "come forward" to depends on the cathedral itself. Keep in mind the concerns of the rite when determining how to use the space for the rite. Another thing to keep in mind is that this "call forward" is not intended for the catechumens to shake the bishop's hand or exchange a greeting with the bishop. Nowhere in the ritual text will we find this diversion from the ritual. Such greetings can occur outside the ritual experience at a reception afterward. This would keep the correct perspective: that the rite of election is not about the bishop but about God's election of these catechumens.

Affirmation by Godparents and the Assembly (RCIA, n. 131)

Once all the catechumens are in place, the bishop addresses the godparents for their testimony. It would be wonderful if the godparents could give spontaneous testimony concerning the catechumens. This could be followed by testimony from people from around the diocese. However, given the large numbers at these rites of election, engaging in the ritual dialogue provided in the ritual text itself seems more appropriate. Godparents need to know clearly beforehand the assent the bishop will ask of them regarding the testimony.

A similar request of the entire assembly follows the testimony by the godparents. The question from the bishop not only focuses on the election of the catechumens, but also on the willingness of the community to continue its support of them.

Invitation and Enrollment of Names (RCIA, n. 132)

The bishop then addresses the catechumens, asking them publicly to declare their intention. Presumably, a great deal of prayer and reflection precedes this moment in the rite for the catechumens. That is why we must include the catechumens in the discernment for election.

Following the public statement of their intention, the bishop invites the catechumens to inscribe their names in the Book of the Elect. How this will be carried out depends on the diocesan practice. If the elect are to sign their names at the rite of election, this is the time to do this and they should come forward with their godparents. Presumably, they are called by parish to do this (since each parish usually maintains its own Book of the Elect).

If the signing of the Book of the Elect already happened in the parish rite of sending, then the Book of the Elect from each parish is brought forward for the bishop—and the assembly—to see. Perhaps in a modified form, the suggestion of holding the Book of the Elect open in the assembly during the rite of sending can be done here. Nonetheless, the books are brought forward and can be held during the next moments of the rite by the persons carrying the books.

It is important to note that neither here nor anywhere else in the ritual text is there included a "signing off" by the presiding bishop. This unusual practice places too much focus on the bishop and takes away from the central focus of God's election of these catechumens. If a parish community wishes to include the specifics of the rite in the Book of the Elect (date, place, presiding bishop), they can include this information after the rite.

Act of Admission or Election (RCIA, n. 133)

The bishop then reflects on the significance of the enrollment and makes a connection to the election by God. Following this, he ritually acknowledges what the community has discerned: that the catechumens are the elect of God, chosen by God for the service of the reign of God. This is an important moment in the rite, and singing an acclamation of praise and thanksgiving is appropriate for the assembly.

Following the words of election, the bishop encourages the newly elected to remain faithful to their call. This is followed by words of support to the godparents as he reminds them of their responsibilities toward the elect. The ritual text recommends that some gesture be done at this time—the rite recommends placing the hands of the godparents on the shoulders of the elect—to signal the acceptance of this responsibility.

An odd custom has developed in some dioceses at this point of the rite of election. They give a small gift—usually a scroll—to the elect as a remembrance of the rite. While this may be a worthwhile gesture, it surely does not belong in the ritual itself. Again, it shifts the focus away from the hard work of responding to God's election. Thus, just as with the other additions to the rite—meeting the bishop and the bishop signing the Book of the Elect—this gesture belongs outside the ritual, perhaps at a reception that follows.

Intercessions for the Elect (RCIA, n. 134)

The community then prays for the elect. Given the solemn nature of this rite, chanting the intercessions with the community singing a response might be appropriate.

Prayer over the Elect (RCIA, n. 135)

The intercessions are followed by a prayer of blessing by the bishop. The assembly can be invited to extend hands in prayer over the elect along with the bishop.

Dismissal of the Elect (RCIA, n. 136)

Following the blessing over the elect, the ritual text prescribes the dismissal of the elect (as usual) and the continuation of the liturgy of the eucharist for the rest of the community. However, since it was noted earlier that the rite of election is more commonly celebrated at a celebration of the Word, the bishop could dismiss the entire assembly to celebrate the great Lenten retreat we are all called to observe.

Liturgy of the Eucharist (RCIA, n. 137)

CATECHESIS FOLLOWING THE RITE

Following the principle that we experience liturgy and then reflect upon the experience to discover its meaning, the major movements and experiences of the rite become the content of the ensuing catechesis.

The focus for catechesis needs to be the word of election by the bishop. This is the significant turning point in the entire process. After hearing the testimony of the community, the bishop proclaims the readiness for the celebration of the sacraments. Not only has the status of these people changed, but the focus and direction of catechesis will shift dramatically.

We must take care to focus on the gracious action of God in this rite—God's free election of these men and women. From that vantage point, the catechesis could unpack the various dimensions of both the rite of sending and the rite of election.

BEGINNING THE LENTEN RETREAT

We now name the unbaptized the elect; we have recognized them as ready and willing to celebrate the initiation sacraments at the Easter Vigil. Their preparation during these final weeks will shift in its focus.

Throughout this process, these men and women have enriched and challenged the parish community. The parish community, too, now enters a new period of prayer and reflection: the Lenten retreat. The Book of the Elect, enthroned in the community's worship space, will be a good reminder for all of the call to a baptismal spirituality.

ADAPTATION WITH CHILDREN OF CATECHETICAL AGE

Curiously, part II, chapter 1 suggests that the rite of election or enrollment of names is optional. This is because this rite was not included in the *editio typica* of the initiation rites; it is an adaptation for use in the United States. Exploring the possible reasons for the exclusion of the rite of election in the original text would not be helpful. It would be helpful, however, to recall the guidelines for implementing part II of the ritual text found in Chapter 3 of this resource. Based on that, we always celebrate the rite of election with children of catechetical age.

An important key to the shape and direction of the rite of sending and rite of election with children of catechetical age can be found in *RCIA,* n. 279. Presumably, the children will be celebrating with the adult catechumens both at the parish rite of sending and at the diocesan rite of election. Thus, the directives for part I are followed.

Two pastoral notes need to be mentioned here. The first deals with the inclusion of parents in the ritual celebrations. *RCIA,* n. 278 notes the importance of the parents' testimony, as well as that of the godparents and catechists. To the extent possible, the parents need to be part of the discernment for election, as well as the testimony. Presumably, they would come forward with their children and the godparents when the children are presented at both rites (*RCIA,* n. 282).

The second pastoral note deals with godparents. Because of the generally accepted practice (though not supported theologically) of asking family and friends to be godparents of infants for ceremonial reasons (and not necessarily for concerns of faith), children can fall prey to the same practice. The same concerns about the appropriateness of serving as a godparent for adults applies even more so for godparents for children. The godparents need to be involved in the faith life of the children—before, during and after the rite of election.

ADAPTATION WITH BAPTIZED CANDIDATES

Rite of Sending the Candidates

The rite of sending the candidates for recognition by the bishop and for the call to continuing conversion (*RCIA,* n. 434 f.) is provided in part II, chapter 4 of the ritual text for baptized candidates. This rite of sending is not used, however, if there are no catechumens going to the rite of election. Instead, we celebrate the rite of calling the candidates to continuing conversion at the parish (*RCIA,* n. 447). As opposed to the rite of election that focuses on God's election of the catechumens, the rite of recognition (and, hence, the rite of sending to recognition) focuses on the decisions of the candidates to complete their initiation within the context of the Catholic Christian community in response to their election by God at their baptism. With different text and different intention, the ritual structure is similar to the rite of sending to election with one major difference: there is no inscription in the Book of the Elect. What this ritual action upholds is already accomplished in the life of the baptized candidate.

Combined Rite of Sending

If the rite of sending the candidates is to be celebrated at the same time as the rite of sending the catechumens to election, then the directive is given in

RCIA, n. 437 to use the combined rite found in Appendix I of the ritual text (*RCIA,* n. 530f.) which is particular to the Church in the United States.

The ritual structure of the combined rite attempts to integrate the two aforementioned rites while maintaining the important distinction between the catechumens and the baptized candidates (see *RCIA,* n. 506). The primary way this is done is by first focusing on the catechumens (up to and including the signing of the Book of the Elect). Then the ritual turns to the candidates and proceeds in a parallel manner, minus the signing of the Book of the Elect. We weaken the intent of the Book of the Elect if baptized candidates also sign it. Similarly, having something else for them to sign (scroll, another book) is inappropriate also. It is important to keep clear what are pre-baptismal gestures and what are gestures that both sets of people can use. Signing the Book of the Elect is one of those pre-baptismal gestures.

Rite of Calling the Candidates to Continuing Conversion

Similar to the rite of sending, part II, chapter 4 of the ritual text provides a rite of calling the candidates to continuing conversion (*RCIA,* n. 446f.). The major difference here is that this is intended as a parish celebration if there are no catechumens in the parish (*RCIA,* n. 447). Presumably, if there are catechumens who are going to the rite of election, the combined rite (to include catechumens and candidates) is followed (*RCIA,* n. 449).

The ritual structure is similar to the rite of election, minus the signing (or presentation) of the Book of the Elect. The reasons for this are given above.

Combined Rite of Election and Call to Continuing Conversion

If the rite of calling the candidates to continuing conversion is to be celebrated at the same time as the rite of election, then the directive is given in *RCIA,* n. 449 to use the combined rite found in Appendix I of the ritual text (*RCIA,* n. 547f.) which is particular to the church in the United States.

The ritual structure of the combined rite attempts to integrate the two aforementioned rites while maintaining the important distinction between the catechumens and the baptized candidates. The primary way this is done is by first focusing on the catechumens up to the act of election. Then the ritual turns to the candidates and proceeds in a parallel manner, minus the signing/presentation of the Book of the Elect and the act of election (instead, there is an act of recognition).

To help facilitate the flow of people in the cathedral, it might be helpful if the elect and their godparents return to their seats before the presentation of the candidates. As with the elect, the presentation of the candidates is not the time to meet the bishop or receive a scroll or other gift.

PREPARATION REMINDERS

❏ Make sure to know the date of the rite of election to be held at the cathedral, and then plan the rite of sending accordingly.

❏ The community needs to know what is going on. Some announcement in the parish bulletin can alert them to the rite of sending.

❏ Godparents need to be contacted early enough so they can plan to participate in the rite of election. Opportunities for formation and support of godparents need to be arranged.

❏ Sponsors need to be informed and consulted in the discernment for election.

❏ Godparents and sponsors need to know the basic direction the witnessing will take at the rite of election. Besides reviewing the ritual, giving them guide questions from which they can formulate their reflections would be helpful.

❏ Consultation with the liturgists and liturgical musicians needs to happen well in advance so they can adapt the ritual and provide acclamations that emerge from the experience of the catechumens.

❏ The final ritual text—with all its adaptations—needs to be housed in a binder or folder that clearly indicates this ritual is important.

❏ The Book of the Elect needs to be retrieved and ready for the rite. Scrapbooks and similar diary-type books fail to represent the importance of this rite. A parish can purchase a leather-bound Book of the Elect through most liturgical supply stores.

❏ If the signing of the Book of the Elect happens at the rite of sending (confirm this with this the diocesan office), be sure that the Book of the Elect and a few pens are in place.

❏ If possible, the group can travel to the cathedral liturgy together. Arrangements will need to be made for transportation to the cathedral.

9

Period of Purification and Enlightenment

Lord,
enlighten your chosen ones with the Word of life.
Give them a new birth
in the waters of baptism
and make them living members of the Church.
—*Opening Prayer for First Scrutiny, Ritual Mass:*
"Christian Initiation: The Scrutinies"

INTRODUCTION

The period of purification and enlightenment begins after the rite of election. The tone of the period of preparation shifts to one more akin to a retreat. It is a period of prayerful recollection, "consisting more in interior reflection than in catechetical instruction" (*RCIA*, n. 139). If the rite intended the previous periods of formation to form disciples into the paschal mystery, this period's intention (presuming the commitment of the rite of election) is to intensify desire by helping the elect to purify their minds and hearts and also to enlighten them with a deeper knowledge of Christ (see *RCIA*, n. 139).

Thus, both the community and the elect begin the Lenten retreat. While the rite does not specify the structure of this Lenten retreat, it does clearly indicate its foundations. Whatever our experiences of retreat we must recognize that the rite emphasizes two important notions about this Lenten retreat: It preserves the element of spiritual recollection, and it places the entire experience within the context of the Church's liturgical prayer. Unlike most retreats, this one has its foundation in liturgy; more specifically, "the celebration of certain rites, particularly the scrutinies and the presentations, brings about this process of purification and enlightenment" (*RCIA*, n. 139).

The Lenten retreat helps the elect step out of the routine of life to prepare better for the life-changing commitment at the Easter Vigil. The elect have made an important choice in their lives: to follow the Lord as disciples in the company of the Christian community. These final days of preparation are not meant to solidify that commitment; instead, they aim to provide the support needed to make this commitment more fully and authentically.

The Lenten retreat is a time for the elect to ponder the significant issues in their lives. The elect serve as prisms for the rest of the community; they serve as a lens through which we reflect on our experience as well. The Christian community discovers anew each Lent that the dynamics of dying and rising continue throughout life. The scrutinies and presentations help all of us to discover the richness of the journey.

Period of Purification and Enlightenment					
	UNBAPTIZED ADULT	CHILDREN OF CATECHETICAL AGE	BAPTIZED, UNCATECHIZED CATHOLIC	BAPTIZED, UNCATECHIZED CHRISTIAN	BAPTIZED, CATECHIZED CHRISTIAN
Reference	*RCIA*, nos. 138–184	*RCIA*, nos.138–184, 291–303	*RCIA*, nos. 459–472	*RCIA*, nos. 459–472	*RCIA*, n. 482
Required	Yes	Yes	Yes, adapted	Yes, adapted	Yes, adapted and modified
Focus	spiritual recollection	spiritual recollection	spiritual recollection	spiritual recollection	spiritual recollection
Goal	purify minds and hearts; enlighten minds and hearts with deeper knowledge of Christ	purify minds and hearts; enlighten minds and hearts with deeper knowledge of Christ	purify minds and hearts; enlighten minds and hearts with deeper knowledge of Christ	purify minds and hearts; enlighten minds and hearts with deeper knowledge of Christ	purify mind and hearts; enlighten minds and hearts with deeper knowledge of Christ
Name	elect	elect	candidate	candidate	candidate
Time	Lent	Lent	Usually Lent	Usually Lent	When ready
Rites	*Scrutinies *Presentations *Preparation Rites	*Scrutinies-Penitential Rite *Presentations *Preparation Rites	*Penitential Rite *Presentations (optional) *Confession	*Penitential Rite *Presentations (optional) *Confession	*Confession

WHAT DOES THE RITE SAY?

Read RCIA, *n. 138.*

The origins of the liturgical season of Lent go back to the early Church's initiatory practice. Lent was the time of final, prayerful preparation for those whom the Church would baptize, confirm and celebrate eucharist at the great Vigil of Easter. With the eventual disintegration of the initiation sacraments, the focus of Lent shifted from preparation for initiation to preparation for recommitment or reconciliation. The reconciliation focus of Lent is the one familiar to most of us.

The restoration of the catechumenal process in the *Rite of Christian Initiation of Adults* brought back an initiatory focus to the Lenten season. Respecting the vast tradition of reconciliation that has emerged over the centuries, the current focus of Lent is twofold: initiation and reconciliation (*SC,* n. 109). What concerns us here is the initiation part of that focus.

Read RCIA, *n. 139.*

This section highlights the important shift that occurs after the rite of election: the formal catechesis is completed and this is now a time for spiritual recollection. The liturgical prayer of this season will guide the Lenten retreat, especially the celebration of the scrutinies and presentations.

Read RCIA, *n. 140.*

This section reminds us of the importance of setting aside Holy Saturday as a day of preparation—as we will see, this includes not only the preparation rites but participation in the paschal fast.

Rites Belonging to the Period of Purification and Enlightenment
Scrutinies

Read RCIA, *n. 141.*

The scrutinies, which include a pre-baptismal exorcism, have a twofold purpose: to uncover, in order to heal all that is "weak, defective or sinful," and to bring out, in order to strengthen all that is "upright, strong, and good." These ritual celebrations, which presume the commitment ritually celebrated at the rite of election, must bring both dimensions into prayer.

Read RCIA, *n. 142.*

Before the rite of election, the determination needs to be made that one has the intention to follow Christ as a disciple. Grounded in this intention, the elect enter this period of preparation that is more intense by nature. This period is not intended for someone who is not resolved in his or her intention.

Read RCIA, *n. 143.*

The rite notes the progressive nature of the scrutinies. Through the praying of the scrutinies, the elect grow in their understanding of the mystery of sin and also their desire for freedom from sin and salvation from Christ. Notice here an important principle in action—liturgical catechesis. It is through the experience of the ritual prayer the elect develop a consciousness about sin and salvation.

Read RCIA, *n. 144.*

The text notes the pre-baptismal nature of the exorcism prayers that are part of the scrutinies. Thus, we only celebrate the scrutinies with the unbaptized.

Read RCIA, *n. 145.*

Throughout the ritual text, we note the important connection with the assembly. This is the case in this section. The important reflection of this season is also the agenda of the baptized community. It is not something we do "to" the elect; it is done "with" the elect.

Read RCIA, *n. 146.*

The ritual text in this section is clear: we celebrate three scrutinies, normally on the Third, Fourth and Fifth Sundays of Lent, which use the lectionary texts of Year A. There is no liberty in this directive to celebrate less than three scrutinies or to use the texts from other lectionary years. The texts from Year A have a long tradition in the community for their use in baptismal preparation. Recall the directive from *RCIA,* n. 20: only the bishop may dispense from celebrating a scrutiny. It is not the prerogative of the pastor or initiation team.

Furthermore, this section notes that if for some reason the preparation for initiation happens outside the normal time, then the community must provide Lent for the elect (and, therefore, for itself).

Presentations

Read RCIA, *n. 147.*

The presentations, expressions of the heart of the Church's faith and prayer (that which we believe, place our hearts upon), are intended to enlighten the elect. Again, we clearly enact liturgical catechesis: the meaning of the event is mediated through the ritual experience itself. Note the pastoral adaptation to anticipate the presentations during the period of the catechumenate. This seems to make sense only if celebrated at the end of that period of formation as the catechumens approach the rite of election.

Read RCIA, *n. 148.*

The first presentation is the Creed, following the first scrutiny. The ritual text makes a wise pastoral directive: the elect are to commit the Creed to memory—the memory of the mind and the memory of the heart. Such an expectation is not unrealistic given the importance of the Creed in the life of the Christian community.

Read RCIA, *n. 149.*

The second presentation is the Lord's Prayer, following the third scrutiny. The elect will proclaim the Lord's Prayer for the first time in communal worship during the celebration of the sacraments of initiation.

CATECHESIS DURING THE PERIOD OF PURIFICATION AND ENLIGHTENMENT

The goal and focus of catechesis during the period of enlightenment is different from that during the period of the catechumenate. During the period of the catechumenate, the focus of catechesis was immersion into the fullness of the Christian community as expressed in the Catholic Tradition—scripture, doctrine, worship, community and service. The period of purification and enlightenment presumes such immersion and the readiness to make the commitment of baptism. Now the focus is akin to a retreat. The elect and candidates, firm in

Lectionary Text for Lent: Year A			
	READING I	RESPONSORIAL PSALM	READING II	GOSPEL
Lent I	*Genesis 2:7–9; 3:1–7* Creation of man and woman; temptation in the garden Eden.	*Psalm 51*	*Romans 5:12–19* If sin and its consequences enter the world through one man, so much more the grace of God through Jesus Christ.	*Matthew 4:1–11* Jesus in the desert, tempted by the devil.
Lent II	*Genesis 12:1–4* Call of Abraham.	*Psalm 33*	*2 Timothy 1:8–10* God saves us and calls us to holiness.	*Matthew 17:1–9* Transfiguration of Christ.
Lent III	*Exodus 17:3–7* Israel grumbling in the desert; God gives water to drink.	*Psalm 95*	*Romans 5:1–2, 5–8* The love of God has been poured into our hearts through the Holy Spirit.	*John 4:5–42* The Samaritan woman at Jacob's well.
Lent IV	*1 Samuel 16:1, 6–7 10–13* David is chosen and anointed.	*Psalm 23*	*Ephesians 5:8–14* Live as children of the light.	*John 9:1–41* The man who had been blind from birth.
Lent V	*Ezekiel 37:12–14* I will put my spirit in you that you may live.	*Psalm 130*	*Romans 8:8–11* If the Spirit of Christ is in you, you will have life.	*John 11:1–45* The raising of Lazarus from the dead.
Passion Sunday	*Isaiah 50:4–7* Suffering servant song; God is my help, therefore I am not disgraced.	*Psalm 22*	*Philippians 2:6–11* Your attitude must be like that of Christ: humbly obedient even unto death.	*Matthew 26:14–27, 66* The passion of our Lord Jesus Christ.

their resolve to embrace the gospel, experience a time set apart for deepened reflection on this gospel way of life, seeking the prayers of the community during these final days of preparation (*RCIA,* n. 139).

If there are both elect and catechumens, the period and process for catechesis will be different. Each group is to be dismissed from the assembly, but they should gather in separate places because the content of catechesis is different. Ideally, the community could dismiss the catechumens (i.e., those who have discerned that it is not the right time to move to the commitment of the Easter sacraments) from one Mass while the elect are dismissed from another Mass.

This, then, is a time of prayer and reflection. This is not the time to cover materials that we may have forgotten during the catechumenate period. Rather, it is a time of focusing on God's gifting presence, and how that presence uncovers and reveals attitudes and lifestyles that are contrary to relationship with God—namely, sin—as well as raising up those attitudes and gifts that deepen the relationship with God.

The content of the catechesis for the first few weeks is the experience of election and the beginnings of this intense period of reflection, using the ritual text and the lectionary as the basis for reflection and prayer. The prayer becomes more focused when the elect celebrate the scrutinies. The experience of the scrutinies provides the material for the remaining catechesis.

THE SCRUTINIES

As mentioned earlier, we celebrate the scrutinies on the Third, Fourth and Fifth Sundays of Lent. The scrutinies take seriously the profound love of God and the desire of God to bring all people to full freedom and salvation. As one deepens in one's awareness of the graciousness of the gift of God's love, one also becomes more sensitive to the barriers that keep this love from transforming and recreating life: the barriers of sin and evil.

The scrutinies raise up and expose whatever keeps the transforming love of God from liberating all forms of oppression. Some of those barriers are freely chosen, the result of personal sin. Others are the result of systemic evil: racism, sexism, ageism, and other forms of discrimination and oppression. Whatever the causes, none of them is rooted in the reconciling and healing love of God. The scrutinies unmask the deception of evil and sin for what they really are: robbers of true and authentic life.

The scrutinies also raise up those dimensions of life that welcome the loving presence of God, thus encouraging full life. These virtues and gifts of God stand as witness to a new way of living in the midst of the destructive dimensions of sin and evil.

Thus, the focus of the scrutinies is toward life, toward freedom, toward salvation. They take very seriously the transforming love of God. Precisely because they do take this love so seriously, the scrutinies also take seriously the reality of sin and evil. However, sin and evil are neither the first word of creation nor the final word of destiny. The scrutinies are one expression of the first and final words of transforming and saving love.

Preparing for the Scrutinies

The best preparation for the celebration of the scrutinies is to help the elect identify and name their areas of strength and weakness in relationship to life with God so that the community may pray with them. The rite clearly indicates that the prayers of intercession during the scrutinies may include the particular needs and concerns of the community (*RCIA,* n. 153). Thus, the community has the opportunity to pray for the elect rather than some general notions about the elect.

There can be many ways to prepare the elect for the scrutinies. Preparation does not mean rehearsal or even instruction about the experience of the scrutinies. Allow the scrutinies themselves to be formative, providing a period of reflection and integration after the celebration. Already the period of purification has been focusing on the need for honesty in naming one's relationship with God and others. It would naturally flow from this that we lead the elect through a reflection process of specifying those areas of their life that need to be raised up for support or healing.

One way of doing this could be to provide a retreat experience with the elect during which time they could raise and address the issues of their life. Another possibility would be to provide a prelude reflection experience for each scrutiny. This would give the elect the opportunity to discern their need from different perspectives, i.e., the symbols of the scrutinies: living waters, light for the world, new life.

Preparing the Intercessions for the Scrutinies

Throughout the period of preparation for the celebration of the scrutinies, the elect have had the opportunity to reflect on the areas of their lives that need to be strengthened so they can be faithful to their commitments, and also the areas of sin and bondage that keep them from truly being free. The team, with the help of the parish liturgists and musicians, can then construct the prayer of intercessions based on these reflections.

If the preparation for the scrutinies happens before each scrutiny, we can form the intercessions based on the discussion and reflection. If the preparation happens during an extended retreat experience for all the scrutinies, then the content of the experience will need to be used for all three scrutinies. The images of the scrutinies—living waters that quench our basic thirst, light for our blindness, and the gift of the fullness of life—suggest an intensification in the prayer of the community that can be reflected in the wording of the intercessions.

What might these intercessions look like? The rite gives us a model text for each of the three scrutinies. The preparer will need to read the scripture text, the scrutiny text—with special note of the intercessions—and then listen carefully to the experience of the elect. Based on the need of the elect, and integrating the intercessions provided in the rite, the cantor can develop intercessions that reflect the experience and prayer of the elect and of the community. For example:

From the blindness of greed and possessiveness, we pray to the Lord.

Response: Lord, hear our prayer.

From the blindness caused by a distorted image of a God of wrath, we pray to the Lord.

Response: Lord, hear our prayer.

To increase our ability to see the gift of God's presence in others, we pray to the Lord.

Response: Lord, hear our prayer.

To increase our ability to see how God's grace has led us to this day, we pray to the Lord.

Response: Lord, hear our prayer.

While preserving the spirit of the scrutiny intercessions, the intercessions can reflect the particular needs of a particular group of elect at a particular time and place. Therefore, another community could never reuse the intercessions, nor could even another group of elect within the same community do so, because their needs and concerns will be very different each time.

At the same time, since we want to avoid an exclusive focus on the needs of the elect, the scrutiny intercessions need also to include the needs of the local community and the world. As with the elect, the scripture texts provide the lens through which we look to construct these intercessions.

The rite suggests approximately eight intercessions. We can extend the listing of intercessions, however, so that we can maintain a rhythm and movement in the intercession prayer. Many communities sing or chant the text to demonstrate the solemnity of the intercessory prayer during these rites.

A word of caution needs to be noted here. The practice has developed which makes the intercessions rather elaborate. While important parts of the scrutiny rite, the intercessions are not the centerpiece of the rite and we should not give them more weight than they deserve. We need to give careful attention to all the dimensions of the rite to be sure that the intercessions do not bear more weight than they should.

Celebrating the Scrutinies

The basic structure for the scrutinies is the same for all three scrutinies. Therefore, we will explore that basic structure, raising some concerns for celebration.

Liturgy of the Word
Readings (RCIA, nos. 150, 164, 171)

The directive reiterates the one stated earlier in *RCIA,* n. 146: the scripture texts come from the lectionary texts for the Third, Fourth and Fifth Sundays of Lent, Year A—the woman at the well, the man born blind, and the raising of Lazarus (*RCIA,* nos. 146, 150, 164, 171). If the scrutiny is celebrated at a time other than those Sundays in Lent, the readings are still used.

Homily (RCIA, nos. 151, 165, 172)

Besides exploring the issues that emerge from the scriptures proclaimed, the homily serves as a preparation for the scrutiny that follows. Therefore, the preacher will need to incorporate the value and purpose of the scrutiny in the preaching.

Note: If the catechumens are present at this liturgy, dismissing them before the celebration of the scrutiny would be appropriate.

Invitation to Silent Prayer (RCIA, nos. 152, 166, 173)

The elect, accompanied by godparents, come forward so the community can pray for them. Use your space in a way that makes clear to the assembly that they are part of this prayer. Place the elect in different places throughout the church.

The presider first turns to the assembly and invites them to pray for the elect, and then turns to the elect and also invites them to prayer. The presider concludes his request by inviting the elect to assume a prayer posture (bow heads or kneel). If possible, kneeling seems appropriate for this rite.

Intercessions for the Elect (RCIA, nos. 153, 167, 174)

After an appropriate period of silent prayer, we pray the intercessions. Simply reading the intercessions may not necessarily create the mood that the rite is calling for at this time. It would be more effective if a cantor sang the intercessions in litany style. Recall that we can adapt the intercessions for the particular needs of the community. When doing that, be sure to maintain the balance of the scrutiny rite: uncover to heal, bring out to strengthen. Also, if the community will not pray the general intercessions later, intentions for the Church and the world should be included.

The elect should remain kneeling or with their heads bowed. The godparents can place their hands on the shoulders of the elect to convey support and acceptance during these intercessions.

Exorcism (RCIA, nos. 154, 168, 175)

The exorcism is the prayer of God's presence; it is a pre-baptismal prayer. Faced with the reality of evil in our world (recall this is a rigorous time of reflection)—the darkness, the void, the emptiness of sin—the exorcism is the acknowledgment of the breath of God being welcomed into those areas that lack life. The exorcism also acknowledges the power of grace over sin; it is a prayer for freedom.

There are three movements to the exorcism prayer, a Trinitarian movement. First, the presider invokes the power and presence of the Creator God to free and protect the elect from sin. Following this prayer, the presider calls upon the power and presence of the Spirit through the ancient symbol of the imposition of hands. Slowly, the presider lays hands on the head of each of the elect, continuing the prayer for freedom. Some communities have expanded the use of this symbol to include the initiation coordinator and the godparents in joining the presider with the laying on of hands. The third movement is the prayer invoking the power and presence of the Christ. We can invite the worshiping community to extend hands over the elect during this final movement.

Note, as with the minor exorcisms in the period of the catechumenate, the exorcisms are not directed toward the Evil One nor do they take a form of command, "Be gone..." Rather, the focus is on the work and presence of God that brings life.

Dismissal (*RCIA*, nos. 155, 169, 176)

We then dismiss the elect from the assembly with words of support and encouragement.

Liturgy of the Eucharist

The liturgy of the eucharist continues as usual. The rite gives pastoral guidance about the general intercessions and the profession of faith, and also a remembrance of the elect and the godparents in the eucharistic prayer.

Some parishes celebrate a litany of prayer similar to the scrutinies at each of the community's liturgies on the prescribed Sunday. Therefore, although we may gather the elect at one Mass, all of the community will have had the chance to struggle with their call to freedom. Following the scrutinies (or the litanies at Masses without the elect present), we can give an invitation to the worshiping community to spend time after Mass to reflect on the experience and look at some implications of the prayer of exorcism. Often parishioners experience great discomfort and confusion about the scrutiny experience. This would provide an opportunity—similar to the catechesis following the scrutinies for the elect—for the parish to process and reflect on their experience.

Catechesis Following the Scrutinies

The experience of the scrutinies is usually a very powerful and moving one. There will be ample material from the experience itself to help the elect integrate and experience empowerment because of the scrutiny. There is a bidirectional focus. First we reflect back on the experience of the scrutiny itself. Then, because the elect recognize their new freedom, they have the grace and courage to continue with the ongoing reflection on conversion that the scrutiny demands.

Inevitably, if we constructed the intercessions with the needs and concerns of the elect in mind, the elect will begin to discuss how they heard their issues, their blockages, their sin named and prayed for. Often this brings about a deepened awareness of God's forgiving love and the level of commitment one is called to in following the gospel.

One would think that after going through one scrutiny, the power and effect of the subsequent scrutinies would diminish. However, if the scrutinies are prepared carefully and honestly, the opposite effect often happens. The elect begin to take even more seriously the need for God and the desire for freedom. The roots of sin—rather than sinful acts—begin to become exposed for what they are. The elect begin to release the illusions and fears that keep them from living full lives. Somehow the excuses that provided comfort and convenience before—"That's just the way I am," "I'm not *really* prejudiced," "I can't give any more than I have already," "I don't have time to worry about those people"— prove to be inadequate, uncomfortable, lies.

The period of catechesis following the scrutinies is primarily a time of support and care for the elect, helping them see God's love operative in the midst of the painful naming of sin. The focus is on God's love, not on our sin. This is not the time to be preoccupied with wretchedness (in fact, there is no wretchedness). Rather, it is the time to be preoccupied with the freedom of being a child of God, and anything that keeps us from living that vocation to its fullness.

THE PRESENTATIONS

Christianity rests on some key fundamental beliefs: (1) That God has revealed Godself completely in the life and teaching of Jesus the Christ; (2) that this revelation happens in human history, i.e., the life, death and resurrection of Jesus the Christ; and (3) that, in the encounter with Christ, men and women experience salvation. How, then, does this fullness of revelation reach ordinary people like us over time? How do we know that through this revelation, we are encountering the Word of God and not someone's particular perspective or viewpoint? The answer: through the Tradition of the Church.

At this juncture, distinguishing between Tradition and tradition is helpful. Basically, when we speak of Tradition, we are referring to the process, guided by the Holy Spirit, whereby the Word of God and gift of God's grace is handed onto subsequent generations through the preaching, teaching and worship of the Christian believers. Alongside this, there are various traditions, i.e., customs and practices for sharing the faith and belief of the Christian community in a particular time and culture. Our concern is with Tradition.

Tradition provides balance. True Tradition gives us roots so that we can withstand the winds of change and transition in our lives and in the Church. When those changes are authentic, they will continue to bear fruit on the tree of Tradition. When they are not, they will wither and die.

This, however, is not so with tradition (customs and practices). These will need to change over time in order to articulate more faithfully the basics of our belief. Otherwise, they will stand in the way of expressing true faith. We will get stuck in them and miss the more important issues.

Tradition also serves as our guarantee that we are faithfully exposed to the fullness of God's revelation in Jesus the Christ. When we stand—personally and communally—in the presence of such revelation, we cannot help but be changed in some way.

Handing On the Faith

One of the primary responsibilities of those entrusted with the formation of catechumens is to hand on the Christian faith faithfully. The basics of this process, while including the sharing of vital information about the Christian life, are outlined in the *Rite of Christian Initiation of Adults* (*RCIA*, n. 75): catechesis, community, liturgical life and apostolic witness. Slowly and deliberately, we form the catechumens in the Christian way of life. This takes time, usually more than a year.

At the conclusion of the catechumenate, while those to be initiated are in the final period of preparation (the period of illumination and enlightenment that coincides with Lent), the community then celebrates two rituals to mark the important shift that has happened in the life of the catechumens. It is now, at the end and not the beginning, that the community hands on what is most dear and cherished in the community: the Creed and the Lord's Prayer. These two proclamations from the community are symbols of the faith to which the catechumens have been awakened, in which they have been formed, in which they now desire to be baptized.

The Creed and the Lord's Prayer

Since the earliest of times, the Tradition was best expressed in the Creed and the Lord's Prayer. Through the celebrations of the presentation of the Creed and the presentation of the Lord's Prayer, the Church hands on the foundations of our faith and life of prayer. On these two key proclamations, the rest of Catholic Christian faith rests. The presentations are often referred to as the *traditio symboli,* the handing on of the symbol tradition.

The presentations of the Creed and the Lord's Prayer can be considered transitional rites: They indicate a movement from one state to another. They presume some tacit knowledge and understanding of that which we are passing on. Thus, the content of each provides direction for the previous periods of formation.

For those still struggling with the "agenda" of the period of the catechumenate, look to the Creed and the Lord's Prayer and ask, "What must we do in order to prepare someone to express this faith and to pray in this manner?" Then, using the guidance of *RCIA,* n. 75, and immersing the catechumens in the Liturgy of the Word and the primary liturgical symbols of our Catholic Christian faith, we will slowly and gradually lead them to an experience of the "mystery of salvation in which they desire to celebrate" (*RCIA,* no. 75.1).

The Creed

What is most important about the Creed is that it is a proclamation of belief: This is what we believe, what we settle our hearts on, what we give ourselves over to. Thus, knowledge of the Creed is more than memorization of words or concepts. Knowledge of the Creed is, in an initial way, exposure to all the movements of salvation it articulates.

The Lord's Prayer

Knowing the words to the Lord's Prayer is not the point here (most already know it because of its popular usage in our culture). Knowing the pattern of prayer it embodies is the point. Once we know the pattern, then we know how to pray as a disciple of Jesus.

Celebrating the Presentations

Week in and week out, we return to these primary proclamations of faith. In effect, the Creed and the Lord's Prayer are the summary statements of our initiation formation and, when one can assent to them with his or her life, then it is a clear indication that the person is ready for the celebration of the initiation sacraments.

That is why we do not celebrate them until the period of purification and enlightenment that follows the rite of election. The presumption is that when someone celebrates the rite of election, that person is ready to celebrate the sacraments. The remaining weeks of preparation become more like a retreat.

In the midst of this retreat, along with the scrutinies, the community celebrates the presentations. While the actual proclamation of the text might be new to the ear of some elect, the meaning behind the text is not new. They have turned these concepts over repeatedly in their minds and hearts over the last few years of preparation. The proclamation/presentation simply brings them together in a coherent manner.

Pastorally, the ritual text allows the option of anticipating the celebration of these presentations in the period of the catechumenate. The primary reason is that the Lenten retreat is already so full (election, scrutinies, preparation rites) that the presentations might get lost.

If a community decides to anticipate the celebration of the presentations, keep in mind their purpose in determining when to celebrate them. It seems reasonable to wait until the final weeks before the rites of sending and election (near the end of the period of the catechumenate) to celebrate them. Then, they can serve as summary rituals and also start the transition into the final period of preparation.

The celebration of the presentations is rather straightforward. Both presume that the presentations happen in a celebration of the Word, in the midst of the assembly and not during a scrutiny. Because of the simple structure for the presentations, a word of caution is necessary. The power behind the celebration of the presentations is in the community's proclamation of faith and its style of prayer. Ritual makers will need to include the community in a robust way.

Avoid the handing out of scrolls with the text of the Creed and the Lord's Prayer, especially during the presentations themselves. We are not presenting this (scrolls) but our expression of faith and prayer. During the ritual itself, the catechumens and community should be focused on the words proclaimed in faith. Scrolls, if given at all, can be given at the following sessions.

Presentation of the Creed

Liturgy of the Word
Readings (RCIA, n. 158)
The ritual text provides scripture texts that support and reinforce the intention of the presentation of the Creed.

Homily (RCIA, n. 159)
The preacher makes a connection between the scriptures proclaimed, the presentation of the Creed and the formation the elect have experienced that leads them to this ritual celebration.

Presentation of the Creed (RCIA, n. 160)
The elect come forward with their godparents after being called. It is important—although the ritual text does not mention this—that the elect face the assembled community because of the ritual action to follow.

The elect then receive a brief instruction as an introduction to the proclamation of the Creed. The proclamation of the Creed by the entire assembly follows this. We should not rush this proclamation; perhaps it can be supported with an antiphon throughout.

Prayer over the Elect (RCIA, n. 161)
The presider invites the community to pray for the elect. Silence follows this. Then, with outstretched hands, the presider prays the prayer over the elect. An adaptation at this point could include inviting the community to extend its hands in prayer.

Dismissal of the Elect (*RCIA*, n. 162)
The elect are dismissed at this time.

Liturgy of the Eucharist (RCIA, n. 181)

Presentation of the Lord's Prayer

Liturgy of the Word
Readings (*RCIA*, n. 179)
The ritual text provides two scripture texts that support and reinforce the intention of the presentation of the Lord's Prayer.
Gospel Reading: Presentation of the Lord's Prayer (*RCIA*, n. 180)
The elect come forward with their godparents after being called. It is important—although the ritual text does not mention this—that the elect face the assembled community because of the ritual action to follow.
The presider then gives a brief instruction/introduction. The proclamation of the gospel text from Matthew—the Lord's Prayer—follows this.
Homily (*RCIA*, n. 159)
The elect and godparents are seated and the preacher explores the importance of the Lord's Prayer.
Prayer over the Elect (*RCIA*, n. 182)
The presider invites the community to pray for the elect. Silence follows this. Then, with outstretched hands, the presider prays the prayer over the elect. An adaptation at this point could include inviting the community to extend its hands in prayer.
Dismissal of the Elect (*RCIA*, n. 183)
The elect are dismissed at this time.

Liturgy of the Eucharist (RCIA, n. 184)

CELEBRATING THE LENTEN RETREAT

The liturgical celebrations of the three scrutinies and the two presentations (Creed and Lord's Prayer) give the direction and time line for the Lenten retreat. What follows is a suggested model for celebrating the Lenten retreat.

A reminder: The celebration of the scrutinies and presentations will be with the elect; any catechumens or candidates who are not celebrating sacraments this Easter Vigil will continue with their own formation.

Ash Wednesday
The catechumens have completed their discernment with the community (we presume this happened weeks ago) in order to celebrate the rite of

election. Today the catechumens gather for this celebration and are dismissed from the assembly as they are normally after the Liturgy of the Word.

The catechesis/reflection based on this day's lectionary texts can lead them into the opening of the Lenten retreat. Help the catechumens see they are beginning a new time in their preparation; they are crossing a new threshold (the rite of election). Invite them to begin the Lenten practices of the parish (e.g., fasting, abstinence, almsgiving) as they journey to Easter with the parish community.

First Sunday of Lent

This is the day most parishes will celebrate the rite of sending to election. It is important that the sponsors and godparents be prepared to give authentic testimony at the community's celebration today.

Following the rite of sending to election, invite the catechumens to reflect on their experience of the lectionary texts and the rite itself. Can they name for themselves (and for us) God's action and work in their lives that bring them closer to their commitment as disciples? Later this day, the catechumens (along with sponsors, godparents and other members of the community) will travel to the diocesan celebration of the rite of election. The parish might choose to provide an extended gathering in the morning, a shared lunch and then a caravan or bus to the rite of election.

In the midst of the excitement, encourage the catechumens to keep their focus on why we come together this day. Their status changes in this rite, and also their title: from "catechumens" to "elect." It would be most appropriate for the diocese to set aside some time for the elect to meet and socialize with the bishop and other members of the elect after the rite of election.

Before the trip home, invite the elect to make the next few weeks a time of truly prayerful reflection. They should take time each day for prayer and reflection. Perhaps supply them with a Lenten prayer journal containing scriptural reflections for each day in Lent.

Second Sunday of Lent

The elect should plan to stay longer on the Sundays of Lent in order to allow ample time for all to reflect together. On this day, there are three concerns to integrate into the prayer time together: a breaking open of the elect's experience of the rite of election, the ways in which today's scriptures move us forward on our Lenten journey, and preparation for next Sunday's scrutiny.

A guided reflection back to the rite of election is an effective way to situate the elect in relation to that event. Use some music and texts from the rite itself and invite all to share their experience. Sponsors and godparents can take the lead here by offering their reflections.

After the elect have spent time speaking about their experience and what it means for them/us, the prayer leader can then move the group forward by proclaiming today's scriptures and helping the group grapple with the meaning of these texts for disciples-on-the-way.

There is no need for an extended catechesis at this time. Remember that the formal catechesis ends with the rite of election. So, after sufficient time in prayer, reflection and discussion, let the elect know that we are moving deeper into the mystery of God's love and that the community will pray with us next week to help the elect deepen that love.

Briefly explain the notion of scrutiny—without explaining away the scrutinies. Thus: scrutinies are prayers of freedom by the community for the elect (and, indeed, also for the community) to uncover for healing in ourselves, our world and our Church what keeps us from the love of God and to strengthen what enables us to remain faithful to that abiding love.

Use the first reading of the first scrutiny (Exodus 17:3-7) as a way to prepare for the celebration. Invite the elect to ponder their thirsts for true life, for freedom, for God. Structure experiences in which the elect and their sponsors/godparents can share these "thirsts." Some communities gather these insights in written form and give them to the parish liturgist as a foundation for the intercession prayer during the scrutiny celebration.

After the elect leave, spend some time with the sponsors and godparents in reviewing the ritual movements and intentions of the scrutiny prayer so they will feel comfortable guiding the elect through the experience next Sunday. If supportive relationships have developed between the elect and their sponsors and godparents, there will be no need to rehearse the rite with the elect. They know they will be guided as they have been throughout the process.

Third Sunday of Lent

Experience the celebration of the scrutinies during Sunday Mass. After the dismissal of the elect, allow the experience to both uncover and heal and also build up and strengthen. Let the elect talk about their experience and their feelings as they were offered living water. Give ample time to allow things to be stirred up. Refrain from giving presentations about the scriptures. Instead, enter into conversation with the elect's experience and also invite them into deeper conversation with the scriptures and the scrutiny texts themselves.

After sufficient time in reflection on the experience of the first scrutiny, begin the preparation for the second scrutiny in the same way as done for the first one. Invite the elect to reflect how, although we have been invited to drink from living water, we need to go deeper into ourselves, our world and our Church to uncover (in order to heal) and hold up (in order to strengthen) what blocks/supports our journey in love. The community will pray with us throughout the week and, again next Sunday, with another scrutiny prayer.

Use the second scriptural text (Ephesians 5:8-14) from the second scrutiny for the reflection together on where the elect experience "light in the

Lord" and where they experience "darkness." Again, after the reflection time, meet with the sponsors and godparents to review the ritual structure and movement of the second scrutiny.

The Week After the First Scrutiny

The community gathers with the elect to celebrate the presentation of the Creed (unless they anticipated this at the end of the period of the catechumenate). Find a time during the week when the community actually does gather—perhaps a midweek parish Lenten meal. After the celebration of the presentation, continue the prayerful reflection on the Creed with the elect, helping them to name various experiences over the years that point to the belief statements in the Creed. Tell the elect to entrust the message and words of the Creed to memory in their minds and hearts. We will ask them to proclaim the Creed at a later time.

Fourth Sunday of Lent

The cycle of celebrating the scrutinies continues this week with the celebration of the second scrutiny. Again, allow the elect to spend some time with their experience of this scrutiny before moving into preparation/reflection on the third scrutiny. Be cautious not to become too didactic during these days; keep the retreat focus always in mind.

Use as preparation the first lectionary text from the third scrutiny (Ezekiel 37:12-14) and invite the elect to name where the graves of death are and where they experience the Spirit that brings life.

Fifth Sunday of Lent

This is perhaps the most powerful of all the scrutinies, especially if the elect have been developing a rhythm of prayer leading up to this event. The reality of sin unto death is truly gripping, so give the elect ample time and space to ponder the message of this day.

The Week After the Third Scrutiny

Again, the elect will gather with the community to celebrate the presentation of the Lord's Prayer. Invite the elect to see the pattern of prayer they have learned over these months together and how this most treasured prayer of the community is also the model of how we are always to pray. As with the Creed, tell the elect to commit this prayer to memory in mind and heart.

Passion Sunday

The scriptural texts of this day give focus to all that has happened during this time for prayer. Invite the elect to reflect on their own experience of death/life and how they experience God's invitation to enter into the paschal mystery. The Lenten retreat ends with the beginning of the Triduum festival (which extends from the celebration of the Mass of the Lord's supper on Holy Thursday through evening prayer on Easter Sunday), a time to immerse ourselves into participation in the death and resurrection of the Lord Jesus and the new life in our midst.

ADAPTATION WITH CHILDREN OF CATECHETICAL AGE

Scrutinies

It is curious that the ritual text in this section makes a major deviation from part I. Instead of identifying this period of purification and enlightenment, the adaptation in the children's section highlights the penitential rite as a second step (in part I, the second step is the rite of election).

Given that, the children who are elect are to enter into the Lenten retreat along with the adults. Instead of the three scrutinies, the ritual text recommends two penitential rites, which are also called scrutinies (the ritual text gives one example in *RCIA,* nos. 295-303). There are four major differences from the structure of the scrutinies found in part I: (1) The scrutiny is not set during the Sunday assembly; (2) The three scrutiny gospels are not mandated, merely listed as one of the options (*RCIA,* n. 297); (3) The adaptation for children includes an anointing with the oil of catechumens (*RCIA,* n. 301; the directive in *RCIA,* n. 33.7 allows its use in the period of purification and enlightenment, though we can presume the community has celebrated it in the period of the catechumenate and, therefore, it is not necessary here; (4) The inclusion of a Liturgy of Penance for the Catholic peer companions (*RCIA,* n. 303). These differences do not enhance the adaptation; rather, they seem to diminish the focus of the scrutinies.

RCIA, n. 291 clearly notes that, since the intention of the penitential rite is the same as the scrutinies found in part I, we can follow the guidelines in *RCIA,* nos. 141-146 with children. This provides a corrective to the proposed adaptation: (1) Celebrate the penitential rite-scrutinies at the Sunday assembly on the Third, Fourth and Fifth Sundays of Lent; (2) Use the Year A texts; (3) Eliminate the anointing (which seems to be linked with the exorcism because of the directive to replace it with a laying on of hands) and follow the exorcism prayer structure of part I; (4) Eliminate the Liturgy of Penance (since it will be Sunday, we can't celebrate it anyway).

One comment needs to be made about the Liturgy of Penance. The inclusion of this liturgy seems to serve two purposes: to include the Catholic peer companions and to expose the elect to the sacrament of penance. We can accomplish both of the purposes in different ways. We can schedule a Liturgy of Penance at another time, and the elect can gather with the peer companions in support and prayer. This ritual experience would be a helpful introduction for the elect to the sacrament of penance, without confusing it with the focus of the scrutinies.

Presentations

The rite gives no directives in part II, chapter 1, so the directives already outlined apply.

ADAPTATION WITH BAPTIZED CANDIDATES

Uncatechized candidates

Penitential Rite

The candidates do not celebrate the scrutinies outlined in part I. The pre-baptismal exorcisms included in those scrutinies are intended exclusively for the unbaptized. Part II, chapter 4 does provide a penitential rite "as a kind of scrutiny" (*RCIA*, n. 459).

The ritual text recommends the penitential rite for the Second Sunday of Lent. When one reviews the ritual structure of the penitential rite, it is strikingly similar to the scrutinies of part I. The pastoral comments for them can be applied to the penitential rite.

The ritual text does not provide for a combined rite here (*RCIA*, n. 463). The combined rites are provided only for the steps in the initiation process.

Some parishes experiment with an attempt at combining the scrutinies with the penitential rite. In this way, the candidates experience the three reflections based on the three great gospels of Cycle A. If this option is explored, care must be exercised to make the appropriate distinctions throughout the rite lest the prayer over the candidates is confused with the exorcism of the elect.

Presentations

Part II, chapter 4 recommends the celebration of the presentations as a way to support their formation (see *NS*, n. 31). If the presentations are celebrated, the pastoral directives given earlier can be used as long as we make the appropriate changes when the text refers to preparation for baptism. We can also celebrate the presentations, in those cases, as an adapted combined rite (with appropriate distinctions).

Sacrament of Penance

RCIA, n. 408 sees the penitential rite as a preparation for the celebration of the sacrament of penance. *RCIA*, n. 482 recommends the celebration of the sacrament of penance before the celebration of the initiation sacraments.

Catechized candidates

The ritual text prescribes no penitential rites/scrutinies or presentations for the catechized candidates. *RCIA*, n. 478 notes that rites used with uncatechized adults may be celebrated if they enhance the pastoral formation of the catechized candidates (see *NS*, n. 31). *RCIA*, n. 482 recommends the celebration of the sacrament of penance before celebrating full communion.

10

Celebrating the Paschal Triduum
Third Step: Celebration of the
Sacraments of Initiation

INTRODUCTION

The liturgical life of the community, and its basic sense of identity, are focused toward the stirrings of the great waters of baptism. On this night of nights, men and women are immersed into the death and resurrection of Jesus the Christ, and the community is also immersed more deeply into this saving event. It is a solemn and holy night. It is a night that empowers all for the call to service.

The sacraments of initiation—baptism, confirmation, and eucharist—are usually celebrated at the Easter Vigil. As the parish community gathers to celebrate the central mysteries of our faith, the paschal event, the community also welcomes men and women into the power and life of Christ's death and resurrection. Through the celebration of the Easter sacraments, the elect receive the forgiveness of sin, celebrate their identity as daughters and sons of God, share in the mission of Jesus, and become full members of the Catholic communion.

CELEBRATING THE PASCHAL TRIDUUM

The Lenten period ends on Thursday of Holy Week before the evening celebration of the Mass of the Lord's Supper. The Paschal Triduum—the three days—is a unitive feast. That is, we both regard and celebrate the Triduum as one extended liturgy. "The Easter Triduum begins with the evening Mass of the Lord's Supper, reaches its high point in the Easter Vigil, and closes with evening prayer on Easter Sunday" (*GNLYC,* n. 19). In effect, we can view it as a stational liturgy: we move through the liturgy at different times and places. We need to be careful, however, not to regard any of the elements of the Triduum as independent of the other parts. All of the Triduum is a celebration of the paschal mystery and our participation in that paschal mystery.

Thus, if one looks at the structure of the liturgies of the Triduum, the continuity is clear. The Mass of the Lord's Supper (on Holy Thursday) ends in

Celebration of the Sacraments of Initiation					
	UNBAPTIZED ADULT	CHILDREN OF CATECHETICAL AGE	BAPTIZED, UNCATECHIZED CATHOLIC	BAPTIZED, UNCATECHIZED CHRISTIAN	BAPTIZED, CATECHIZED CHRISTIAN
Reference	*RCIA*, nos. 206–243	*RCIA*, nos. 206–217, 304–329	*RCIA*, nos 409	*RCIA*, nos. 409, 487–504	*RCIA*, nos 478, 487–504 (NB: *RCIA*, n. 473)
Rite	Celebration of the Sacraments of Initiation (baptism, confirmation, eucharist)	Celebration of the Sacraments of Initiation (baptism, confirmation, eucharist)	*Rite of Confirmation*	Rite of Reception into the Full Communion of the Catholic Church	Rite of Reception into the Full Communion of the Catholic Church
Combined Rite	Celebration at the Easter Vigil of the Sacraments of Initiation and of the Rite of Reception into the Full Communion of the Catholic Church				
Required	Yes	Yes	Yes	Yes	Yes
Time	Easter Vigil	Easter Vigil	Easter Vigil (if delegation to confirm granted); at parish or diocesan celebration of the *Rite of Confirmation*	Easter Vigil	When needed

silence...and the celebration of the Passion of the Lord (on Good Friday) begins in silence and ends in silence...and the community gathers in silence and darkness to proclaim Christ as Light of the World at the Easter Vigil....This silence is a grand thread woven through the fabric of the Triduum celebration to help us recognize that, though we gather over three days, we are gathering for one event.

As we do each time we Christians gather, we remember and celebrate the saving death and resurrection of the Lord Jesus and our participation in that paschal mystery. The purpose of the Triduum is not to reenact historically the events of the last days of Jesus' life. This would be what we call "historicizing," that is, narrating the events as history, placing the focus on the past. While the Triduum recalls those great memories and remembers the events that shape the Christian imagination, its celebration focuses on our immersion in the paschal event: how we live the saving death and resurrection of the Lord Jesus today.

This focus on our participation in the saving death and resurrection of the Lord Jesus is risky business. We conjure up a rather dangerous memory. That may be why many find it easier to spend their energies over these days in attempting to relive Jesus' experience; but our interpretation of Jesus' experience gives these events a skewed bias. The problem is that these engaging reenactments keep us an arm's length from the very mystery we celebrate. In its best liturgical tradition, the Church gives us a different way of celebrating which places us right at the center of the paschal mystery rather than on the margins. Into this way of life we immerse both the catechumens and the elect.

On Holy Thursday, it is not Jesus at the Last Supper long ago washing the feet of his disciples. No, it is Christ present washing our feet and calling us to wash the feet of the world. On Good Friday, it is not Jesus suffering on the cross and groaning in agony. No, it is Christ present crucified in our midst and offering us the cross as the source of our life and hope that we, too, might die for others. On Easter Sunday, it is not the apostles running from the empty tomb announcing that Christ has been raised. No, it is the risen Christ present in our midst inviting us into the gift of eternal life. The great stories serve as conduits for our participation in Christ's death and resurrection.

Celebrating with catechumens and elect

The *Rite of Christian Initiation of Adults* does not provide any directives for celebrating the full Triduum with either catechumens (who will not be celebrating the sacraments at this Easter Vigil) or the elect (who did celebrate the rite of election at the beginning of Lent and who will celebrate the sacraments this Easter Vigil). It does give ritual directives for the preparation rites on Holy Saturday and the celebration of the sacraments at the Easter Vigil (both of these for the elect, of course), but says nothing about Holy Thursday and Good Friday.

Yet we must make it clear to both catechumens and elect that the celebration of the Triduum—the full Triduum—is of primary importance in their Christian life. How we celebrate with them will provide the pastoral foundation and formation for their continued celebration in the future.

Holy Thursday

Holy Thursday: Mass of the Lord's Supper			
Reading I *Exodus 12:1–8, 11–14* Israel and the Passover.	Responsorial Psalm *Psalm 116*	Reading II *1 Corinthians 11:23–26* St. Paul's testament of the eucharist: I received from the Lord what I hand on to you.	Gospel *John 13:1–15* The washing of the feet of the Twelve.

The pastoral questions for the Mass of the Lord's Supper are these: Do the elect participate in the *mandatum?* Do we dismiss the elect on this night? If we do dismiss the elect, who will lead their reflection time? Do we invite them to participate in the prayer before the reserved sacrament of the eucharist?

Do the elect participate in the mandatum?

"What I just did was to give you an example: As I have done, so you must do"—Jesus' statement gives us the term *mandatum* (Latin, "commission"), meaning literally "something given into another's hand." The gospel reminds us that we who call ourselves followers of Jesus the Christ are first of all servants of God's reign, servants of all in true need.

Our celebration this night gives us a rich symbol to drive the message home: The presider washes the feet of members of the community (or, in some communities, the assembly's members wash each other's feet). Be careful here not to fall back into historicization. This is not a role-playing of Jesus' washing feet. Rather, with this symbolic action, we embrace the life style of the servant Jesus.

The focus is our participation in the servant mission of Jesus that both precedes and flows from our eucharistic gathering. This night reminds us that eucharist and service are inextricably intertwined. The elect, therefore, participate in this ritual action along with the community

Do we dismiss the elect on this night?

If our pastoral practice has been consistent with the directives of the ritual text— "ordinarily…[the catechumens] should be kindly dismissed before the liturgy of the eucharist begins…" (*RCIA,* n. 75.3)   then why would we change this practice tonight? The reason we have dismissed the catechumens (now elect) was due primarily to their inability to participate in the priestly prayer of Christ (which they will share in through baptism, cf. *RCIA,* n. 75.3). Hence, though we have mutually discerned readiness for celebrating the sacraments of initiation (that readiness was ritually celebrated at the rite of election), the elect continue to be dismissed from the assembly until after their baptism.

Some people argue that this is a "special night" for the community, and therefore we should make a change in our practice. After all, there is something important about linking the Last Supper institution narrative with the liturgy of the eucharist. We need to be careful in this line of thinking that we do not fall prey to "historicizing" this liturgy. Furthermore, such thinking does not justify diminishing the soon-to-be-baptized elect's immersion at their baptism into the royal, priestly, and prophetic mission of Christ—and we will diminish that immersion if we introduce them into a passive role as observers during the liturgy of the eucharist on Holy Thursday. After all, they will participate in the directive of the eucharist—go and serve—through the ritual mandatum (washing of the feet).

Perhaps the desire to keep the elect present because of some objective eucharistic practice betrays a community's misunderstanding of its priestly role in the great prayer of thanksgiving.

If we do dismiss the elect, who will lead their reflection time?

If the elect have "faithfully listened to God's word proclaimed by the Church...responded to that word and begun to walk in God's presence... [and] shared the company of the Christian brothers and sisters and joined them in prayer" (cf. *RCIA*, n. 131B), then why couldn't they lead their own reflection on their experience of the liturgy of the word? After all, they will be doing it for themselves (and we hope with others) for the rest of their lives. Catechumenal formation has provided both a method and an expectation for such reflection. There is no need to have members of the parish community be dismissed with them this night.

In keeping with the retreat theme of the season, simply ask the elect to be especially attentive to the evening's celebration and then give them some reflection questions to get started. It seems the experience of the liturgy of the word with the *mandatum* ritual is powerful enough to be a rich source for prayerful reflection. At the end of the celebration members of the team and sponsors can meet with the catechumens and elect for some final thoughts.

Do we invite them to participate in the prayer before the reserved sacrament of the eucharist?

This question is referring to the practice in most parishes of placing the reserved eucharist (to be used for the sick and homebound) in a chapel or other place with the opportunity for public prayer until midnight. There is not room here to explore the theological implications of such a practice. However, it is important to note that any eucharistic adoration (in whatever form) only makes sense within the context of the experience of the eucharistic assembly praying the eucharistic prayer together (liturgy of the eucharist). Therefore, introducing the elect to adoration of the eucharist before their participation in the eucharistic prayer can lead to great distortions and misunderstandings about the eucharist. There will be ample opportunities in their life to participate in such gatherings (if they choose) in the future; it does not seem to be a wise practice to do so at this time.

Good Friday

The Paschal Fast

"On Good Friday and, if possible, also on Holy Saturday until the Easter Vigil, the Easter fast is observed everywhere" (*GNLYC*, n. 20). Furthermore, the ritual text prescribes that the elect "be advised that on Holy Saturday they should refrain from their usual activities, spend their time in prayer and reflection, and, as far as they can, observe a fast" (*RCIA*, n. 185.1; see *NS*, n. 15).

The paschal fast is a different kind of fast than the ones we are accustomed to. Recall that Lent—with its observances, including the penitential fasts—concludes just before the Mass of the Lord's Supper on Holy Thursday. We are no longer in a penitential mode, and therefore our paschal fast is not penitential. It is an anticipatory fast: the fast that prepares us for a great event (like a wedding or an anniversary celebration). Therefore, the Church invites all of the faithful to refrain from food and normal activities (such as work and entertainment) and to focus, instead, on the paschal mystery they participate in. The elect, in a special way, participate in this paschal fast throughout the period before the celebration of the Easter Vigil.

Given the significance of this time, recommending that the elect take off from work during these days is appropriate (as, we would hope, all of the faithful would). The parish community could provide space for personal reflection and prayer throughout these days, and also support (financial, perhaps), for those who would experience a hardship by not working these days. The parish needs to send an important message: this paschal fast is so important that we are willing to put our resources behind it to support you. Sponsors, godparents, spiritual directors, or someone from the team may want to be available to them at various times over these days for support and shared prayer.

Celebration of the Passion of the Lord

Good Friday: The Passion of the Lord			
Reading I *Isaiah 52:13–53:12* The suffering servant is ever faithful; through his suffering, we are made whole.	Responsorial Psalm *Psalm 31*	Reading II *Hebrews 4:14–16; 5:7–9* Christ, who identifies with us, is the source of salvation for all.	Gospel *John 18:1–19, 42* The passion of our Lord Jesus Christ.

Concerning the celebration of the passion of the Lord, questions that we face are: Do we dismiss the elect before the communion rite? Do we invite the elect to participate in the veneration of the cross?

Do we dismiss the elect before the communion rite?

Given what was said for the Mass of the Lord's Supper, dismissing the elect before the communion rite at this liturgy is consistent. Recall why we dismiss the elect. It is not simply that they do not participate in eucharistic communion with the community. It is broader: they do not yet participate in the priestly prayer of Christ that members of the Body of Christ participate in. Similarly to the directives given for the Mass of the Lord's Supper, we would dismiss the elect on their own to reflect on the experience of the Word. This dismissal happens before the intercessions.

Do we invite the elect to participate in the veneration of the cross?

This ritual gesture will occur during the remainder of the celebration of the passion of the Lord. Remember that the veneration of the cross is not about mourning Jesus' death. Rather, it is about acknowledging our participation in that saving death today. It seems appropriate, especially as we view this as a unitive feast (connected with Holy Thursday and the Easter Vigil), that the elect participate in this ritual action with sponsors after the community's celebration.

Holy Saturday

The rite encourages that the elect set Holy Saturday apart for prayer and reflection (*RCIA,* n. 185.1). The team may choose to use this opportunity to gather for the day with the elect (and sponsors, whenever possible). Rather than having a structured day of prayer, give the elect the opportunity to have a quiet space for the day. Members of the parish can contact the elect to take care of any needs they may have at home during that day. For most of us, if no one takes us from our homes and gives us a place to pray and rest, we won't. There will be so many distractions for the elect at home—and so many preoccupations.

The parish community may gather on Holy Saturday morning for morning prayer. This would be a good opportunity to incorporate the preparation rites for the elect with members of the community gathered. Following the preparation rites, the elect can then remain at the parish center—or in another designated place—in prayer and reflection. The texts from the Vigil readings can be used for reflection. At lunch time, the elect and sponsors can share a simple meal—soup, cheese, bread, fruit—with their godparents, team members and parishioners. The afternoon can include more time and space for private prayer and reflection. Midday, all the elect can gather for a prayer experience and faith-sharing, and then return home for the final preparations before the Vigil service.

Some people react adversely to the notion of asking the elect to stay for most of Holy Saturday with the team in prayer and reflection. However, many members of the elect who have done just that have been positive and supportive of the idea. Most admit that they would have found it difficult to create this space in their own home. They felt relieved of anxieties and could focus on the true meaning of the Vigil experience. There wasn't time to worry, only to pray and to keep watch with God.

Preparation Rites

The *Rite of Christian Initiation of Adults* provides various rites that begin the initiation ritual: presentation of the Lord's Prayer if the parish has deferred it, the recitation of the Creed, the ephphatha rite, and the choosing of a baptismal name.

Read RCIA, *n. 185.*

This is a reminder of the importance of the paschal fast, and also of noting the preparation rites to be celebrated in anticipation of the celebration of the sacraments of initiation at the Easter Vigil.

Read RCIA, *n. 186.*

This section provides direction for the order of worship when using the various preparation rites. These directives will be incorporated in the model below.

Read RCIA, *nos. 187-192.*

The recommended model for the celebration of the preparation rites is as follows (with appropriate adjustments reflecting *RCIA*, n. 186):

Gathering Song (*RCIA*, n. 187)

Greeting (*RCIA*, n. 188)

Reading of the Word of God (*RCIA*, n. 189)

— If celebrating only the recitation of the Creed, see *RCIA*, n. 194 for texts.

— If celebrating only the ephphatha rite, see *RCIA*, n. 198 for text.

— If celebrating both the ephphatha rite and recitation of the Creed, see *RCIA*, n. 194 for texts.

— If celebrating the presentation of the Lord's Prayer, use the gospel text and ritual presentation in *RCIA*, n. 180.

Homily (*RCIA*, n. 190)

Celebration of the Rites: Following is the order of celebrating if using all the rites; if a rite is not used (or had been previously celebrated), eliminate from this listing.

— [Choosing a Baptismal Name (RCIA, n. 202). Note that *RCIA*, n. 33.4 indicates that the directives for the U.S.—except when the diocesan bishops chooses otherwise—is that there is to be no giving of a new name.]

— Ephphatha rite (*RCIA*, n. 199)

— Recitation of the Creed (*RCIA*, nos. 195-196) [Note: Celebrate only if the presentation of the Creed has been celebrated earlier.]

Concluding Rites (*RCIA*, nos. 192, 204-205

Recitation of the Creed

Read RCIA, *n. 193.*

This preparation rite—often called the *redditio symboli:* the return of the symbol (i.e., Creed)—serves two purposes: immediate preparation for the public profession of faith at the celebration of the sacraments of initiation, and also a catechetical purpose. Of course, if there has not been a previous celebration of the presentation of the Creed, this preparation rite would not be celebrated.

Reciting the Creed from memory is customary for the elect. While there

194 The RCIA: Transforming the Church

is no statement in the rite either way, it seems appropriate that the words that symbolize the life of the community are engraved in the hearts and minds of the newly initiated. Of course, if the elect are too nervous to recite from memory, we can provide a copy of the Creed.

Ephphatha Rite
Read RCIA, *n. 197.*

The ephphatha rite (see Mark 7:31-37) is an appropriate complement to the scrutinies. Throughout the period of purification, the elect have prayed for freedom from sin.The ephphatha is the prayer for God to open the ears of the elect truly to hear God's Word and to open the mouth of the elect that they may proclaim it. The rite focuses on the fact that the very ability to hear and respond to God's Word is a gift of grace and not something we can earn or manipulate.

If both the recitation of the Creed and the ephphatha rite are to be celebrated at the same ritual, then the ephphatha rite precedes the recitation of the Creed (*RCIA,* n. 194). It is the grace of God that empowers one to hear the message of the gospel and then to proclaim it. The Creed that they proclaim flows from the experience of God's grace.

Choosing a Baptismal Name
Read RCIA, *n. 200.*

Except when allowed by the diocesan bishop, it is the practice in the United States not to give a new name (see *RCIA,* n. 33.4). If the elect are to choose new names, the presider will need to reflect on the importance of being named by another. Naming denotes some sense of relationship and intimacy. It suggests that one knows another. To give another a name expresses the transformative quality of the relationship. The same is true of our experience of God, especially in baptism. We are transformed in the experience of baptism.

CELEBRATION OF THE SACRAMENTS OF INITIATION

Read RCIA, *n. 206.*

In this section, the text reminds us about the integrity of the initiation sacraments— baptism, confirmation, eucharist—as well as the effects of celebrating the sacraments: forgiveness of sin, sharing in the people of God, adoption as children of God, and sharing in the fullness of the reign of God (already but not yet). Note well that the concern of the sacraments is not membership-related but disciple-focused: sharing in the life and mission of the Body of Christ (see *NS,* n. 14).

Read RCIA, *n. 207.*

This text situates the "when" and "by whom" of the celebration: at the Easter Vigil following the blessing of the water, with the bishop as presider.

There is no obstacle to implementing the first part of the directive (the "when"). The second part of the directive will normally be extended to parish celebrations presided over by the pastor.

Read RCIA, *n. 208.*

In the extraordinary circumstance that initiation for unbaptized persons occurs at a time other than the Easter Vigil (e.g., serious illness), the celebration (and final preparation) needs to maintain the paschal character outlined throughout the rite: the sharing in the death and resurrection of the Lord Jesus and our responsibility as disciples.

A pastoral note is in order here. It requires a great deal of energy—physical, psychic, spiritual—to celebrate the Lent-Triduum-Easter celebrations of a community. It does not make sense to try to replicate that again during the year (given the other demands of the liturgical cycle) except in grave circumstances. The decision to celebrate initiation outside the usual time must be made very carefully.

Celebration of Baptism

Read RCIA, *n. 209.*

The ritual dimensions of the first movement in the celebration of the initiation sacraments (baptism) are discussed in this section. In summary fashion, the ritual text outlines the structure of the rite and demonstrates the important link between the baptismal washing and the explanatory rites. Note that it is through ritual action and symbol that we give the meaning of baptism to the newly baptized, not by speeches or lectures.

In the next sections (*RCIA,* nos. 210-214), we explore the various dimensions of the baptism rite.

Read RCIA, *n. 210.*

Besides giving clear directives about the necessity of the blessing of the water (and what water to use) if we celebrate initiation outside the normal time, this section gives a synthesis of a theological reflection on the importance of water in the baptism rite. This will be a helpful section for the catechist to review for the period of mystagogy when reflecting back on the experience of the baptism rite.

Read RCIA, *n. 211.*

This section is helpful not only for its explanation of the meaning of the renunciation of sin and profession of faith, but for its use in discernment for election and mystagogy. Here we have the clear statement on the central importance of an explicit faith in the paschal mystery. This is why the rite expects a prolonged formation of catechumens (one year) and prescribes a particular type of formation (*RCIA,* n. 75) which has less to do with "knowledge" of the faith and more to do with coming to an explicit profession of faith in the paschal mystery.

Whenever we fear we are losing the focus of our initiation preparation, we need to review this section of the ritual text. How do we create the environment to lead people to the concerns expressed here? A faithful implementation of the rite as described in the periods and steps seems a sure route.

Read RCIA, *n. 212.*

Here it is clear: baptism and its effects are the work of God. In the ritual action of baptism, the elect (those chosen by God) become children of God and members of the Body of Christ. This is not membership in the casual sense; here we are talking about discipleship. It is important to note again that God gives this new status as child of God and disciple, while calling forth responsibility from each of us.

Read RCIA, *n. 213.*

The rite places particular focus on the baptismal rite and the paschal mystery: one enters into the waters of death and new life. This section highlights the importance of the symbolic action to bear the weight of such an important proclamation: immersion or pouring of water. Both actions speak of an abundance of water—there should be no missing the implications of the ritual action due to an absence of flowing water. The *National Statutes* note that baptism by immersion is the preferred option (*NS,* n. 17).

Read RCIA, *n. 214.*

This section keeps the clear link between the baptismal washing and the explanatory rites. Normally, the anointing with chrism will not be celebrated because sacramental confirmation will now follow.

Celebration of Confirmation

Read RCIA, *n. 215.*

This is a very strong statement about the importance of celebrating baptism and confirmation at the same ritual celebration. It would be wise to read and reread this section to be clear that only "serious reasons" (e.g., emergency baptism by a lay person) would prevent celebrating these sacraments together.

Read RCIA, *n. 216.*

This notes when the celebration of confirmation occurs in the sequence of the liturgy. Note that if the bishop is not the presider at this liturgy, the presider who baptized also has the faculty to confirm (see *CIC,* canon 883; *NS,* nos. 12-13).

The Neophytes' First Sharing in the Celebration of the Eucharist

Read RCIA, *n. 217.*

This section clearly notes the importance of the active participation and celebration of the newly baptized in the eucharist at this celebration. Now the newly baptized participate in the priestly prayer of the Body of Christ: general intercessions, the eucharistic prayer and communion, the dismissal of the faithful. The explicit connection of this priestly responsibility of all the baptized to the baptism-confirmation sacraments can be lost if we did not dismiss the catechumens/elect during their formation (*RCIA*, n. 75.3). Dismissal of the catechumens/elect is not simply to provide time for them to reflect on the Word of God; the rite connects it with preparing them for their celebration of the eucharist (*RCIA*, n. 75.3).

THE EASTER VIGIL

Keeping in mind the directives noted in *RCIA*, nos. 206-217, the following will give a broad outline of the celebration of the sacraments of initiation during the Easter Vigil as found in *RCIA*, nos. 218-243 with some pastoral recommendations for the celebration.

We celebrate the vigil after nightfall on Holy Saturday night. It is a time of prayer and celebration, a time of welcome to those who will be baptized, confirmed and share in the eucharist. It is also a time for the community to rededicate itself to the mission of the reign of God. Communities that do not have women and men who will enter the waters of baptism during the Vigil will have a more difficult time exposing themselves to the power of these symbols.

There are four basic movements to the Vigil service: the service of light, the liturgy of the Word, the liturgy of baptism, and the liturgy of the eucharist.

Service of Light

As a continuation of the major liturgies of the Triduum, the Easter Vigil begins in silence in the dark outside around a fire. Whenever we gather to pray as a community, we light the fire (candles), keeping in mind the presence of Christ, the light of the world. This night, the fire is large. The mood is anticipatory.

The service of light needs to be celebrated in a place where the community can gather. It serves little purpose to celebrate the service of light in the church vestry where no one but the ministers can be present. If there is no place to gather for the community, then the service of light needs to be adapted for the worship space of the community.

The movement of the service is simple—and it is the simplicity of these rites that heightens the power for the symbols to speak. Fire is blessed. The Easter candle is blessed and lighted. In the darkness of the night, one light shines bright, shattering the darkness, offering hope. The candle is carried in procession through the community with the proclamation: "Christ our Light!" Candles lit from the great candle begin to be passed among the assembly as they solemnly process into the worship space. The Easter candle is enthroned and usually incensed. After the community has assembled, there is silence. With only the light from the Easter candle—and its extension to the candles held by the community—the Easter proclamation is sung. The Exultet is a prayer of blessing and thanksgiving.

Liturgy of the Word

Following the Easter proclamation, the community sits for the liturgy of the Word. Environment and mood are created with dim lighting, allowing the burning Easter candle to stand as witness to the proclaimed texts.

Easter Vigil: The Resurrection of the Lord		
Reading	Text	Responsorial Psalm
1	*Genesis 1:1–2:2* The Creation story.	*Psalm 104* or *Psalm 33*
2	*Genesis 22:1–18* The sacrifice of Isaac by Abraham.	*Psalm 16*
3	*Exodus 14:15–15:1* The passing of Israel through the sea of reeds, Escaping from Egypt.	*Exodus 15:1–6, 17–18*
4	*Isaiah 54:5–14* God's eternal love serves as the foundation.	*Psalm 30*
5	*Isaiah 55:1–11* All who are thirsty, come to the water, and receive life.	*Isaiah 12:2–6*
6	*Baruch 3:9–15, 32–4:4* Follow God's way and you will always dwell in peace.	*Psalm 19*
7	*Ezekiel 36:16–28* God will give you a new heart and a new spirit.	*Psalm 42* or *Isaiah 12:2–6* (if not used above) or *Psalm 51*
8	*Romans 6:3–11* Are you not aware that we were baptized into Christ death?	
9	Year A: *Matthew 28:1–10* Year B: *Mark 16:1–8* Year C: *Luke 24:1–12* Christ is risen from the dead!	

There are a total of nine readings prescribed for the Vigil. In the early Church, the community kept vigil all night, recalling the great deeds of God and of God's love in the community. They told stories of salvation. While the community remained in prayer and proclamation all night, they gathered the elect in the baptistery for their initiation. Thus, the newly initiated—when brought to the community who had been praying and listening to the scriptures throughout the night—became the concrete enfleshment of God's continuing salvation in our midst.

Many parishes have reduced the number of readings for the Vigil. The instruction in the lectionary states that at the very least two readings from the Hebrew scriptures (one of which must be the Exodus account) and the two prescribed texts from the Christian scriptures are to be used. With the renewed interest in the Vigil liturgy, especially because of the central focus of initiation, more and more parishes are beginning to restore the full Vigil experience. One way of doing this is to begin with the Easter fire and then move into the cycle of readings. Perhaps a reader could proclaim a new text every half hour, with the intervening time for a response and private prayer.

The Liturgy of Baptism

The liturgy of baptism follows the homily and is celebrated in full view of the community. If the baptismal font is not situated where the community can participate, then a portable vessel will need to be used in the sanctuary (*RCIA*, n. 218).

Presentation of the Candidates for Baptism (RCIA, n. 219)

The rite prescribes three options for the presentation of the candidates depending on the place of baptism. The order of worship for each option follows:

1. Option A: Baptism Is Celebrated Immediately at the Baptismal Font

This option does not include an extended procession to the baptismal font; it is used if the baptismal font is nearby (but not in the sanctuary, Option C)
— Celebrant and assisting ministers go to the baptismal font.
— Elect are called forward and godparents present them.
— Elect and godparents take places around the font, not blocking the view of the community. If there are a large number of elect, they can take their places during the singing of the Litany of the Saints.
— Invitation to prayer (*RCIA*, n. 220)
— Litany of the Saints (*RCIA*, n. 221)

2. Option B: When Baptism Is Celebrated after a Procession to the Font

— Elect are called forward and godparents present them. If there are a large number of elect, they can begin to form the procession.
— Procession is formed:
  • minister carrying the Easter candle
  • elect with godparents
  • presider and assisting ministers

— Litany of Saints (*RCIA*, n. 221)
— Elect and godparents take places around the font, not blocking the
  view of the community.
— Invitation to prayer (*RCIA*, n. 220)

3. Option C: When Baptism Is Celebrated in the Sanctuary
—Elect are called forward and godparents present them.
—Elect and godparents take places around the font, not blocking the
  view of the community. If there is a large number of elect, they can
  take their places during the singing of the Litany of the Saints.
—Invitation to prayer (*RCIA*, n. 220)
—Litany of the Saints (*RCIA*, n. 221)

Invitation to Prayer (RCIA, n. 220)
The presider invites the community to pray for the elect as they prepare
to enter into the waters of baptism. There follows a period of silent prayer.

Litany of the Saints (RCIA, n. 221)
The litany of the saints is sung. We can adapt the litany to include other
petitions: names of patron saints of the parish community, the elect; names of
our brothers and sisters of the covenant at Sinai such as Abraham, Sarah,
Jonathan and David; names of other members in the communion of saints not
yet formally recognized, such as Thomas Merton, Dorothy Day, or John
XXIII. The litany should move and not be dragged out.

Blessing of Water (RCIA, n. 222)
The rite prescribes five options depending on circumstances:
    — At the Easter Vigil: Option A
    — Outside the Easter Vigil with water not blessed at the Easter Vigil:
      Option A, B or C
    — During the Easter Season with water blessed at the Easter Vigil:
      Option D or E
Because of the presumption that the normative time to celebrate is the
Easter Vigil, we will continue with option A. The rite prescribes that the
presider sing the blessing of the water. This may cause a concern for presiders
who cannot sing. In those instances, it seems appropriate that the blessing be
sung by a cantor or schola. If the presider should choose to recite the blessing
(although the text does seem to be a hymn and not a pronouncement), an
appropriate antiphon could be sung by the community at various points during
the blessing.
    The blessing of the water recounts the various uses of water in the history
of salvation. After asking God to unseal the fountain of baptism, the presider low-
ers the Easter candle into the still waters. This rather graphic and deliberate ges-

ture seems to have ancient roots—the impregnation of the primordial waters with new life, breaking open the waters with fertility. The symbol of the candle breaks the seal of the water with the enlivening grace of God's Spirit so that all who enter these waters can be filled with this same Spirit. We now have the first stirrings of the water—the waters will move again when the bodies of those to be claimed in baptism are immersed in them. Thus, these men and women will become the bearers of this new life. Though the movement of the symbol—the immersion of the Easter candle into the waters, stirring them up—may be subtle (or even lost if done poorly), it makes a powerful statement of the sacramental dimension of life.

Profession of Faith (RCIA, nos. 223-225)

The presider then invites the elect to reject sin (*RCIA*, n. 224) and make a profession of faith (*RCIA*, n. 225). Recall the importance of this explicit profession of faith for baptism (see *RCIA*, n. 211).

The renunciation of sin takes the form of responses to a series of inquiries (three options are given). The questions are directed to the elect as a group, and they respond in unison.

The profession of faith, also in the form of responses to a series of inquiries, is given individually by each of the elect. Immediately after the profession of faith, we baptize the elect. If the baptism is in a baptismal pool, the elect can enter the waters before the profession of faith, followed by the proclamation of the profession of faith and baptism.

The rite does provide this adaptation for large groups: the profession of faith may be made together or in smaller groups, followed by the individual baptism. Given the importance of what was said in *RCIA*, n. 211, the individual profession of faith should be preferred even with a large number of elect.

During the baptismal liturgy of the early Church, the elect turned and faced the west, the darkness, and rejected sin and evil. They were then instructed to face the east, the rising sun, and to accept the new life of baptism. The elect can similarly be involved in the turning from west to east. The presider can ask them to face the west, the direction of darkness, and begin to question them on their desire to renounce sin and evil. Then as they enter the baptismal pool (or approach the font) we can invite them to turn (with the assistance and support of their godparents) to face the east, the rising sun and morning star, and profess faith in Christ Jesus.

Baptism (RCIA, n. 226)

The rite offers two options for baptism: option A: immersion (full body or the head only); or option B: the pouring of water over the head of the elect. A directive about large numbers is given which allows the group to be divided into smaller groups with the baptism presided over by assisting ministers. This adaptation does not seem reasonable unless there is a very large space for one grand font—or for "extensions" of the font. In either case, it is not a preferred option and appears rather cumbersome to execute.

The ritual text and action is simple: triple immersion (or pouring) along with the Trinitarian formula. The directives for immersion state the godparents should touch the candidate—this will need to be thought through carefully because of the immersion action. For the pouring option, the godparents place the right hand on the shoulder of the elect.

It seems reasonable to suggest that full body immersion most fully expresses the symbol of the water bath in baptism. The elect will enter into the fullness of the death and resurrection of the Lord. They are dying to the old to embrace the new. They enter into the waters of life and death to emerge transformed by God's Spirit. The power of that symbol—for the one being baptized as well as for the baptizing community—is best expressed with full body immersion.

Some churches have constructed baptismal pools in the entrance way of the church—a clear reminder of the responsibility of the baptized. Usually the baptismal pools are of two types: either one with running waters, or one that can be covered with a brass plate. For those churches with baptismal pools, the choice for baptism is obvious.

Explanatory Rites (RCIA, n. 227)

Following the baptism, there are a series of rites that help expand and explain—through symbol—the meaning of the baptism experience. If there will not be a celebration of confirmation during this celebration, the baptism is followed by an anointing with chrism on the crown of the head (*RCIA*, n. 228).

We clothe the newly baptized with the baptismal garment—usually a white robe, although it can be of a different color depending on local custom (*RCIA*, n. 229). This is followed by the presentation of a candle (lit from the Easter candle) by their godparents.

Celebration of Confirmation

Confirmation follows (unless it is to be deferred; then the renewal of baptismal promises of the faithful would be placed here; see *RCIA*, n. 230, final directive). Confirmation will take place at the same place where we celebrated baptism (*RCIA*, n. 231). In the absence of the bishop, the minister of baptism is authorized to confirm (*RCIA*, n. 232).

Invitation (RCIA, n. 233)

The newly baptized, along with their godparents, are instructed in the meaning of confirmation and its association with baptism. Following this, we invite the community to pray in silence for the newly baptized.

Laying On of Hands (RCIA, n. 234)

The presider then extends his hands over the newly baptized and says a prayer of invocation, asking God to send forth the Spirit in a new way in their lives.

Anointing with Chrism (RCIA, n. 235)

The laying on of hands is followed by the anointing with chrism, the sealing of the sacrament. This sealing—traditionally associated as the indelible mark of the Spirit—sets the newly baptized apart for service for the mission of the reign of God. They are now, as it were, branded or marked for charity and justice.

The chrism used for the confirmation and the action of confirming needs to be visible to the community. A simple but elegant procession of the chrism before the celebration of confirmation could help focus this part of the ritual. Or the chrism could be carried in by liturgical dancers who gracefully present the chrism to the presider. The chrism, which can be carried in a crystal container, can then be poured by the presider into a glass bowl for the confirmation rite.

During the anointing, the godparents place their right hand on the newly baptized's shoulder. The presider dips his finger (or hand) into the chrism and marks the sign of the cross on the forehead of the newly baptized while reciting the formula of confirmation, followed by the first exchange of the kiss of peace. They should not wipe the chrism away from the foreheads after the confirmation rite.

Renewal of Baptismal Promises

Invitation (RCIA, n. 237)

The candles used earlier are relit and each of the faithful holds his or her candle, just as the newly baptized hold their newly-lit candles.

Renewal of Baptismal Promises (RCIA, nos. 238–239)

We now call upon the community, having witnessed the baptism of the elect, to renew its own baptismal promises through a renunciation of sin and a profession of faith. If the neophytes turned toward the west and east in their renunciation and profession of faith, it seems to overwork the symbol to repeat it again. If they did not, perhaps this could be included at this time.

Sprinkling with Baptismal Water (RCIA, n. 240)

Following the renewal of baptismal promises, the presider sprinkles the community with the blessed water. Before the service, an appropriate branch can be cut for use at this time. The presider may wish to test out the branch before the ritual. While we do not want to drown people, we do want them to experience the waters of baptism. A slight mist of water does not convey the message.

Another option would be to invite the community to come forward to the baptismal pool and to sign themselves with the baptismal waters. This procession to the waters need not be organized. In fact, it should have the quality of spontaneity. Some people will sign themselves, others will touch the water, and others will actually dip part of their body into the water. During this time, the community can sing an appropriate hymn.

The Liturgy of the Eucharist

The newly baptized now take part in the community's celebration at the table of the eucharist (*RCIA,* nos. 241-243). They join, for the first time, in the community's prayer during the general intercessions or prayers of the faithful. Perhaps they may be part of the presentation of the gifts. We mention them during the eucharistic prayer.

Before the breaking of the bread, the presider may wish briefly to mention the importance of the eucharistic meal in terms of our sacramental initiation. The neophytes and newly received are then welcomed to the table to share in the community's communion with the Lord and with each other.

The community can continue the celebration of the initiation with a reception and party following the Easter Vigil. The parish community can have the opportunity personally to welcome the newly baptized into the Catholic Church, as well as into this parish community.

EASTER SUNDAY

As noted earlier, the Feast of the Triduum continues through Evening Prayer on Easter Sunday. Most probably, the neophytes will not return for the Masses of Easter Sunday. However, after spending time in celebration with family and friends, the neophytes should gather again with the community during its solemn celebration of Evening Prayer.

ADAPTATION WITH CHILDREN OF CATECHETICAL AGE

Children should participate in the parish celebration of the Triduum as much as possible, following the directives noted earlier in this chapter. They also should celebrate the preparation rites as noted.

Part II, chapter 1 is clear: children of catechetical age should celebrate their full sacramental initiation at the Easter Vigil (*RCIA,* n. 304). Presuming unbaptized adults also, this would be an integrated celebration of adults and children. Thus, all the directives noted above apply for celebrating with children.

The ritual text provided (*RCIA,* nos. 309-329) is for use when celebrating only with children of catechetical age. The basic structure is the same, with some language modifications. For reasons unknown, some directives of part I are missing from this section. Therefore, for ease of use, following is the ritual schema that includes sections from part I.

Service of Light (unless not at Easter Vigil)
Liturgy of the Word (*RCIA*, n. 309)
Celebration of Baptism
—Presentation of the elect; recall the three options (*RCIA*, n. 219).
— Invitation to Prayer (*RCIA*, n. 310)
— Litany of the Saints (*RCIA*, n. 221)
— Blessing of the Water (*RCIA*, n. 311)
— [Community's Profession of Faith (*RCIA*, n. 312). It is unclear why the text moves this here. It seems reasonable to follow the normal order of worship and celebrate this later in the liturgy.]
— Profession of Faith of the Elect (*RCIA*, n. 313)
Renunciation of Sin (*RCIA*, n. 314)
[Anointing with the Oil of Catechumens (*RCIA*, n. 315). Since the directives for the United States are clear that this anointing is to happen during the period of the catechumenate (*RCIA*, 33.7), we eliminate this from the liturgy.]
Profession of Faith (*RCIA*, n. 316)
— Baptism (*RCIA*, n. 317)
— Explanatory Rites (*RCIA*, n. 318)
[Anointing after Baptism if no Confirmation at this celebration (*RCIA*, n. 319)]
Clothing with Baptismal Garment (*RCIA*, n. 320)
Presentation of a Lighted Candle (*RCIA*, n. 321)
Renewal of Baptismal Promises
— Renewal of Baptismal Promises
Renunciation of Sin (*RCIA*, n. 238)
Profession of Faith (*RCIA*, nos. 312 or 239)
— Sprinkling with Baptismal Water (*RCIA*, n. 240)
Celebration of Confirmation
Note: Recall that children of catechetical age are to celebrate the rite of confirmation just as the adults do. Both the *Code of Canon Law* (*CIC*, canons 852, 866, 883, 885) and the *Rite of Christian Initiation of Adults* (*RCIA*, nos. 305, 322) are clear about this. The delegation prescribed is given in favor of the children, that is, the children have a right to the sacrament and, therefore, he must confirm. Only emergency situations warrant the delay of confirmation, as with adults.
— Invitation (*RCIA*, n. 324)
— Laying On of Hands (*RCIA*, n. 325)
— Anointing with Chrism (*RCIA*, n. 326)
Liturgy of the Eucharist (*RCIA*, nos. 327-329)

ADAPTATION WITH BAPTIZED CANDIDATES

Candidates should participate in the parish celebration of the Triduum as much as possible, following the directives noted earlier in this chapter. They do not celebrate the preparation rites because of their focus on preparation for baptism.

Uncatechized Catholics

Uncatechized Catholics complete their initiation by renewing their baptismal promises, making a profession of faith, and celebrating confirmation and eucharist. There is no special rite for this.

This completion of initiation can happen at any time. Because the normal presider at confirmation is the bishop, it usually happens at either a parish or a diocesan celebration of the *Rite of Confirmation.* In some instances, the argument can be made to include the Catholic candidates with the catechumens and other candidates for celebrating initiation. In those cases, the pastor must request and receive delegation from the bishop to confirm the Catholic person.

If delegation is given, the pastoral staff should review the *Rite of Confirmation* for direction in celebrating the completion of initiation. If the Catholic candidates are celebrating completion of initiation with catechumens and/or candidates, then either the combined rite (Appendix I, noted below) or the rite of reception (adapted) is used depending on the candidates (use the former for when catechumens are included; use the latter for when celebrating only with other candidates).

Uncatechized and Catechized Christians

Apart from celebrating a combined rite (as will be discussed below), both uncatechized and catechized Christians coming into the full communion of the Catholic Church celebrate the rite as outlined in part II, chapter 5 of the ritual text. The formation and preparation for the celebration will differ depending on the candidate—we will enroll the uncatechized in a longer formation process (*RCIA,* n. 402) whereas the catechized candidate will have a limited period of preparation (*RCIA,* nos. 473, 477). The rite recommends that both should also be prepared for and make a confession of sins before the rite of reception (*RCIA,* n. 482).

Part II, chapter 5 provides the rite of reception as celebrated within Mass and outside Mass. In keeping with all that we have said about the central role of the assembly throughout the formation of candidates, it seems that reception outside Mass would happen in very rare circumstances. Directives are given in *RCIA,* n. 487 (within Mass) and n. 499f. (outside Mass) regarding lectionary and sacramentary texts. The *National Statutes* prefer that the reception into full communion not take place during the Easter Vigil (see *NS,* nos. 33-34).

The actual rite of reception is rather simple. After the homily, the candidates come forward with their sponsors. Following the invitation by the presider, the candidates and community proclaim the Nicene Creed, followed by the text of affiliation found in *RCIA*, n. 491. This is followed by the declaration of reception (*RCIA*, n. 492).

This is followed by the rite of confirmation. *RCIA*, n. 481 notes that confirmation is celebrated unless the candidate has been validly confirmed. Currently, the Roman Catholic Church only recognizes confirmation in the Orthodox churches. The presider is given the delegation by law (*RCIA*, n. 481; *CIC*, canon 883§2; *NS*, n. 35) to confirm.

A sign of welcome then follows the rite of confirmation (*RCIA*, n. 495). This gesture of welcome should not be confused with the exchange of peace (which comes later). The community then prays the general intercessions (*RCIA*, n. 496) and may anticipate the exchange of peace (*RCIA*, n. 497). If the exchange of peace occurs now, we omit it before the communion rite. The liturgy of the eucharist continues.

Combined Rite of Sacraments of Initiation and Reception into Full Communion

Taking into account the directives for celebrating the Rite of Reception into the Full Communion of the Catholic Church, following is a schema of the combined celebration at the Easter Vigil of the Sacraments of Initiation and of the Rite of Reception into the Full Communion of the Catholic Church (Appendix 1, *RCIA*, nos. 566-594).

Service of Light

Liturgy of the Word

Celebration of Baptism

— *RCIA*, n. 566 reminds us of the importance of keeping the distinctions between the unbaptized and baptized candidates.

— Presentation of the elect (recall the three options). If a procession is used, the baptized candidates for full communion do not take part in the procession.

— Invitation to Prayer

— Litany of the Saints

— Blessing of the Water

— Profession of Faith of the Elect
  Renunciation of Sin
  Profession of Faith

— Baptism

— Explanatory Rites
  [Anointing after Baptism if no Confirmation at this celebration]
  Clothing with Baptismal Garment

Presentation of a Lighted Candle

Renewal of Baptismal Promises

— Invitation. The baptized candidates stand with the rest of the community with lit candles.

— Renewal of Baptismal Promises

    Renunciation of Sin

    Profession of Faith

— Sprinkling with Baptismal Water

Celebration of Reception

— Invitation. Before celebrating this rite, if the presider is still at the font, he is to return to the sanctuary for the rite of reception. Then the candidates for full communion come forward with their sponsors. Note that the uncatechized Catholic candidates do not come forward; they have renewed their baptismal promises with the rest of the community (as have these candidates). This ritual action is about communion in the Catholic Church.

— Profession by the Candidates. The rite prescribes that the text be said in unison. Some parishes adapt this into a question-response format.

— Act of Reception. This is done individually.

Celebration of Confirmation

— Invitation. The newly baptized, the newly received, and Catholics completing their initiation (if delegation has been received by the bishop) come forward together.

— Laying On of Hands

— Anointing with Chrism

[*Newly Baptized Change Clothes.* This is not written in the ritual text, but at some point the newly baptized need to leave to change from their wet clothes into something new. If the newly baptized left before now, we could be sending messages we did not want to send: they might miss the renewal of the community's baptism or the rite of reception. Furthermore, by leaving and returning now, we might end up reinforcing the separation of the confirmation rite from the baptism rite. People who come to the Vigil know that this is a long night into morning; perhaps a ritual "pause" is appropriate here.]

Liturgy of the Eucharist

PREPARATION REMINDERS

❏ If immersion is used—either full body or immersion of the head only—the elect will need to know this ahead of time so they can dress appropriately and bring along a change of clothes. They can be advised to wear a simple outfit—one that cannot be seen through when wet.

❏ Plenty of towels will need to be readily available for the newly baptized, especially if they are baptized by immersion. A quick toweling of excess water is all that is needed at the time of the ritual. Standing dripping in the waters of new life is a rather strong statement to the community.

❏ We can assign someone for each person to be baptized to help them with the changing of clothes after they leave the assembly.

❏ If baptismal robes are to be used, they will need to be ready for the Vigil. A simple poncho-style robe would suffice.

❏ The vessel of chrism for confirmation can be carried into the community in a glass container for everyone to see. As with the gospel procession, there can be a procession or liturgical dance to carry in the chrism.

❏ The names of those initiated, along with the date and place, should be recorded in the appropriate registry in the parish.

11

Period of Postbaptismal Catechesis or Mystagogy

INTRODUCTION

Sacramental initiation does not end with the celebration of the sacraments of initiation. The *Rite of Christian Initiation of Adults* provides for the final period, the period of postbaptismal catechesis or mystagogy (that is, reflection on the mysteries). This formal period of reflection and prayer continues until the Pentecost festival at the end of the Easter season (see *NS,* n. 22).

WHAT DOES THE RITE SAY?

Read RCIA, *n. 244.*

The ritual text outlines both the goal and the direction of mystagogy in a broad way in this section. Including the community and the newly baptized, the Church sets out before us the task of both deepening our understanding and integrating more effectively in our lives the experience of initiation (immersion in the paschal mystery). Reminiscent of *RCIA,* n. 75, the text prescribes the primary way to do this.

Read RCIA, *n. 245.*

"Mystagogy" means to reflect on the mysteries, to savor the mysteries. By mysteries, we do not mean something to be solved or a puzzle. Rather, it is the experience of God that is both alluring yet causes us to stand back in awe. Our word "sacrament" comes from the same Greek root as "mysteries" (see *NS,* n. 23).

Recall earlier that we noted that, in our Catholic Christian Tradition, we lead one into the experience of the mystery (*RCIA,* n. 75.1) through word and sacrament (symbol). This section reaffirms that foundational stance. Thus, through the experience of the mysteries, we experience a shift in life: new perceptions and ways of living—ongoing conversion.

Read RCIA, *n. 246.*

This section highlights the close connection between the community of the faithful and the neophytes—something that has been growing throughout the initiation process. Clearly, the experience of sacrament focuses the neophytes from looking within to looking around them, outside themselves in the community.

	NEWLY BAPTIZED ADULT	CHILDREN OF CATECHETICAL AGE	BAPTIZED, UNCATECHIZED CATHOLIC	BAPTIZED, UNCATECHIZED CHRISTIAN	BAPTIZED, CATECHIZED CHRISTIAN
Reference	*RCIA*, nos. 244–251	*RCIA*, n. 330	*RCIA*, n. 410	*RCIA*, n. 410	*RCIA*, nos. 473, 478.
Required	Yes	Yes	Yes	Yes	Yes, adapted and modified
Focus	*Meditation on the gospel *Sharing in the eucharist *Doing works of charity	*Meditation on the gospel *Sharing in the eucharist *Doing works of charity	*Meditation on the gospel *Sharing in the eucharist *Doing works of charity	*Meditation on the gospel *Sharing in the eucharist *Doing works of charity	*Meditation on the gospel *Sharing in the eucharist *Doing works of charity
Goal	Grow in deepening grasp of paschal mystery and make it part of their lives	Grow in deepening grasp of paschal mystery and make it part of their lives	Grow in deepening grasp of paschal mystery and make it part of their lives	Grow in deepening grasp of paschal mystery and make it part of their lives	Grow in deepening grasp of paschal mystery and make it part of their lives
Name	neophyte	neophyte	—	—	—
Time	Initial mystagogy: Easter Season; extended mystagogy: one year to anniversary of initiation	Initial mystagogy: Easter Season; extended mystagogy: one year to anniversary of initiation	Initial mystagogy: after completion of initiation; extended mystagogy: one year to anniversary of initiation	Initial mystagogy: after completion of initiation; extended mystagogy: one year to anniversary of initiation	Initial mystagogy: after completion of initiation; extended mystagogy: one year to anniversary of initiation
Rites	Sunday eucharist; Mass with the bishop	Sunday eucharist; Mass with the bishop	Sunday eucharist; Mass with the bishop	Sunday eucharist; Mass with the bishop	Sunday eucharist; Mass with the bishop

*(Table title: **Period of Postbaptismal Catechesis or Mystagogy**)*

Authentic immersion in sacramental life fosters community. The parish community needs to provide avenues for encouraging this interaction.

Read RCIA, *n. 247.*

This section affirms the primary place of mystagogy: with the liturgical assembly at the Sunday eucharist. The texts from Year A are recommended (though not required, as with the period of purification and enlightenment), as they assist in the process of mystagogy. The readings from Years B and C, however, are similar enough also to accomplish this. Letting the Easter Season truly be lived in the community is essential for effective mystagogy. This includes, but is not limited to, effective preaching.

What is striking is that the rite gives no direction for additional sessions. These, as we will discuss, are helpful and, presumably, now normative in the life of the neophyte—we trained them into a pattern of life that includes a regular reflection on the Sunday experience with other members of the community.

Read RCIA, *n. 248.*

Keeping the close relationship between neophytes, godparents and the community, this section supports the earlier section. Because of the special role they play in the life of the community during the Easter Season, the neophytes may sit in special places in the community. This is a rare directive in the Catholic Church — normally no one gets a "better place" or "special seating." Yet, for the sake of the community, we give the neophytes special seating within the community as clear reminders (icons) of God's continued presence in the community.

Read RCIA, *n. 249.*

This section highlights the importance of gathering for a special festival near the close of the period of mystagogy.

Read RCIA, *n. 250.*

This section notes the importance of coming back after living within the community of the faithful: for support, to share experiences, to deepen and renew their commitment. There is pastoral wisdom in this—not always will neophytes experience Catholic communities who live faithfully the rhythms of Catholic life they were formed by (*RCIA,* n. 75). It is easy to become disillusioned or out of practice. The *National Statutes* direct monthly gatherings up to the one year anniversary (*NS,* n. 24).

Read RCIA, *n. 251.*

This section directs the bishop to both meet the neophytes and celebrate the eucharist with them during this year following initiation.

UNDERSTANDING MYSTAGOGY

Mystagogy is similar to what most of us do around significant moments in our lives: the death of a loved one, being alone for a holiday, celebrating our 50th birthday, sending our daughter off to her first day of school, our son's first date, our first profession of vows, our ordination to the priesthood, or just a long afternoon alone with a special friend. To move forward, we look back to gain meaning and understanding. When we look forward, we can anticipate and hope; when we look back, we can appreciate and learn. Looking both ways is essential for creative and rich human living.

The period of mystagogy is the time during the initiation process when the newly baptized do look back to move forward. First the newly initiated needed to live the experience of entering into the death and resurrection of the Lord Jesus through the sacraments of initiation. Now it is time to explore the meaning of that experience to have a perspective for Christian living—the life of the disciple.

The Mysteries

But what are the "mysteries" that we look back upon and savor? Saying what the mysteries are not would be helpful.

We are not talking about mysteries as in the Agatha Christie genre: They are not problems that elude us but for which we can find a solution. Nor are the mysteries some kind of hidden pleasure of God that we need to entice out from God so we know our definite future. Finally, the mysteries do not refer to whatever we simply do not understand and want to attribute to God's will. The mysteries here refer to two special notions, one of which is more-or-less irrelevant to us today, but the second of which is fundamental.

The first notion of the mysteries deals with revealing to people things kept hidden. For various reasons, in the early Church they did not inform people preparing for initiation in any of the rituals of initiation. Part of the mystagogical catechesis was to help explore that experience for them. While most people today know about the Christian celebrations of baptism, confirmation, and eucharist before the actual ritual, there is something worth retaining in this earlier practice of keeping secrets.

For example, rather than "rehearsing" rituals with the elect, allow the sponsors to lead them into the experience. The elect know that we will immerse them in water for baptism, anoint them lavishly for confirmation, and bring them to the table of great feasting for the eucharist. But rather than burdening them with all the details of the ritual, allow the elect to experience the ritual. Walk through the details with the sponsors and godparents, who can guide the elect.

The second meaning of the mysteries also has deep roots: It is a way of speaking of sacraments. The mysteries (or sacraments) are experiences of the Holy that both draw us closer in intimacy and, simultaneously, cause us to pull back in awe. Such an understanding of sacrament moves us away from sacrament as something we get to sacrament as experience of God. Mystagogy, then, is the process wherein we ponder the saving experience of the Holy—in this case, through the celebration of the initiation sacraments—in order to understand better who we are and whose we are. No one can truly be touched by the presence of the Holy and not be changed in some way. Mystagogy helps us give a name and some meaning to that change.

Savoring the Mysteries

Thus, we can return to the process of mystagogy: savoring the experience of the mysteries, reflecting back on the experience of the mysteries. This looking back is not nostalgic. Rather, it sharpens our perceptions to see in new ways and move forward into God's promised future. We look back to glean meaning from our experience. Rooted in the experience of the Holy, we have the courage and conviction to be about the mission of the reign of God.

THE CHARACTER OF MYSTAGOGY

When we look at the rite itself, the guidance and direction we get for this period of critical reflection and integration on how to deepen the grasp on paschal mystery is simple and reminiscent of something we heard earlier in the rite: meditation on the gospel, sharing the eucharist and doing works of charity along with the community of the faithful (see *RCIA*, 244). There are no surprises here; it is the agenda of *RCIA*, n. 75, which serves as the foundation for catechumenal formation. The process of becoming Christian provides guidance and direction for remaining Christian. Here, the concern is to focus those skills so that indeed the neophytes and the community will be faithful to such a way of life.

How, then, is the work of mystagogy different from the period of the catechumenate? The *Rite of Christian Initiation of Adults*, n. 246 helps us here: Now the neophytes are different. Having been formed and led into the experience of the mystery in which they desire to participate (*RCIA*, n. 75.1) through "the gospel message they have learned and above all through their experience of the sacraments they have received" (*RCIA*, n. 245), the neophytes develop new ways of viewing life. The experience of the mystery of God changes how they view faith, Church, the world (see *RCIA*, n. 245). They do not see new things; rather, they see things in new ways—isn't that what radical conversion means?

Going Backward To Move Forward

During the period of the catechumenate, the community provides an apprenticeship in the Christian way of life. We go back to the basic skills outlined in *RCIA*, n. 75 again and again until they are carved deeply in the hearts and imaginations of the catechumens. Now during mystagogy, presuming such skills are in place, we help the neophyte move from a posture of preparing for the Christian life to one of living fully the Christian life by showing how we exercise these skills in our daily lives. We do this not as an exercise or extension of the neophyte's learnings; we do it because we, too, have been awakened in new ways by our experience of the paschal mystery this Easter season. Thus, we, too, need to look back to garner new meaning for today so we can move forward on our mission. By this time in the initiation process, a significant shift has occurred. The neophytes are not in formation for discipleship. They are disciples, one with us in our shared participation in the paschal mystery. Everything we do during mystagogy is for all of us, enabling us to move forward.

Such a basic understanding of mystagogy, then, places priority on the gathering of the assembly rather than on additional meetings of the neophytes. The neophytes discover anew their baptismal identity when they gather in common worship with the community. Together, we rediscover ourselves as the body of Christ for the world. It is in such worship, especially during the Easter season, that we corporately look back to the mysteries celebrated during the Triduum that marked our transition from death to life. How is this done? It is done through the liturgies of the Easter season (*RCIA,* n. 247, and *NS,* n. 22). This does not mean building a catechetical session on the lectionary texts and orations for these Sundays; it means the actual praying of the Easter liturgies—the performance—in that we come face to face again and again with the meaning of the mysteries experienced during the Triduum. These liturgies are themselves expressions of the Holy, providing, in turn, new experiences on which to look back and reflect, and the cycle continues. While the Easter season provides a privileged experience of mystagogy for the Easter feast, it also reminds us of the weekly cycle of mystagogy we enter whenever we gather to celebrate the eucharist, the ongoing sacrament of initiation.

Does this lessen the effectiveness of coming together with the neophytes at a separate time for more explicit and critical reflection? No, but it does put such gatherings into a different perspective.

Mystagogical catechesis is different from the dismissal catechesis of the period of the catechumenate. We aimed those events at forming the catechumens into a priestly, prophetic and royal people. To that end, such gatherings served almost as extensions of the liturgy of the word of the larger assembly. Now that they have assumed their places in the community, the primary gathering is always the celebration of the liturgy.

Gatherings for critical reflection do indeed enhance the celebration of the liturgy, but they do not replace it. If a community schedules such gatherings, they can focus on how the celebration of the liturgy helps us integrate the various threads of Christian living in our daily lives. Then the catechist can go back to the experiences of the Sunday Liturgy of the Word and Liturgy of the Eucharist as a source for reflection and also as a way of making explicit connections with the experience of the Triduum and the celebration of the initiation sacraments.

Thus, the work of the community (and pastoral staffs in particular) is to examine how the liturgies of the Easter season are, indeed, mystagogical. How do such gatherings of the community enable all to reflect back to move forward? The Church provides help by its selection of lectionary texts and orations. This needs to be supplemented by effective preaching (see *RCIA,* n. 248). From these gatherings that enable their full, conscious and active participation, the neophytes are redirected into the world—along with the rest of us—on mission.

The following captures the essence of the character of mystagogy: The success of mystagogy is not in how many people show up for mystagogy sessions (here referring to gatherings besides the Sunday assembly) but in how ordinary men and women—teachers, carpenters, nurses, doctors, social workers, designers, dressmakers, plumbers—are living the gospel way of life and giving witness to that way of life.

IMPLEMENTING MYSTAGOGY

How, then, does mystagogy happen? Our first impulse may be to schedule another meeting of the newly initiated so we can help them reflect on their experience.While that might be helpful, it misses the point of initiation. These persons have not been initiated into an extended adult religious education program. Rather, initiation is into the eucharistic community, where they are sent as disciples to serve the mission of the reign of God. The entire initiation process has provided the foundation and formation needed to be such a disciple in today's world. Now it is time to go forward in a new way.

As noted earlier, the *Rite of Christian Initiation of Adults* directs mystagogy to be done by meditation on the gospel, sharing in the eucharist, and doing works of charity (RCIA, n. 244).

The neophytes, along with the community, reflect together on the celebration of the Easter mysteries—the paschal event—and begin the process of making it a full and active part of their lives. The neophytes continue to gather weekly, supported by the community and their godparents, until Pentecost.

The entire community celebrates the Easter season, the season of feasting. The neophytes gather at the Sunday eucharist with the community, witness to their experience of God for the community, and participate in the planning and celebration of the eucharist. They are leaven for new life in the community; they are the source of renewal for the community. Together, the neophytes and the community discern their gifts and recognize their responsibility to serve the mission of the reign of God. Mystagogy is the final period of the initiation process, but it is also the beginning of the responsibility of discipleship.

Meditating on the Gospel

Primacy of the Sunday Liturgy of the Word
The proclamation and preaching of the Easter Season scriptures help the neophytes (and community) to explore the meaning of the paschal mystery. But how will they know these things? Who will tell them?

If our initiation process has immersed them in a rich breaking open of

God's Word for at least one year (as the rite prescribes), then the neophytes will know how to hear that Word and explore its meaning in their lives, especially in the light of the great mysteries just celebrated at the Easter Vigil.

The preaching moment during the period of mystagogy is extremely important for the neophytes and for the community. While it is unreasonable to expect the preaching moment to explain and expand all the richness of the initiation experience, the preacher can continually interpret and connect the experience of initiation with the texts of the Easter season, thus providing a primary form of mystagogy. To facilitate this end, the ritual text recommends that the readings from Year A be used during the Easter season at the Masses celebrated with the neophytes because of the nature of those readings.

Supplemental Gatherings

Perhaps the neophytes may meet weekly with the catechetical team to uncover and explore the richness of the initiation commitment, and also to begin to integrate themselves in the parish community. Though the primary experience of mystagogy is the community's breaking open and sharing of the Word and eucharist (*RCIA*, n. 247), the continued weekly gatherings help the neophytes more explicitly "unpack" their experience.

With the help of the catechetical team, the neophytes can begin to internalize and appropriate the experience of initiation. They will need to reflect on the power and message of the Easter symbols. What was it like to stand in the darkness of the church with the one light of the Easter candle? What meaning did the stories of God's deeds throughout history have for you? How were you able to enter the prayer with the entire Church as sung through the litany of the saints? What was it like to go into the waters of baptism? How do you understand yourself now that you are sealed with the Spirit? What was it like to remain with the community for the eucharistic prayer rather than being dismissed? What meaning did sharing in the eucharist have for you? If an appropriate catechesis for symbols occurred during the initiation process, then the fifth movement of this catechesis can be done now (see Chapter 7 of this resource).

The reflection on the mysteries—the experience of God in the sacraments, in the Word proclaimed and in the community—can easily be integrated in the reflection on the Sunday texts, especially if Year A readings are used. The focus of catechesis now is integration and preparation for mission.

Personal Prayer and Reflection

The neophytes can be encouraged to read and pray the scriptures daily, if this is not already part of their lives. We could make resources for exploring the Sunday texts available to them so they can begin to prepare for each Sunday's gathering of the community to listen to the Word of God. Also, we can make opportunities for varieties of prayer experiences available to them—or,

The Easter Season—Year A				
Feast	**Reading I**	**Responsorial Psalm**	**Reading II**	**Gospel**
Easter Sunday	*Acts 10:34, 37–43* All who believe in Christ have forgiveness of sin.	*Psalm 118*	*Colossians 3:1–4* Your life is hidden now in Christ or *1 Corinthians 5:6–8* Celebrate the feast with the new unleavened bread of sincerity and truth.	*John 20:1–9* They went to the tomb and found it empty.
Easter II	*Acts 2:42–47* The life shared in common.	*Psalm 118*	*1 Peter 1:3–9* We have a new birth in the Risen Christ.	*John 20:19–31* Thomas' profession of faith.
Easter III	*Acts 2:14, 22–28* Peter's proclamation on the day of Pentecost.	*Psalm 16*	*1 Peter 1:17–21* Christ ransomed us from sin.	*Luke 24:13–35* The story of the disciples on the road to Emmaus.
Easter IV	*Acts 2:14, 36–41* Reform, be baptized and receive the Holy Spirit.	*Psalm 23*	*1 Peter 2:20–25* By his wounds we are healed.	*John 10:1–10* Christ is the sheepgate; all who enter will be safe.
Easter V	*Acts 6:1–7* Seven were elected to serve the needs of the community.	*Psalm 33*	*1 Peter 2:4–9* God called you from darkness into God's marvelous light.	*John 14:1–12* Christ, the way, the truth and the life.
Easter VI	*Acts 8:5–8, 14–17* They received the Holy Spirit through the laying on of hands.	*Psalm 66*	*1 Peter 3:15–18* Christ died to lead us to God.	*John 14:15–21* Christ will not leave us orphaned, but will send a new Advocate.
Ascension Thursday	*Acts 1:1–11* Jesus ascends into heaven.	*Psalm 47*	*Ephesians 1:17–23* Christ is raised to the right hand of the Father.	*Matthew 28:16–20* Baptize all nations and know that Christ is with us always.
Easter VII	*Acts 1:12–14* The disciples devote themselves to constant prayer.	*Psalm 27*	*1 Peter 4:13–16* Your identification with Christ will bring you suffering.	*John 17:1–11* Christ entrusts the disciples to God's care.
Pentecost	*Acts 2:1–11* The Holy Spirit comes to the disciples gathered in the upper room.	*Psalm 104*	*1 Corinthians 12:3–7,12–13* There is one Spirit who gives varied gifts for the one body.	*John 20:19–23* Receive the Holy Spirit; go and forgive sins and unbind others.

at the very least, we can give information about different prayer forms to them. Each neophyte will approach the experience of God in a different way because of the unique relationship with God, as well as the unique personality of the neophyte. Discerning appropriate personal and communal prayer forms with the neophytes will be a great service, as well as highlighting the ongoing importance of liturgical prayer.

Sharing in the Eucharist

The sharing in the eucharist—from the great prayer of the community, to the communing of the assembly, to the mandate of mission and service from the table—provides the model for the Christian lifestyle for the neophyte. But who will explain the Mass parts and all the things we do during Mass?

If that is our concern, we are misguided. Rather, we have immersed the neophytes for over a year in the rich foundations of our liturgical life: blessings, anointings, celebrations of the Word, and exorcisms. Along with other members of the community they have discovered the real presence of God in our communal worship. Now they can join in the community's great prayer of thanksgiving, the eucharist. But they do not need to be taught the prayer if we have tutored them in a eucharistic posture all along.

Keep the Easter Season Alive!

The Sunday eucharist during the *Magna Dominica* (the Great Sunday, i.e., the Easter Season) is the place of mystagogy, beginning with the Easter Sunday celebration. But this can happen only if the neophytes feel part of the local community because the true catechist is the community. We must avoid minimalism, thus avoiding no change: this is an important period in the life of the whole Church. The environment should be festive: fresh spring flowers, decorative wall hangings, rich vestments, incense and beeswax candles. The music should be rich—keep the Easter brass and strings to keep the Alleluia alive! Flood the senses: rich and bright sights, clear and joyful sounds, renewing and fragrant smells, fresh and appealing tastes, warm and embracing touch.

Liturgy Preparation·

The neophytes are encouraged to be a part of the liturgy planning during the *Magna Dominica.* Pastorally, this can be problematic because usually the Easter Season is prepared well before Easter. However, as part of that preparation, the liturgy committee may choose to designate specific dimensions of the preparation to be taken care of by the neophytes, such as preparation of the general intercessions one week, or presentation of the gifts another week, or baking the eucharistic bread another week. Then the director of liturgy can participate with the neophytes during the catechetical gatherings to help better prepare them for liturgical prayer.

Public Witness of Newly Baptized

The neophytes are introduced again to the community and welcomed. They are to be remembered by name during the homily and the general intercessions. They continue to wear their white baptismal albs and sit in their reserved seats without leaving after the Liturgy of the Word.

One of the greatest gifts the neophytes give to the community is the witness of their presence. The community deepens its own awareness of God's loving concern and gift of salvation as it sees these new members of the community embrace the way of life of the gospel. The Easter Sunday eucharist is when the neophytes begin their witness to the parish by their presence as well as through witnessing. The neophytes can be given the opportunity after communion to strengthen the community by giving witness to the experience of God they have celebrated. Sponsors and godparents can also be included to witness before the parish. By Pentecost, each of the neophytes and godparents and sponsors will have had the opportunity to speak if any so choose.

Works of Charity

Focused on Mission

Finally, the gospel way of life summons the neophytes to do works of charity. For it is only in spending themselves for the other that they truly discover their own identity as sons and daughters of God. Who will tell them how to do this, or where to do this?

If we have postured their initiation formation toward service of others (as *RCIA*, n. 75.4 prescribes as a constitutive part of the formation process), then they will know in their hearts that the true response to the experience of the living God is service for the authentic needs of others. John Paul II in his 1979 World Day of Prayer for Peace said, "We are beginning to see that the parish catechumenate is a rich and fertile soil in which to plant the seeds of justice and peace." Their experience of the initiation sacraments propels them into this way of life; their experience of initiation formation provided the foundation. Hopefully the neophytes have discovered that the commitment to discipleship is a commitment to mission for the reign of God. Concretely, it is to stand in solidarity against oppression and announce the liberation of God with one's life.

Discerning Charisms

We invite the neophytes to discern how the Spirit has gifted them to serve the mission of God in this community and in the larger Church and world. Various presentations aid this discernment: experiential witnesses of the sacramental life by married couples, the ordained and other ministers; needs of the parish presented by the parish team and ministry development committee of the parish council; and reflections on personal and communal conversion to justice.

The community also needs to discern its needs and how the community invites new people to serve the community. Once the community can articulate specific areas of service, representatives of the various organizations, such as the parish council, can invite the neophytes to consider using their gifts in service in these particular ways.

The neophytes and the community need to learn the art of ministerial reflection to manifest the basic motivations behind their service. Unfortunately, charity and condescension sometimes become mixed together. Condescension is looking down on others, recognizing their need, and giving them assistance—because they cannot do it and we can. We give them what they need because there but for the grace of God go I. Sometimes our motivation is tainted by our own guilt and our desire to free ourselves through contributing to others. As St. Vincent de Paul reminds us: May the poor forgive us for our charity to them (when this charity comes from motives of condescension and relieving of guilt).

Charity, on the other hand, recognizes the complexity of the human person and recognizes one's solidarity with the other person. It is not a case of "I have to give," but rather "We stand together in need." Compassion is knowing how to suffer with others in their true need: physical, psychological, and social. For charity and compassion to be authentic, they must include all three levels of solidarity. Charity and compassion are the willingness truly to stand with another, whatever the cost.

Support and Care of the Community

Deepening the Immersion in Community Life
The newly baptized are now full members of the community, and the period of mystagogy is concerned with helping them become more integrated into this community. Their status has changed and now they need to find more ways of being aligned and involved in the community's life. Here are a few ideas of how to achieve this:

— After the Easter Vigil, the parish community can celebrate with a party to welcome the neophytes into the community.
— The sponsors and godparents continue to meet with the neophytes on a regular basis to help them become more acquainted with the parish community and the Catholic way of life.
— We can invite the neophytes to join new-forming and existing support groups in the parish to continue to share faith with others and to be assisted in living the gospel in the ordinariness of their life: their families, neighborhoods, work, and the world.
— At some time during the Easter season, the neophytes gather with the

other neophytes of the diocese around the table of the Word and eucharist with the bishop.

— At some time during the year after initiation, the neophytes gather with the bishop to celebrate the eucharist.

— At some time during the year after initiation, the neophytes meet with the bishop to reflect together on their experience.

Sorting It All Out

Mystagogy presumes that the neophytes have had an extended period of formation that has prepared them to be part of the eucharistic assembly. This preparation is not about knowing the what of Catholic Christian life (anyone can learn the information) but mentoring into a way of life. Using the guidance the rite gives throughout each of the periods and stages, the celebration of the initiation sacraments at the Easter Vigil serves as a nexus: It all comes together. The weeks following the Vigil are meant to help sort out this coming together to move forward as disciples.

ONGOING MYSTAGOGY

The writers of the national statutes for implementing the initiation rites in the United States were very wise in their inclusion of *National Statute*, n. 24, which calls for regular gatherings of the neophytes until the anniversary of initiation. After the intensity and immediacy of the initiation experience and the following mystagogy, it is easy for the neophytes to become disenchanted when things return to "normal" (though we know nothing can ever be the same again). For over a year—perhaps several years—the newly initiated have received the focused attention and care of the community. Weekly, there have been explicit signs of concern, direction and support. Then, following the Pentecost festival, all that changes, or at least it appears so at first glance.

The roots planted in the soil of Christian discipleship throughout the initiation process were, it is hoped, strengthened and deepened during the period of immediate mystagogy. The transition from being in preparation to being on mission was accomplished in a way that, again it is hoped, helped the neophytes recognize that the basic skills for Christian living are readily available. Finally, it is hoped that the community itself is discovering again and again the rich rhythm of catechesis grounded in the Word of God, the celebration of liturgy and the generous self-gift of service (see *RCIA,* 75). The task of ongoing mystagogy is to help the newly initiated live this rhythm as an ordinary member of the faithful.

While the primary place of the immediate mystagogy of initiation is at the Sunday liturgy, gathering with the newly initiated in special gatherings to explore how they are integrating the various dimensions of the Christian way of life now seems appropriate. The format of such gatherings can be rather simple: a celebration of the Word (perhaps using the Sunday readings) that includes an opportunity for shared reflection on the scriptures. During this time together, the newly initiated and their sponsors can be allowed the opportunity to speak about their experiences since the last gathering. Ideas and insights can be shared for support. As a discipline, keep returning to the four dynamics outlined in RCIA, n. 75.

ADAPTATION WITH CHILDREN OF CATECHETICAL AGE

The guidance given in *RCIA,* n. 330 is that a period of mystagogy be provided for children that is an adaptation of the directives given in part I. In other words, the children who are neophytes gather with the Sunday assembly for the Sunday eucharist weekly and, as with the adults, enter into reflection on their experience.

One possible adaptation of ongoing mystagogy could be the enrollment of the children in the parish's formal religious education program. Presumably, during the initiation preparation and celebration, we did not enroll them in the formal religious education program, though they were affiliated with it through their peer companions. A caution needs to be made, though, that the monthly gathering not be eliminated if integration into the religious education program happens. The monthly gatherings are important times to attend to the specific needs of the children and their families.

ADAPTATION WITH BAPTIZED CANDIDATES

RCIA, n. 410 recommends that uncatechized adults would benefit from mystagogy and, since they will normally celebrate initiation at or near the Easter Vigil, can do so with the newly baptized.

The ritual text notes nothing specific about catechized candidates completing initiation. However, if we continue to use part I of the ritual text as normative for initiation, some form of mystagogy—both immediate and ongoing—should be provided.

MYSTAGOGY: BEGINNING OR END?

Is mystagogy an end? Perhaps it is an end to this ritual of initiation. But it is a beginning for the rest of one's life—a model of how we need again and again to pause during our story and to remember, to renew and recommit, to be challenged and stretched because of our belief and trust in the gospel of Jesus Christ.

Part Three

Other Important Considerations

12

Some Pastoral Issues

INTRODUCTION

A variety of pastoral issues emerge during the implementation of the *Rite of Christian Initiation of Adults,* such as the question of annulments, validity of baptism, and ecumenical sensitivity, to name a few. Besides attending to the specific needs of the catechumens and candidates during the initiation process, the initiation team will need to be sensitive to some of these issues. Following are some comments on areas of pastoral concern that seem to emerge regularly in parishes implementing the rite.

EVANGELIZATION

How do inquirers come to our communities? Do we advertise? Do we make direct contacts? What are the issues of evangelization?

Evangelization is bringing the message of the gospel to those who may not have heard this good news, and also continuing to proclaim the gospel so that those already familiar with it hear it in new ways. While this proclamation of the kerygma does happen through verbal witness, the most effective evangelization is the manner and quality of an individual's and community's lifestyle. People see how we live, how we relate, how we pray. They begin to ask questions about it. This is the primary form of evangelization for the *Rite of Christian Initiation of Adults.*

This does not exclude the possibility of inviting people to come and see our community, or running some kind of local advertisement. However, such attempts should be secondary to the community's own renewal and witness to the gospel. It is often the experience that communities expend great efforts at evangelization. People come forward and some enter the *Rite of Christian Initiation of Adults* process. However, when the process of sacramental initiation is completed, there is not much of a community for the neophyte to live in. The process of evangelization needs to be intimately connected with the vision of the parish community and its own call to conversion. What have we to offer as a parish? Why do we want people to join with us?

LITURGICAL MUSIC IN THE *RITE OF CHRISTIAN INITIATION OF ADULTS*

The role and purpose of liturgical music is to help the community in its prayer, and to enhance the experience of the prayer (some might call this "to pray better," but it is difficult to place such qualitative judgments on the experience of prayer—what does it mean "to pray better?"). "Music should assist the assembled believers to express and share the gift of faith that is within them and to nourish and strengthen their interior commitment of faith" (*MCW*, n. 23). Liturgical music can do this in many ways: by adopting an attitude toward liturgical music as a ministry of service to the community, by corresponding with and reflecting the liturgical action, and by facilitating participation in the liturgy.

Adopting an attitude toward liturgical music as a ministry of service to the community. For too long and for too many, liturgical music (and musicians) have been viewed as the after-thought in liturgical planning and ministry. This attitude, unfortunately, has often been perpetuated by some musicians themselves. "Music should assist the assembled believers to express and share the gift of faith that is within them and to nourish and strengthen their interior commitment of faith" (*MCW*, n. 23). Musicians need to be part of the liturgy preparation. Music—and its performance—needs to be of a high quality. "The musician has every right to insist that the music be good" (*MCW*, n. 29).

Corresponding with and reflecting the liturgical action. Liturgical music is not an appendage attached to the ritual. Rather, it complements and flows from the liturgical experience. The criterion for selecting music and acclamations is not because we like the piece, or because we always sing this piece. Rather, it is because it reflects and brings the community to encounter the essential dimensions of the liturgical action. "Does the music express and interpret the liturgical text correctly and make it more meaningful? Is the form of the text respected?" (*MCW*, n. 32).

Facilitating participation in the liturgy. Liturgical prayer is not performance, either by the ministers of prayer or by the musicians. The *Constitution on the Sacred Liturgy* asks that "all the faithful be led to that full, conscious, and active participation in liturgical celebrations which is demanded by the very nature of the liturgy," thereby encouraging the community "to take part by means of acclamations, responses, psalmody, antiphons, and songs, as well as by actions, gestures, and bodily attitudes" (*SC*, nos. 14, 30). Composition and choice of liturgical music need to empower the worshiping community for full and active participation in the rites.

Throughout the implementation of the *Rite of Christian Initiation of Adults,* the appropriate use of liturgical music enhances the ritual experience.

This presumes the active participation of the musician, to some degree, in the hearing of the journey of faith of the catechumens. The beauty of the rituals of the *Rite of Christian Initiation of Adults* lies in their ability to disclose the conversion experiences of the catechumens and the community. The musicians need to be sensitive to this both in their own lives and in how this is manifested in the community.

ENVIRONMENT AND ART

In addition to music, the environment we create is an important communicator to both the catechumens and the parish community. This includes the sense of warmth and hospitality we offer to people who come to our community, as well as the basic decor of our worship space and the symbols of our celebrations.

The U.S. Bishops' Committee on the Liturgy published a statement in 1978 entitled *Environment and Art in Catholic Worship* as a companion piece to *Music in Catholic Worship.* In this statement, the bishops offer principles for preparing liturgical space for worship. Highlighting a few of these principles would be helpful as they apply to the *Rite of Christian Initiation of Adults.*

The concern of environment and art is to draw people together to celebrate, not to distract or alienate. "The environment is appropriate when it is beautiful, when it is hospitable, when it clearly invites and needs an assembly to complete it" (*EACW,* n. 24). The place of worship will be an important evangelizer to those seeking a faith community.

The celebrations of the *Rite of Christian Initiation of Adults* lend themselves to the use of rich and powerful symbols. Symbols evoke a response from various levels and dimensions of the person and the community. "[T]he liturgical celebrations of the faith community involve the whole person. They are not purely religious or merely rational and intellectual exercises, but also human experiences calling on all human faculties: body, mind, senses, imagination, emotions, memory" (*EACW,* n. 5). Signing of the senses and passing on of the cross, handing on the gospel book, the laying on of hands, the presentations of the Creed and the Lord's Prayer, the waters of baptism, the anointing with oil, the breaking of the bread, the light in the darkness, the community assembled, and so on: these symbols—gestures, word, art—need to be pronounced yet simple. They need to be easily recognizable. They need also to carry the message that this is important. "One should be able to sense something special (and nothing trivial) in everything that is seen and heard, touched and smelled, and tasted in liturgy" (*EACW,* n. 12).

Other forms of visual art are also appropriate during the *Rite of Christian Initiation of Adults.* Wall hangings, banners in procession, liturgical vestments—all can change or detract from the celebration. The lighting during the Vigil service, the mood created during the scrutinies, the decor around the water font for baptism, the flowers during the eucharist, the dancer who processes with the oil in a glass bowl, the simplicity of the Easter candle, the bread torn during the eucharist—all of these and more are art. All these necessarily communicate certain attitudes about the ritual celebration. What we choose and how we choose it reveals something about the value we place upon it. Therefore, liturgy places two demands on art: quality and appropriateness (*EACW,* n. 19): "Quality means love and care in the making of something, honesty and genuineness with any materials used..." and appropriateness means that the work of art "must be capable of bearing the weight of mystery, awe, and wonder...and it must clearly serve (and not interrupt) ritual action which has its own structure, rhythm and movement" (*EACW,* nos. 20, 21).

PREACHING

Sometimes we are of the misunderstanding that we base the catechetical gatherings only on the scriptures proclaimed in the assembly. These texts are formative and central. However, the preaching that builds and develops this proclamation is also very important. It is the whole Liturgy of the Word experience—which includes the preaching moment—that becomes the foundation for the catechesis.

For many people in our communities, the only formal moment of catechesis is the experience of preaching. People will often choose the Mass during which to celebrate depending on who is preaching. Unfortunately, the preaching moment has often been a weak link in the assembly's worship. The reasons for this vary: poor training, inability to keep theologically current, inability to keep socially current, lack of preparation time, and so on. As in the catechetical moment, the preaching moment is an attempt to integrate the proclaimed Word of God in a meaningful and credible way in the ordinary lives of people. The preaching moment is a time of invitation and challenge.

Sometimes the preaching moment becomes an instructional moment—and when it does, when its concern becomes the transmission of information, then it is no longer preaching. Preaching is proclamation.

This would suggest, then, there can be an ongoing working relationship between the preacher and the catechists. If the catechetical gathering flows from the experience of the word—both the text and the ensuing proclamation—then it would be a helpful resource for the catechist to know the basic direction and emphasis of the preaching. We could expand and develop the issues and insights raised in the preaching moment in the catechetical moment.

We can then relocate the passing on of information that is transformative in the catechetical moment and out of the preaching moment.

The integration of the preaching and catechetical moments are quite clear when we celebrate the rituals of the *Rite of Christian Initiation of Adults.* The preacher is hard pressed to make a proclamation on the scriptures and the rite of acceptance and welcome if the preacher has not somehow shared in the experience of the candidates, even if only through conversation with the catechists. This becomes clearer during the scrutinies. The intercessions and exorcisms of the scrutinies need to build on the preaching moment if they are to be addressed to both the elect and the gathered community.

The "how" of working together—preacher and catechists—can only be determined by those involved. Perhaps a regular gathering—weekly or monthly—between them for prayer, sharing of faith and the initial development of the preaching-catechetical moments would be both a good discipline and service: discipline because it will force all involved to spend an appropriate period of time with the Word, letting it make a claim, and service because both the preacher and the catechist will be able to glean insights from each other in preparing their respective part of the experience.

In some situations, it may not be possible to gather regularly to pray the scriptures and to prepare the preaching-catechetical moments (but when it does happen, it usually makes a remarkable difference in both moments). At the very least, there needs to be a commitment to find some time before the celebration of the Liturgy of the Word to discuss—even if only by phone—the issues that will be addressed in the preaching moment. When the two moments are not working together, we can suffer from a schizophrenic presentation. This is not to suggest that the preaching moment dictates the direction of the catechesis. However, it makes for a more integrated approach to work together.

ECUMENICAL SENSITIVITY

The *Rite of Christian Initiation of Adults* was restored for the sacramental initiation of unbaptized adults into the Catholic Christian communion. However, it has been the experience of most parishes that the largest number of adults seeking full sacramental initiation are baptized Christians in another ecclesial community. In light of this reality, the pastoral implementation of the *Rite of Christian Initiation of Adults* demands a high level of ecumenical sensitivity.

We have already discussed the need to make explicit in the ritual celebrations the distinction between the unbaptized and the baptized in the initiation process. Following are additional principles that can help inform initiation praxis.

◆ The process of celebrating full communion in the Catholic community needs to be a positive experience, respecting the experiences of baptism
and formation which have already taken place. The posture is one of respect
and welcome: respect for the individual's previous religious affiliation, and
welcome into the continuation of their journey of faith in the Catholic tradition. Any manner of triumphalism is to be avoided (*RCIA*, nos. 475.2, 479).

◆ The process of formation usually requires a prolonged period of
preparation that corresponds to the one prescribed for the unbaptized (*RCIA*,
nos. 401, 402). Catechetical formation (doctrinal and spiritual preparation)
needs to be coordinated with the liturgical year (*RCIA*, nos. 408, 477), and
includes the period of mystagogy (*RCIA*, n. 410).

◆ The previous formation and Christian life of the already baptized
need to be taken into consideration and will affect the length of the period of
formation (*RCIA*, nos. 400, 473, 474, 478).

◆ The community supports these men and women throughout the
process (*RCIA*, nos. 403). Sponsors from the community accompany them and
give witness for them (*RCIA*, nos. 404, 482).

◆ Liturgical rites mark the various periods of preparation, similar to
those for the unbaptized, yet clearly noting the distinctions (*RCIA*, nos. 405,
406, 407, 478). "Anything that would equate candidates for reception with
those who are catechumens is to be absolutely avoided" (*RCIA*, n. 477).

◆ Before the celebration of reception, the candidate, according to his
or her conscience, may celebrate the sacrament of reconciliation. It is advisable that the candidate inform the confessor that he or she is a candidate for
full communion (*RCIA*, n. 483).

◆ We usually celebrate reception into full communion at the Easter
Vigil through a profession of faith and celebration of confirmation and the
eucharist (*RCIA*, n. 409). The priest who presides at the celebration of full
communion has the faculty for confirming the candidate (*RCIA*, n. 481). If celebrated at another time, it is preferred that the reception into full communion
occur within the celebration of the Mass (*RCIA*, nos. 475, 476).

◆ Baptism is not to be repeated. Only in the case of reasonable doubt concerning the fact or validity of the baptism should baptism be administered condi-
tionally, and only after we give a full explanation to the candidate (*RCIA*, n. 480).

VALIDITY OF BAPTISMS

Being able to distinguish between valid and invalid baptisms is important for discerning the appropriate initiation journey for an individual.

A valid baptism is one that
• is conferred with true water

• through immersion or pouring
• with the Trinitarian formula
• with the minister having the intention to baptize
• and the recipient, if adult, having the intention to receive baptism.

Most of the baptisms in other Christian traditions are considered valid. However, there are some that are not, and initiation teams will need to ascertain validity before celebrating the rite of acceptance or rite of welcome.

EASTERN NON-CATHOLIC CHRISTIANS

It would be impossible to provide in this resource a history of the relationship between the Eastern Churches and the Roman Catholic Church. After centuries of separation that date back to the early Christological arguments of the fifth century, some Churches in the East sought reunification with the Roman Catholic Church after the Council of Trent. Thus, there are Eastern Churches that are Catholic and those that are non-Catholic. The Catholic Church, therefore, is a communion of twenty-two different churches. The Roman Catholic Church is the largest. However, all the Catholic Churches share an equal status with each other. For more information about Eastern Catholic Churches, see John D. Faris, *Eastern Catholic Churches: Constitutions and Governance According to the Code of the Canons of the Eastern Churches* (New York: Maron Publications, 1992).

A person baptized in an Eastern Non-Catholic Church who makes a profession of faith (see *RCIA,* n. 474) before a Roman Catholic priest does not become a member of the Roman Catholic Church. Rather, he or she becomes a member of the corresponding Eastern Catholic Church.

A person baptized in an Eastern Non-Catholic Church who wishes to become a Roman Catholic must request a transfer of rite directly through the Apostolic See. Once the permission is given, he or she makes a profession of faith. If the rite is not transferred to the Roman Catholic Church, the person becomes a member of the corresponding Eastern Catholic Church.

CANON LAW

At some point during the catechumenate process, the question of the appropriate role and function of canon law will need to be addressed, if for no other reason than that it is a reality in the life of the Church.

The *Code of Canon Law* makes explicit reference to the initiation in various sections. It will be helpful to see, within the context of the law of the Church, the responsibility of the Church to provide a full and adequate formation process.

◆ Full Christian sacramental initiation requires the celebration of baptism, confirmation, and eucharist (*CIC,* canons 842 §2; 866).

◆ Adults desiring baptism are to enter the catechumenate process (*CIC,* canon 851, 1°). They are to be prepared through liturgical rites, instructed in the truths of the faith, and formed to a life in accordance with gospel values (*CIC,* canons 788 §1 and 2; 851, 1°; 865 §1).

◆ Children of catechetical age preparing for baptism are to follow the same process (appropriately adapted) as adults (*CIC,* canon 852 §1).

◆ Sponsors must be fully initiated members of the Church who are leading the Catholic way of life (*CIC,* canon 874 §1, 3°).

◆ A sponsor or godparent of another Christian denomination may be admitted as a witness only if there is also a Catholic sponsor or godparent (*CIC,* canon 874 §2).

◆ A catechumen has the right to a Christian burial (CIC, canon 1183 § 1). When two catechumens are married, or when a catechumen marries an unbaptized person, the appropriate rites are to be used (cf. *RCIA,* n. 47).

◆ Those who are fully in communion with the Catholic Church are those baptized persons who express this intention within the structures of the Church through profession of faith, participation in the sacramental life, and adherence to ecclesiastic governance, i.e., union with the hierarchy (*CIC,* canon 205).

◆ The *Code of Canon Law* does not specify procedure for those already baptized and preparing for full communion. The norms established in the 1988 ritual edition of the *Rite of Christian Initiation of Adults* are to be invoked. Their baptism in another Christian community is to be recognized and respected (*CIC,* canon 869 §2).

◆ Those already baptized can be admitted to the sacraments of penance, eucharist and anointing under certain circumstances (*CIC,* canon 844 §3).

◆ The norms established with the rites of the Church retain their force unless they are contrary to the Code (*CIC,* canon 2). Hence, the liturgical norms established and approved in the *Rite of Christian Initiation of Adults* are supported by the *Code of Canon Law.*

PREPARING FOR INITIATION AND MARRIAGE

The process for sacramental initiation is an intense period of formation in faith. Often people come to the initiation process because of their intention to marry a Catholic and the desire to share a common faith. The process of preparing for marriage, just as with the *Rite of Christian Initiation of Adults,* is a long and intense formation process. Marriage preparation makes a great number of demands on the couple—explicitly and implicitly. Explicitly, there are the variety of arrangements ranging from participation in marriage preparation sessions, working out various dimensions of the married life (such as budget, where to live, and so on), and the arrangements for the wedding itself. Implicitly, there are a variety of changes and challenges that the couple—as individuals and as a couple—need to deal with prior to the formal marriage ceremony. The demands of loving, sharing life, surrendering some dimension of autonomy, and the necessary growing that happens as love deepens to the level of a life commitment—all of this is rather intense and demands much time and energy.

Both experiences—preparing for full sacramental initiation and preparing for marriage—require a high level of commitment, time and dedication to the formation necessary to prepare oneself for the witness of celebrating the sacrament. Therefore, not enrolling individuals in the initiation process who are also preparing for marriage seems pastorally prudent. As we discourage children from preparing for reconciliation and eucharist at the same time—albeit for different reasons—the same fundamental insight that each sacramental celebration demands the necessary time and focus for preparation also holds true here. Often the experience of preparing for marriage and full sacramental initiation is overwhelming. In such circumstances, it seems more helpful to the individual to encourage that he or she give fully to the process of preparing for marriage, and then, after having had a chance to celebrate God's presence in matrimony, begin the process for full sacramental initiation.

ANNULMENTS

One difficult dimension of the initiation process is working with candidates who will need to enter the annulment process. This is difficult because it requires entering what is often a painful discussion early in the relationship. Once the formal annulment process has begun, however, it often becomes a period of healing for the individual. If the individual is a catechumen (i.e., unbaptized), then the possibility of the Pauline or Petrine privileges (to be discussed below) might apply. These are dissolutions of the marriage bond in favor of the practice of the faith.

Being aware of some basic issues concerning annulments is helpful for team members. An annulment is the formal decree that a marriage was never a sacramental union (which is indissoluble). It does not claim there was no marriage—but that there was no sacramental marriage. By the Catholic Church's canon law 1137, a declaration of nullity does not affect the legitimacy of children. In order for someone to petition for an annulment, he or she must have already received a civil divorce.

People who are divorced and remarried (without the previous marriage being annulled) are not excommunicated from the church. This penalty, which originated in 1884 and existed only in the United States, was removed by the United States bishops in 1977.

The pastoral minister will need to place the annulment question within the larger picture before beginning the process with the catechumen. Is the person already remarried? Does the person plan to enter a new marriage, especially in the near future? How recent was the experience of the divorce? Giving the catechumen the time needed for some preliminary healing from a recent divorce seems pastorally sensitive. Unless it is absolutely necessary, they can address the annulment process later.

Without diminishing the uniqueness of the marriage relationship there are some basic situations that can help the team determine the need to discuss the necessity for an annulment. The annulment process helps to determine if the marriage was valid and, therefore, still binding before the Church. Generally speaking, the Catholic Church presumes all marriages are valid—civil and religious. The marriage between baptized Christians is considered sacramental. Therefore men and women who are divorced and plan to remarry (or are remarried) who are entering the Catholic community, either through baptism or a profession of faith, will need to enter the annulment process.

Valid Marriages				
	UNBAPTIZED	BAPTIZED CATHOLIC[1]	BAPTIZED EASTERN NON-CATHOLIC	BAPTIZED OTHER CHRISTIAN
Unbaptized	Public exchange of vows	Catholic service[2]	Eastern non-Catholic service	Public exchange of vows
Baptized Catholic[1]	Catholic service[2]	Catholic service[2]	Catholic service[2]	Catholic service[2]
Baptized Eastern Non-Catholic	Eastern non-Catholic service	Catholic service[2]	Eastern non-Catholic service	Eastern non-Catholic service
Baptized Other Christian	Public exchange of vows	Catholic service[2]	Eastern non-Catholic service	Public exchange of vows

[1]Roman Catholic who has not formally left the Catholic Church, see *Code of Canon Law,* canon 1124.
[2]Catholic service: Exchange of vows in a Catholic Church before priest and two witnesses (unless one receives a dispensation from the bishop).

The following situations can help clarify whether there will be the need to begin the annulment process for a particular individual. Of course, it is presumed that the individual is presently divorced. However, for clarity's sake, we will list the situations in terms of the previous marriage relationship. The first spouse mentioned will be the catechumen or candidate.

Unbaptized person married to unbaptized person in either civil or religious service	Annulment needed. The catechumen could also investigate the possibility of the Pauline privilege. The Pauline privilege, a privilege of the faith, may be relevant when both parties are unbaptized (and therefore there is no sacramental marriage because a sacramental marriage presumes baptism). This bond can be dissolved in favor of the newly baptized person entering into a sacramental marriage (see *Code of Canon Law,* canons 1143–1147).
Unbaptized person married to Catholic in Catholic service	Annulment needed. The catechumen could also investigate the possibility of the Petrine privilege. The Petrine privilege, another privilege of the faith, refers to the marriage between a baptized Christian and an unbaptized person. If the marriage is consummated after the unbaptized person becomes a baptized Christian, then this cannot be invoked. The privilege is granted by the pope in Rome.
Unbaptized person married to Catholic in other than Catholic service (with no dispensation from the bishop)	No formal annulment is needed because there was never a valid marriage in term of Catholic "form." The bishop of each diocese determines the procedures for handling these cases. In general, these procedures are much simpler than formal cases. Catholic form is a marriage in the presence of a delegated Catholic priest and two witnesses. The usual exception to this is when the bishop grants permission to be married before a minister, rabbi or civil official in what is called an interfaith (mixed) marriage (see *Code of Canon Law,* canons 1124ff.) If this form is lacking in a marriage where one or both partners is Catholic, there is no valid marriage. Note: A person baptized in the Catholic Church (or received into full communion) who leaves the Catholic Church (after November, 1983) by a formal act is no longer bound by the Catholic form of marriage (see *Code of Canon Law,* canon 1124).
Unbaptized person married to baptized Eastern non-Catholic in Eastern non-Catholic service	Annulment needed. The catechumen could also investigate the possibility of the Petrine privilege (see above).

Unbaptized person married to baptized Eastern non-Catholic not in Eastern non-Catholic service	No formal annulment is needed because there was never a valid marriage in terms of Eastern non-Catholic "form." Contact your local chancery or tribunal for procedures.
Unbaptized person married to baptized Christian (neither Catholic nor Eastern non-Catholic) in either civil or religious service	Annulment needed. The catechumen could also investigate the possibility of the Petrine privilege (see above).
Baptized Eastern non-Catholic married to unbaptized person in Eastern non-Catholic service	Annulment needed. The possibility of the Petrine privilege can also be investigated (see above).
*Baptized Eastern non-Catholic married to unbaptized person no*t *in an Eastern non-Catholic service*	No formal annulment is needed because there was never a valid marriage in terms of Eastern non-Catholic "form." Contact your local chancery or tribunal for procedures.
Baptized Eastern non-Catholic married to a Catholic in a Catholic service	Annulment needed.
Baptized Eastern non-Catholic married to a Catholic in other than Catholic service (with no dispensation from the bishop)	No formal annulment is needed because there was never a valid marriage in terms of Catholic "form." Contact your local chancery or tribunal for procedures.
Baptized Eastern non-Catholic married to an Eastern non-Catholic in an Eastern non-Catholic service	Annulment needed.
Baptized Eastern non-Catholic married to an Eastern non-Catholic not in an Eastern non-Catholic service	No formal annulment is needed because there was never a valid marriage in terms of Eastern non-Catholic "form." Contact your local chancery or tribunal for procedures.
Baptized Eastern non-Catholic married to baptized Christian (not Catholic) in Eastern non-Catholic service	Annulment needed.

Baptized Eastern non-Catholic married to baptized Christian (not Catholic) not in an Eastern non-Catholic service	No formal annulment is needed because there was never a valid marriage in terms of Eastern non-Catholic "form." Contact your local chancery or tribunal for procedures.
Baptized Christian candidate married to unbaptized person in either a civil or religious service	Annulment needed. The possibility of the Petrine privilege can also be investigated (see above).
Baptized Christian candidate married to Catholic in Catholic service	Annulment needed.
Baptized Christian candidate married to Catholic in other than Catholic service (with no dispensation from the bishop)	No formal annulment is needed because there was never a valid marriage in terms of the Catholic "form." Contact your local chancery or tribunal for procedures.
Baptized Christian candidate married to Eastern non-Catholic in Eastern non-Catholic service	Annulment needed.
Baptized Christian candidate married to Eastern non-Catholic not in an Eastern non-Catholic service	No formal annulment is needed because there was never a valid marriage in terms of Eastern non-Catholic "form." Contact your local chancery or tribunal for procedures.
Baptized Christian candidate married to baptized Christian (neither Catholic nor Eastern non-Catholic) in either a civil or religious service	Annulment needed
Baptized Roman Catholic married to an unbaptized person in a Catholic service	Annulment needed. The possibility of the Petrine privilege can also be investigated (see above).
Baptized Roman Catholic married to an unbaptized person in other than Catholic service (with no dispensation from the bishop)	No formal annulment is needed because there was never a valid marriage in terms of the Catholic "form." Contact your local chancery or tribunal for procedures.
Baptized Roman Catholic married to baptized Catholic in Catholic service	Annulment needed.

Baptized Roman Catholic married to baptized Catholic in other than Catholic service (with no dispensation from the bishop)	No formal annulment is needed because there was never a valid marriage in terms of the Catholic "form." Contact your local chancery or tribunal for procedures.
Baptized Roman Catholic married to baptized Eastern non-Catholic in Catholic service	Annulment needed.
Baptized Roman Catholic married to baptized Eastern non-Catholic in other than Catholic service (with no dispensation from the bishop)	No formal annulment is needed because there was never a valid marriage in terms of Catholic "form." Contact your local chancery or tribunal for procedures.
Baptized Roman Catholic married to baptized Christian (neither Catholic nor Eastern non-Catholic) in Catholic service	Annulment needed.
Baptized Roman Catholic married to baptized Christian (neither Catholic nor Eastern non-Catholic) in other than Catholic service (with no dispensation from the bishop)	No formal annulment is needed because there was never a valid marriage in terms of the Catholic "form." Contact your local chancery or tribunal for procedures.

NB: Roman Catholic candidates listed pertain to those referred to in Part Two, Chapter 4 of the *Rite of Christian Initiation of Adults.* Eastern Catholics are not listed because they would not be considered with this rite.

Processes dealing with prior marriages fall into several categories: formal cases, documentary cases, privilege cases and others. Talking with a member of the pastoral team to determine initially the probability of the annulment process will be necessary for the individual. Furthermore, the member of the pastoral team working on the annulment process needs to obtain good advice from the diocesan tribunal at the beginning of the process.

Formal cases declare there is adequate evidence that there was no sacramental union. There are many categories of formal cases, including psychological incapacity, lack of due discretion, simulation of consent, force and fear, fraud and error. Some examples include: lacking in sufficient use of reason; intoxication at the time of consent; chronic alcoholism or drug addiction at time of marriage; premarital pregnancy and immaturity; serious personality disorders or mental illness. Simulation of consent refers to the conscious decision at the time of the marriage to place conditions on the marriage consent or to exclude an essential aspect of marriage, such as entering marriage only to

Summary: Annulments				
	UNBAPTIZED CATECHUMEN	BAPTIZED EASTERN NON-CATHOLIC	BAPTIZED CHRISTIAN CANDIDATE	BAPTIZED ROMAN CATHOLIC CANDIDATE
FORMER SPOUSE: UNBAPTIZED	*Public exchange of vows:* Annulment needed OR Pauline privilege.	*Eastern non-Catholic service:* Annulment needed OR Petrine privilege. *Outside Eastern non-Catholic service:* No annulment needed.[2]	*Public exchange of vows:* Annulment needed OR Petrine privilege.	*Catholic service:* Annulment needed OR Petrine privilege. *Outside Catholic Church without permission:* No annulment needed.[1]
FORMER SPOUSE: BAPTIZED CATHOLIC	*Catholic service:* Annulment needed OR Petrine privilege. *Outside Catholic Church without permission:* No annulment needed.[1]	*Eastern non-Catholic service:* Annulment needed. *Outside Eastern non-Catholic service:* No annulment needed.[2]	*Catholic service:* Annulment needed. *Outside Catholic Church without permission:* No annulment needed.[1]	*Catholic service:* Annulment needed. *Outside Catholic Church without permission:* No annulment needed.[1]
FORMER SPOUSE: BAPTIZED EASTERN NON-CATHOLIC	*Eastern non-Catholic service:* Annulment needed OR Petrine privilege. *Outside Eastern non-Catholic service:* No annulment needed.[2]	*Eastern non-Catholic service:* Annulment needed. *Outside Eastern non-Catholic service:* No annulment needed.[2]	*Eastern non-Catholic service:* Annulment needed. *Outside Eastern non-Catholic service:* No annulment needed.[2]	*Catholic service:* Annulment needed. *Outside Catholic Church without permission:* No annulment needed.[1]
FORMER SPOUSE: BAPTIZED CHRISTIAN	*Public exchange of vows:* Annulment needed OR Petrine privilege.	*Eastern non-Catholic service:* Annulment needed. *Outside Eastern non-Catholic service:* No annulment needed.[2]	*Public exchange of vows:* Annulment needed.	*Catholic service:* Annulment needed. *Outside Catholic Church without permission:* No annulment needed

[1] Contact your local chancery or tribunal for procedures.

[2] The marriage is not valid unless the Roman Catholic partner left the Catholic Church by a formal act after November, 1983 (see *Code of Canon Law,* canon 1124). Contact your local chancery or tribunal for procedures.

obtain citizenship, the expressed intention of not remaining faithful to one's partner, or the refusal of children. Force and fear would limit the ability of the individual to make a free and full consent—for example, the typical "shotgun" wedding.

Documentary cases fall into two major categories: absence of form and previous bond. Absence of form refers to the lack of the proper Catholic form for the marriage. This only applies to marriages that include at least one Catholic. The necessary procedures can be handled locally. Previous bond means that one of the parties had already been validly married prior to the marriage in question.

Finally, there are dissolutions, which are invoked either through privileges of the faith or because of nonconsummation. In terms of privileges of the faith, there presently exist two options: the Pauline privilege and the Petrine privilege. We have already described both above. Nonconsummation—that the marriage was never consummated in sexual intercourse—needs to be petitioned through Rome.

There are other impediments to a valid marriage: lack of the age of consent, impotence, one person in canonical orders or vows, murder of former spouse to marry the present one, and so on.

When helping a catechumen apply for an annulment, it is often in the best interest of the catechumen to allow the tribunal to assess the case and propose the appropriate direction the case needs to go. Whatever the situation, however, the pastoral minister will need to be sensitive to the various avenues for healing available through the pastoral care of the church.

VALIDATION OF MARRIAGE

The validation of a marriage (or, more technically correct, the convalidation) is the act of making valid a marriage union. There are two situations wherein the need to convalidate a marriage would affect a catechumen or candidate for full communion. The first is if the spouse of the catechumen or candidate is Catholic but they were not married in a Catholic service (or had received the permission of the bishop for an interfaith service). The second is if the catechumen or candidate is in a second marriage and the first one is annulled. The annulment nullifies the previous bond and allows the present marriage to be recognized as valid.

13

Discernment

INTRODUCTION

The *Rite of Christian Initiation of Adults,* when fully implemented, respects the unique journey of faith of the individual within the structures provided by the rite. A key dimension of this balance between individual conversion and the structured periods of the catechumenate is discernment. Before each transition to a new period of the process—marked by a ritual celebration—there is a prolonged period of discernment to help the catechumens identify their readiness to make the commitments required of the next period of formation.

Throughout this resource, we have reflected on the specific concerns and issues of discernment proper to each step of the *Rite of Christian Initiation of Adults.* At this point, it would be helpful to examine the art of Christian discernment in general to situate the particular focus that discernment has in the *Rite of Christian Initiation of Adults.*

A CONTEMPORARY APPROACH TO DISCERNMENT

Life is full of decisions. And there is never a guarantee that the decisions we make will indeed be the right decisions. However, we can be open to a posture of decision-making that reflects a God-focus. We can enter the process of discernment.

The word "discernment" comes from the Latin *discernere* and means "to separate out," "to distinguish," "to recognize what is distinct and different." Discernment is the art of clearing away what is not worthwhile and life-giving from that which is indeed authentic and life-promoting. Discernment is about recognizing and responding to God's invitation to embrace the reign of God.

Distinguishing two types of discernment is important. The first type is moral discernment. Basically, moral discernment deals with issues of right and wrong, explicit good and evil. The material in this chapter presumes the ability to discern between good and evil in this way.

The second type of discernment is life-centered discernment. This type of discernment is usually between two apparent goods, between two (or more) viable options or choices. This type of discernment struggles to hear God's invitation to a fuller experience of life. Sometimes the choice is between good and evil, but it is a very subtle form of evil (as opposed to the obvious distinction in moral discernment). It is this life-centered discernment that will be the focus of these reflections.

THEOLOGICAL PRESUPPOSITIONS

The reflections in this chapter on discernment presume the following theological concepts:

♦ Revelation is the active process of God's self-communication to us, our response in faith, and the resulting change in our lives or conversion.

♦ An important center of God's revelation is within human experience, i.e., the religious depth dimension of human experience, as reviewed in Chapter 2 of this resource.

♦ God's will or plan, as articulated in Ephesians 1:9-10 and affirmed in *Dei Verbum,* chapter I, n. 2, is that all creation be drawn up into God's eternal embrace of love. The fulfillment of this plan is when Christ is the all in all. Since God's will is to bring all creation into God's embrace of love, God desires the well-being of all creation, especially the human community. Whatever facilitates authentic love can be seen as in accord with God's will.

♦ Such a notion of God's will, then, is dynamic and takes seriously the particularity of the human experience. It eliminates the notion of a predefined blueprint or map of God's will. Rather, God is actively involved in the now of our life, inviting us to fuller life.

♦ Furthermore, the human person is created for God, open for fulfillment only by infinite love.

♦ The fulfillment of human desire is God. A theology of grace articulates God's self-gift of love to us. God's love empowers us to seek the truly authentic and valuable. Therefore, we strive for true self-transcendence through self-sacrificing love.

♦ God's free gift of self—grace—empowers us to make decisions congruent with responsible living. Therefore, the decisions and choices we make need to be within the responsibilities of our present state in life.

♦ An understanding of discernment, therefore, is an exploration into the wonderful mystery of God-present-in-love. In that sense, it is messy. There are no clear-cut answers, no pre-set agendas. It is the continual awakening to God's invitations to deepened love and authentic life in our concrete, historical situation.

DISCERNMENT: RIGHT OR WRONG?

Before exploring some basic criteria for a contemporary discernment, it is necessary to address the question of the "right" judgment based on a discernment process. Discernment is not a foolproof set of directions one follows to come to the perfect solution. Rather, it is a surrender into a process of coming to fuller self-knowledge and responding out of that experience. While the practical judgment made is of definite value, it is the whole process of trust and surrender that is of greater importance. Such a process affirms the basic theological assertions mentioned earlier: God's loving presence within the human person, and the human person's striving to come to a sense of wholeness and congruence with the gifted presence of love already given. We will never achieve fullness of all we are and can be while we are pilgrims on the way to God. There will always be an element of incompleteness. Therefore, we can never know if the decisions we make are "right" decisions because we see now "only as in a glass darkly." However, we can know we made a "good" decision if we have been faithful to the demands of the discernment process.

FOOLISH EXPECTATIONS

Considering briefly what the discernment process is not before considering some contemporary criteria for discernment will be helpful.

◆ Discernment does not occur only through gut-level responses such as feelings or emotions. This is not to belittle the role and importance of affectivity in the discernment process. But rather it is to affirm that affectivity, however integrated, cannot be the sole criterion for a discernment. For example, someone feels good after a period of prayer during which time the individual has asked for God's guidance in a life-direction. The person presumes God's guidance in the warm feeling and makes a decision based on that confirmation of God's will to be done. So the person enters religious life or considers marriage, based on this gut-level instinct. But what happens when the "feelings" are gone?

◆ Discernment does not in essence happen through a systematic and logical process, a step by step approach whereby a clear, correct and precise answer can be guaranteed because of faithfully "following the directions." Such a notion is simply a new form of secular decision-making. Discernment is more than decision-making. It is an adventure that faces the mystery of

God's stirrings. While there is order to God's movement, such order is holistic and not totally rational and logical.

◆ Discernment usually does not occur through private revelations to an individual. We are men and women within a world community and, more specifically, within the Christian community. Private revelations are prone to self-deception and therefore need the corrective of the community's confirmation. God's revelation is within human experience. Such revelation is always interpersonal, and calls forth the necessary guidance and support from the larger community. Otherwise, we would feel justified in establishing a privatized religion with a privatized God. Prophets (which may be of the "private revelation" vein) always remained within the community, though it was often to this very community the prophet spoke the difficult Word of God.

GUIDELINES

We have already mentioned that there is no clear-cut method to follow for a correct discernment. Such an "easy" method would be a welcome sight for many. However, such a method would negate several fundamental Christian beliefs: the uniqueness and individuality of each man and woman; the inability to determine another's "level" of spiritual development (i.e., we do not know the hearts of others); the impossibility to grasp the fullness of God's love and justice; and the resistance to a domestication of God, faith and the spiritual life (i.e., making it neat, organized, controllable and, ultimately, boring).

However, there are certain guidelines that have emerged from the Christian community's struggle to be faithful to God's call that can be used as a measuring stick to our experience of discernment. Again, such guidelines will not assure an infallible response but will serve as a barometer of sorts. These guidelines are not listed in any order of importance. No attempt has been made to prioritize any of them for fear they will become a new set of "easy rules" to follow. Hopefully these guidelines will offer a balanced and thorough approach to the process of discernment.

◆ An important center of God's continual revelation is our concrete historical situation. Therefore, discernment is the art of finding meaning in our daily lived lives as it reflects God's revelation. Discernment is about a new quality of vision. It is not about seeing new things but seeing things in a new way. We root Christian discernment, therefore, in the revelation of God in Jesus, the Christ. Of the many things we could say about such revelation, one key dimension is the question of relationship. Jesus reveals a God who is deeply involved in the life of people. The God of Jesus is not a removed and distant observer. The life-praxis of Jesus illustrates the commitment one must be willing to embrace in order for the values of this already near God to emerge. The question becomes "What is God inviting me to do and how do I respond to this invitation?"

◆ Often we can discern the ways of God by using common sense supported by informed and prudent judgment. The use of common sense may also serve as a preliminary moment in the discernment process. Caution needs to be exercised, however, as to the extent of the use of common sense. The drawback lies in the extension of common sense: we sometimes presume to be experts in areas we only have basic knowledge of. We overextend our competence, and therefore blind ourselves to the need for further investigation and consultation.

◆ Discernment is a holistic process: intellect, psychological state, affectivity, spiritual, volitional, physical. All elements of our embodied person can play a role offering cues. For example, the intellect can gather and sort the necessary data. Our psychological state affects the process: under duress or high levels of anxiety, we can suspect the origin of the process. Feelings, though not absolute indicators of discernment, contribute to the process by signaling either uncomfortableness or a sense of congruence. From a spiritual perspective, we enter mystery beyond human comprehension, a journey of faith. The volitional dimension, or will, affects the discernment in how we eagerly accept and respond to the decision as "ringing true." The body also plays a significant role: if the mind is saying "yes" but the body is breaking down, we need to reconsider the process in light of what the body is saying. Discernment, like conversion, affects the various dimensions of our lives.

◆ We recognize that the gift of God's love centers us, and therefore one can approach this process with confidence that God will guide us in our faithful searching. Such a level of trust presumes a developing relationship between us and God. Discernment is not the "quick fix" solution to life's worries: we "fill up" with God and run around until we reach empty, and then we "fill up" again, stopping in at the garage whenever we have a problem. The great mechanic God solves it all. Discernment presumes the rigors and joys of willingly entering relationship with the One who is greater yet chooses to love us. We acknowledge that we are often unfaithful in this relationship. And yet God continues to come to us where we are and forgive us, love us, reconcile us to renewed relationship. Such a relationship demands vulnerability, risk, the "leap" into the darkness of faith, truly believing that the arms of God will hold us and embrace us. When we live in this mystery ever-so-near-yet-ever-so-much-more, we give ourselves to love, we foster a level of trust and confidence that believes that God's desire is truly the good of all. We can then freely submit to the rigors of striving, searching, sometimes wandering because the Beloved is always there, even in apparent absence.

◆ We also must be comfortable with the possibility of a wrong decision. However if we are faithful to the process of discernment, we can rest in the certitude of a good decision, knowing that God will use whatever our falterings are to bring about good.

◆ Time is an important dimension in discernment. We can differentiate between time as *chronos* and time as *kairos*. *Chronos* is measured time, the time of a clock. It is our accustomed way of keeping time, of "clock-watching," of knowing when someone is early or late. Such measured and calculated time is human time with human expectations. *Kairos* is God's time, the appointed time, the time that best serves the building of God's reign. God's time breaks in silently like a thief in the night, or a master returning from a feast. It is not calculated and cannot be measured except in terms of the fidelity of the night watch. It takes trust to allow God's time to emerge, to know the right moment and not rush into any discernment.

◆ The process of discernment leads us to a sense of true detachment, i.e., to remove ourselves enough to be able to accept whatever is asked of us. Without the pressure of calculated time, we can allow God's Spirit to emerge and invite us toward the greater good. Such detachment teaches us to make room to welcome whatever is given. We learn to accept all as gift. We are not a stingy heart, but rather a heart that is opened with room for all God asks of us.

◆ Two underlying values in discernment are obedience and surrender. Obedience means truly to listen to the words of life, and then respond to such words. Surrender means to turn over private expectations and desires for the greater gift that we can receive if we open our hearts to God. Both are active postures based in trust.

◆ We should always approach discernment with a contemplative posture, i.e., a heart opened to God's stirrings and movements. Such a heart is listening in love to all inner impulses. This posture is most enhanced through prayer. It is important to note that simply because we have prayed is no guarantee that the decision we make is correct and reflective of God's will. Another important dimension is not only that we pray, but also how we come to this prayer. We have already discussed the importance of obedience, surrender and loving trust that is necessary to attune our hearts to God's call.

◆ The place to begin in discernment is true self-knowledge. We must be continually willing to search our hearts and confront the illusory and celebrate the gifted dimensions of ourselves to facilitate invitations to deepened awareness of the self. The path to self-knowledge, however, is not simply an intellectual exercise. It is an exercise of both the head and the heart. This dynamic tension gives a depth and breadth to our self-understanding. As Pascal says: "The heart has reasons reason does not know." To speak of the heart, we need to include the symbolic and affective dimensions of the person. Imagination and memory are important vehicles for coming to this level of self-knowledge. But we cannot stop there. In order for conversion to take place continually, we must let the story of Jesus have an impact on our stories, transforming the imagination and personal symbols.

FOUR MOVEMENTS

Four movements can characterize the discernment process itself: deliberation, reflection, insight, and decision and action.

(a) *Deliberation:* There are two forms of deliberation we need to be available for in order to give balance to a discernment. The first deliberation or consultation is to ourselves. We need to take seriously the call to true self-knowledge, which helps us come to terms with our gifts and also our limitations. Second, we need to consult with others. When looking for someone to consult, certain qualities are important. We need someone who will help us work (and talk) the discernment through—someone who is objective (who does not have personal gain at stake or is too personally involved), and someone who leaves us free ultimately to make our own decisions, even if they are poor ones. In addition to another person, we need to consider consulting other authorities: the scriptures, Tradition, books and articles.

Deliberation includes the acquiring of the necessary information to make an informed decision, assessing our current situation honestly, and visioning the resolution. Additionally, it includes hearing all sides of the issue, weighing the pros and cons, and honestly surveying the possibilities.

Here are some helpful reflection questions for use during deliberation: Am I open to consult other persons in this process, especially my spiritual director? Do I consult with my legitimate authorities for feedback and direction? Do I find time for silence and solitude in this decision-making process? Can I bring this decision to my prayer?

(b) *Reflection:* There are at least two types of reflection. One type infers certain expectations. We have already made up our minds, have already decided what meanings we will discover. Our own desires, goals, and needs dictate what we will discover because we already know what we want to discover. We close our eyes to anything that might threaten the planned meaning. We impose meaning on life rather than uncovering the meaning that emerges. Such reflection does not sponsor an honest discernment.

The second type of reflection is the opposite. During this type of reflection, we try to see and accept whatever meanings that emerge. We do not protect ourselves from the uncomfortable. Rather, we are open to the truth in whatever way we can at a given moment. Such a posture demands that we not be possessive or frightened; rather, we can trust divine providence and can wait.

During an honest discernment, we will allow the issues and ideas raised during the deliberation to be begin to work from the inside out. Slowly and respectfully, we will listen to the word of truth and value that emerge, whatever the cost. There is a level of disinterested involvement: we give ourselves over to the process without making a previous claim on the vision that begins to take shape.

Here are some helpful reflection questions for use during reflection: Where is God for me in all of this? How does this relate to my life in community? How will Christian love be advanced? Can I recognize the limits and also the possibilities in the decision? How does the decision promote Christian values? Is this a responsible course to take?

(c) *Insight:* The theologian Bernard Lonergan claims that insight is the release of the tension of inquiry. We give ourselves to the discernment process, opening ourselves to whatever gifts that will be given to us because of the process. We slowly purge ourselves of any urgency or desire to "short-cut" and simply can *be* with the process. On a deeper level, something is happening. Images are being transformed, symbols reinforced, awareness of ourselves made more explicit. All of this can happen because the self has received the message from us that we respect and reverence both the process and the person. We can wait through the labor of birthing. It is the gift of the Spirit.

Here are some helpful reflection questions for use during the period of insight: Do I give this time to settle, to seep into my person? What feelings do I have while making this decision? How might these affective responses influence my choice? How is this related to my life—my history and my vision for the future? Whom do I experience myself to be in relationship to God in this process of decision-making? Is there a sense of inner peace and quiet with the decision? Can I honestly say that this decision "fits" with my true sense of myself?

(d) *Decision and Action:* After prayerful reflection and consultation, we can come to a posture of liberation and hence decision. This decision will affirm and promote gifts given for the building of the reign of God. We should resolve to follow the decision made until evidence presents itself that the decision needs to be reevaluated.

EVALUATION OF DISCERNMENT

True discernment leads to the truth, and from the truth into freedom. St. Paul offers some criteria for discerning the presence of the Spirit in Galatians 5:22-23 in his discussion on the fruits of the Spirit. Because discernment is a Spirit-based activity, we can include this listing to evaluate our experiences of discernment. We can recognize the presence of the Spirit through the Spirit's fruits: love, joy, peace, patience, kindness, goodness, faithfulness, gentleness, and self-control. Paul also lists in Galatians 5:20-21a the works of those who do not walk with the Spirit: fornication, impurity, licentiousness, idolatry, sorcery, enmity, strife, jealousy, anger, selfishness, dissension, party spirit, envy, drunkenness, carousing and the like. When we live by the Spirit and the decisions of the Spirit, we will reflect in our way of life the fruits of that same Spirit.

DISCERNMENT AND CHRISTIAN INITIATION

Throughout the initiation process, the candidate and team, along with the parish staff and community, are called upon to discern the various movements and invitations from God to enter the commitment of sacramental initiation. In addition to helping the catechumen to come to an honest decision, the team can also help the catechumen to develop a basic life posture of discernment rooted in the providential love of God. We accomplish this through the modeling offered throughout the initiation process, but most especially through the manner and style of the discernment at the various periods and steps of the *Rite of Christian Initiation of Adults.*

What might this discernment "look like" at each period of the initiation process? This resource addresses the specifics of the discernment appropriate to each period or step in the corresponding chapter. Keeping those specifics in mind, following is a model that can be used for such discernment. Of course, the particulars will differ in each community.

◆ *The initiation team and sponsors meet to review the concerns of the discernment.* Weeks before entering into the formal discernment, there needs to be a careful review of the discernment concerns (ideas for this are outlined in the corresponding chapters in this resource). This will also give the initiation team and sponsors an opportunity to review and understand the upcoming ritual celebration, which serves as the foundation for the discernment.

◆ *The initiation team gives sponsors guidelines for preparing for the formal discernment.* Clearly, sponsors cannot simply walk up to the candidates or catechumens and start asking questions. Rather, the initiation team can provide guidance on entering pastoral conversations with the candidates and catechumens, using the discernment issues as the primary content of the conversations.

◆ *The sponsors meet informally with the candidates or catechumens to make an initial assessment.* As with any pastoral assessment (discussed in chapter 5 of this resource), the concern is to come to an initial sense of the needs of the candidate and catechumen. Here, it is in terms of the upcoming celebration of the particular rite. Together, the sponsors and candidates or catechumens try to articulate where the candidates or catechumens are on the journey of faith.

◆ *The sponsors and candidates or catechumens spend time together in prayer and reflection.* If the initial assessment suggests movement toward celebrating the upcoming ritual, the sponsors and candidates or catechumens need to schedule time together for prayer and reflection to review the expectations of the upcoming rite (but not the specifics of the rite). Those concerns are outlined in the corresponding sections of this resource. After this quality time together, the sponsors and candidates or catechumens make an initial discernment regarding the readiness to celebrate the rite. The sponsors are then responsible for sharing this initial discernment with the person (or persons) responsible for such discernment (usually the pastor or initiation coordinator). Of course, the sponsors need to clarify with the candidates or catechumens what is confidential and what is permissible to be discussed.

◆ *The community gathers for a more formal discernment.* Since initiation is not a one-sided process, both the candidates or catechumens and the larger community need to be in prayerful conversation during this discernment. Usually, the concerns of the community are represented through the initiation team and pastoral leadership, though there is nothing to prevent other members of the community from gathering during this discernment. It is important not to plan any discernment reflection at this point without the presence of the sponsors and the candidates or catechumens. If we cannot say something directly to the candidates or catechumens, then we need to evaluate if we should say it at all.

The process and the format of this gathering need to include the following: prayer for guidance, short reflection on the "criteria" for discernment (preferably in non-technical and non-jargon language), and the opportunity to prayerfully consider each candidate's or catechumen's request to celebrate this rite. Perhaps we can invite the candidates and catechumens to share the summary of their initial discernment, and we can invite sponsors to give appropriate testimony based on their ministry with the candidates or catechumens. We can then expand this prayerful conversation to include others gathered: other members of the initiation team, etc. These people can offer their reflections and insights.

Time needs to be included for silent reflection. Perhaps we can bring someone to the discernment to offer an objective reflection of what he or she heard regarding the candidate or catechumen. We should address concerns of a minor nature now; concerns of a major nature perhaps are best addressed in a subsequent pastoral conversation. Nonetheless, the community then needs to come to that moment of insight, that near-clarity of what is appropriate at this time. If this insight does not emerge, then the community needs to continue the conversation. That is why it is important to plan this discernment well before the rite being celebrated to provide adequate time for prayer and reelection.

◆ *We inform the full community of the discernment.* Clearly, the entire community needs to know the fruit of the discernment. Specifically, through various mediums, we need to make the community aware that Jane and Ed and Mark are celebrating the rite of acceptance into the order of catechumens on a certain date. This then begins the reeducation of the community in its role and responsibility regarding the candidates or catechumens. If the discernment is clear that someone is not celebrating the upcoming rite, there is no need to bring this to the community at this time. Presumably, the candidate or catechumen will continue in the formation process the community provides.

◆ *The initiation team begins to prepare for the next discernment.* It is important for the initiation team to keep before them the demands of the rite concerning discernment and look to the next formal opportunity.

14

Evaluation

INTRODUCTION

It is important to step back on a regular basis and examine what we are doing and why we are doing it. This is also true for implementing the *Rite of Christian Initiation of Adults.* Following is an evaluation tool for use with initiation teams. Like the remainder of this resource, it requires a critical reading of the ritual text.

At various times during this reflection process, the initiation team may find itself feeling affirmed in the parish's current practice; at other times, it will feel that what the parish is doing and what the rite calls for are two entirely different things. The only way any of us can move toward the full implementation of the initiation process is by keeping the vision of the *Rite of Christian Initiation of Adults* clearly in front of us. Sometimes, that vision will seem larger than life. Rather than letting it overwhelm us, let it invite us forward.

The initiation team will need to schedule time together for this review—perhaps a day of reflection together away from the parish. Even in a day, they probably cannot do all the exercises presented in these pages, but it will help them move forward. The team can be advised to do as much as they can in the allotted time and then make a commitment to come together again for further reflection.

PRIMARY ASSUMPTIONS

Before the team starts exploring various aspects of the parish's initiation practice, it is helpful to take time initially and name some primary assumptions that direct that initiation practice. In other words, why does the parish do the things that it does? Here are a few reflection questions for the initiation team to respond to:
- Who is *primarily* responsible for initiation?
- What phrase best describes your initiation practice (e.g., "learning about the Catholic faith")?
- How similar/dissimilar is your initiation of children compared with your initiation of adults?

254

After responding to these questions, the team should turn to the *Rite of Christian Initiation of Adults* to see how the rite presumes we answer these questions: for who is responsible, see *RCIA,* n. 9; on how to describe initiation, see *RCIA,* nos. 1, 5, 8; about children, see *RCIA,* n. 252f.

How does the parish's current practice fare compared to the vision given in the ritual text? What needs to happen to move closer to this vision?

PERIOD OF EVANGELIZATION AND PRECATECHUMENATE

After naming some presumptions about initiation, the team can begin by taking a moment to describe the current model in the parish for the period of the precatechumenate:
- What does the parish do when people ask about Catholicism?
- When and where do the precatechumenate gatherings meet?
- How often do they meet?
- What happens during the gatherings?
- What is the role of the sponsors during the precatechumenate?
- What determines the "agenda" of the precatechumenate gatherings?
- How does the parish know when it is time for someone to move from the precatechumenate?
- Does everyone move from the precatechumenate together?

After discussing these questions together (i.e., the current practice of the parish), the team can review the following sections from the *Rite of Christian Initiation of Adults,* nos. 36-40. What is the vision of the ritual text for the period of the precatechumenate? To answer this, each member of the team can take each paragraph noted above and write a summary of it in his or her own words in answer to the question, "What is this saying to us about initiation?" Then each person writes one final summary of all the paragraphs: "The ritual text says that the period of the precatechumenate... " After completing this exercise, the team members can share their responses with each other.

After reviewing the ritual text, the team can now explore some future possibilities together (each corresponds to the questions asked earlier):
- Strategies for providing welcome and support to inquirers whenever they come.
- Precatechumenate gatherings meeting in households all year long.
- Establishing a rhythm of inquiry gatherings every week or every other week.
- Strategies for evangelization that start with people's experiences and needs.
- Active and early involvement of sponsors from the parish community with inquirers.

• Critical reflection on the rite of acceptance as setting the agenda for this period.
• Process for discerning readiness based on *RCIA,* n. 42, not on a calendar.

RITE OF ACCEPTANCE INTO THE ORDER OF CATECHUMENS

Next, the team takes time to reflect on the parish's experiences of the rite of acceptance:
• How often and when does the parish celebrate the rite?
• Have sponsors been prepared for the celebration?
• How has the team prepared the candidates?
• Does the rite include candidates that are unbaptized and those baptized in other Christian traditions?
• Does the rite include children of catechetical age?
• How is the community prepared for this rite?
• On whom is the rite focused: the candidates or the assembly?
• How is the prayer space used? Does everything happen in the "front," or is the whole liturgical space used (including the outside)?
After celebrating the rite of acceptance:
• Is there an opportunity for the parish community to meet the catechumens and candidates?
• How does the team help the catechumens and candidates reflect back on their experience?
• How does the team help the community reflect back on its experience?
Now the team needs to spend some quality time with the ritual text itself to explore the dynamics of the rite of acceptance into the order of catechumens (*RCIA,* nos. 41-68). To achieve that, this reflection will continue in two parts. The first will be similar to what was suggested with the period of the precatechumenate.

Each team member takes *RCIA,* nos. 41-47 and writes a summary of each section in his or her own words: "What is this saying to us about initiation?" Then each team member writes one final summary of all the paragraphs: "The ritual text says that the rite of acceptance ..." The entire team can share their responses with each other.

For part two, each person takes a sheet of paper, turns it sideways and divides the sheet into four columns headed, (1) "number," (2) "symbol and ritual action," (3) "meaning," and (4) "preparation." Then, using *RCIA,* nos. 48-68, each team member places the following information in each appropriate column:

- *Number:* note the section number of the ritual text.
- *Symbol and ritual action:* what does the rite say is happening and what object or action is prescribed to achieve this? (e.g., marking people with the sign of the cross, community in procession, etc.).
- *Meaning:* what is the meaning of this symbol and/or action, especially as it relates to other parts of the celebration?
- *Preparation:* what needs to have happened in the precatechumenate to celebrate this moment of the rite with authenticity (e.g., the promise to follow the gospel way of life presumes some basic exposure to the gospel way of life)?

One option may be to divide the ritual text between various team members so that people focus on one section. After sufficient time to explore the ritual, the team comes together and talks about each section to arrive at a shared understanding of the ritual action and its meaning.

The team has helped each other grasp the vision of the rite. At this point, the team goes back to its earlier reflection on *RCIA,* nos. 41-47. How does this vision confirm its reflection? How does it expand its understanding?

The team now rewrites the initial summary statement "The ritual text says that the rite of acceptance…"

Before proceeding, there are two final notes about this rite that can help this evaluation. The parish might be celebrating the combined rite of acceptance and welcome with adults who are already baptized, with some adults unbaptized and some already baptized, or with children. Guidance for these adaptations is given elsewhere in the ritual text. However, before the team can explore them, it needs to know the primary vision (which is for the unbaptized). Then it can look at those sections of part II of the ritual text or appendix I that include those adaptations needed in the parish community.

PERIOD OF THE CATECHUMENATE

Next, the team takes time to reflect on the parish's experiences of the period of the catechumenate:
- When and how often do the catechumens meet?
- Describe the catechesis of this period.
- What involvement do the catechumens have with the community?
- How is moral and spiritual formation included in their preparation?
- What is the place of ritual prayer in this process?
- How is apostolic service included?

After discussing these questions together (i.e., the parish's current practice), the team needs to review the following sections of the *Rite of Christian Initiation of Adults,* nos. 75-80. What is the vision of the ritual text for the period of the catechumenate? To answer this, the team follows the same process outlined earlier, with the members taking each section and writing a summary of it, each in his or her own words: "What is this saying to us about initiation?" Then write one final summary of all the paragraphs: "The ritual text says that the period of the catechumenate ..." Again, the team shares their personal reflections.

Unlike the period of the precatechumenate, the period of the catechumenate is ritual-based, that is, every gathering of the catechumens is within the context of a ritual. The team will need to spend time coming to understand the shape and structure of the various ritual moments of this period to use them frequently throughout.

During the period of the catechumenate, the ritual text calls for frequent and ample use of liturgical prayer (see *RCIA*, nos. 75.1 and 75.3), especially celebrations of the Word, minor exorcisms, blessings and anointings.

The team can form four groups and each group can review one of the four types of liturgical prayer listed above. Here are the guidelines for each group:

Celebrations of the Word (RCIA, nos. 81-89)

What is the purpose of these celebrations? How often do we celebrate them? What is their ritual shape or structure?

Minor Exorcisms (RCIA, nos. 90-94)

What is the purpose of the minor exorcisms? When (and by whom) do we celebrate them? Take one of the examples given in *RCIA*, n. 94 and examine its structure (i.e., what is being prayed at each section), and then take another example (the rite gives eleven) and see if the structure is consistent.

Blessings of the Catechumens (RCIA, nos. 95-97)

Why do we bless? Who blesses? Take one of the examples given in *RCIA*, n. 97 (the rite gives nine) and follow the directions for minor exorcisms, as immediately above.

Anointing of the Catechumens (RCIA, nos. 98-103)

What is the purpose of the anointing? When (and by whom) would we celebrate it? Look at the structure of the prayers in *RCIA*, nos. 102 and 103, and describe what is going on in each prayer.

After working with the particular type of liturgical prayer, the team can come back together and share their insights with the other members of the team. Then the team can explore together some future possibilities (each item below corresponds to one of the questions asked earlier):

• Sunday dismissal catechesis

• A catechesis based on the Sunday Liturgy of the Word that breaks open the Sunday readings but also enters into conversation with the Catholic Tradition that emerges from an experience of those readings

• Active role of sponsors to integrate catechumens into the ordinary life of the parish

• Helping catechumens to discover moral and spiritual guidance from the "book of the community," that is, from living with the community.

• Rich and regular (i.e., always) celebrations of liturgical prayer when catechumens gather so we will immerse them into a sacramental way of life.

• Regular discernment of how God is gifting each catechumen for unique service to the world community as an expression of the ministry of Jesus the Christ.

RITE OF ELECTION OR ENROLLMENT OF NAMES

There is little a parish initiation team can do to shape the celebration of the rite of election since it is a diocesan-wide celebration. However, it is important to come to a better understanding of the rite to celebrate better the rite of sending to election (*RCIA*, nos. 106-117). Because the specifics of the rite of sending and the rite of election differ in each diocese, this reflection time will explore the vision of the rite of election, presuming appropriate adjustments based on particular diocesan directives.

The team can begin this part of the reflection process by reviewing the following questions:

• What is election?

• What difference does this ritual make?

• Why celebrate it with the rest of the diocese?

After discussing these questions together, the team will need to review the sections of the *Rite of Christian Initiation of Adults* that deal with the rite of election. The team can follow the discussion format outlined above for the rite of acceptance. For part one of the reflection, the team uses *RCIA*, nos. 118-128. For part two of the reflection, the team uses *RCIA*, nos. 129-137. Then the team writes one final summary of all the paragraphs. "The ritual text says that the rite of election..."

PERIOD OF PURIFICATION AND ENLIGHTENMENT

Next, the team reflects on the parish's current model for celebrating the period of purification and enlightenment:

• How does this period differ from the period of the catechumenate?

• Does the parish celebrate the scrutinies? How often?

• How does the team prepare the elect for the scrutinies?

• Does the parish celebrate the presentations? When?

Even more so than with the period of the catechumenate, the period of purification and enlightenment will rely on the public rituals of the period to give it shape and direction. Specifically, we are concerned with the celebration of the scrutinies and the presentations.

To explore the vision of this period, the team can move in three steps. The first step will be to explore together the overall vision of the period as outlined in *RCIA,* nos. 138-140. The second and third steps will focus on the two types of ritual celebrations during this period.

Scrutinies

Three scrutinies are celebrated on the Third, Fourth and Fifth Sundays of Lent. They are progressive in their reflection on sin, and we must celebrate all three (recall that we need the bishop's permission not to celebrate one of the scrutinies; see *RCIA,* n. 20). To appreciate the vision about the scrutinies, the team can separate this part of the reflection into two sections (as with the rite of acceptance). Part one of the reflection is the same as for the rite of acceptance, using *RCIA,* nos. 141-146. Part two will look at the three scrutinies. The team can divide into three smaller groups, with each group reviewing one of the scrutinies (first scrutiny, *RCIA,* nos. 150-156; second scrutiny, *RCIA,* nos. 164-170; third scrutiny, *RCIA,* nos. 171-177) using the following questions:

> • What do the scripture readings assigned for this scrutiny tell us about the nature of this celebration (note: the team will need to have the lectionary readings assigned to the three scrutinies)?
> • What are the primary symbols from these readings and how do they speak of both sin and grace?
> • What purpose do the intercessions serve?
> • What is the structure of the exorcism prayer (the three movements) and how does it tie in with the scripture readings of the day?

Each group can then share its reflection on the meaning of the scrutinies. With the larger vision of all three scrutinies, the larger group can continue with completing the sentence: "The ritual text says that the scrutinies ... "

Presentations

The rite also provides ritual presentations during this period of formation. Recall that the rite also allows the anticipation of these presentations during the end of the period of the catechumenate (see *RCIA,* n. 104f.). As with the scrutinies, the team will continue in two stages. The first is a large group reflection on *RCIA,* nos. 147-149. For the second step, the team can separate two groups, with each reviewing one of the presentations: presentation of the Creed, *RCIA,* nos. 157-163, and presentation of the Lord's Prayer, *RCIA,* nos. 178-184. As with previous rituals, the groups should divide their sheet of paper into four columns ("number," "symbol/ritual action," "meaning," "preparation") and explore the meaning and dynamics of the ritual.

After discussing their findings together, the team can then explore together some future possibilities (each item below corresponds to one of the questions asked earlier):

- Make this a retreat time different from previous periods.
- Celebrate the three scrutinies using the Year A readings.
- Spend time in a retreat-style recollection to prepare for the scrutiny, perhaps using the first reading of Year A, and elicit from the elect their own needs and concerns for themselves, the world and the Church (which can then be used for the intercessions during the scrutinies).
- Consider anticipating the presentations during the final weeks of the catechumenate, being sure they are verbal proclamations of these cherished treasures.

CELEBRATION OF THE SACRAMENTS OF INITIATION

The initiation team begins this section by reviewing the parish's current experience of the celebration of the sacraments of initiation:

- When and where does the parish celebrate the sacraments of initiation?
- Does this celebration include both adults and children of catechetical age?
- How full is the use of symbols (assembly, light, water, oil, bread and wine, new garment, etc.)?

The team can then follow the same process outlined above in the section on the rite of acceptance. Part one will deal with *RCIA,* nos. 206-217; part two will deal with *RCIA,* nos. 218-243.

After this reflection, the team writes out a final summary: "The ritual text says that the celebration of the sacraments of initiation ... "

Then together, the team can explore some future possibilities (each item corresponds to one of the questions asked earlier):

- Celebrate full sacramental initiation at the Easter Vigil.
- Include all who are ready (adults and children) at this primary festival of the community.
- Consider possible ways of using the liturgical symbols of this ritual in fuller and richer ways: a large, gathering fire; the single flame of the paschal candle in the midst of darkness; full body immersion for baptism; etc.

PERIOD OF MYSTAGOGY

The team now reflects on the parish's experience of the period of mystagogy:
  • What is mystagogy?
  • When does the parish "do" mystagogy?
  • When does it end?

After discussing these questions together (i.e., the parish's current practice), the team reviews the following sections of the *Rite of Christian Initiation of Adults,* nos. 244-251. What is the vision of the ritual text for the period of mystagogy? To answer this question, each team member takes each section one by one and writes a summary of it in his or her own words: "What is this saying to us about initiation?" Then each person writes one final summary of all the paragraphs: "The ritual text says that the period of mystagogy . . . " Together, the team discusses the personal reflection on mystagogy.

After coming to a common understanding of mystagogy, the team can then explore together some future possibilities (each item corresponds to one of the questions asked earlier):
  • Mystagogy as a means of deepening the experience of the paschal mystery within the context of the assembly by reflecting on the gospel, celebrating the eucharist and participating in service.
  • Mystagogy "happens" primarily during the Sunday eucharist; preachers break open the paschal mystery for all, following the pattern of Year A.
  • Initial mystagogy is completed at the Pentecost festival (now they are fully integrated into the life of this Christian community); but the National Statutes for implementing the rites in the United States indicate that there needs to be continuing mystagogy for a year (see *NS,* n. 24).

RECLAIMING THE VISION

Hopefully, this reflection provides the initiation team with enough affirmation to know that they are on the right track—and enough dissatisfaction with things as they are to cause them to want to develop and change the current practice of the parish to be more faithful to the vision of the *Rite of Christian Initiation of Adults.*

Here is one possible model for developing a plan to move forward. What is important about this planning process is that the full initiation team all work on it together and make a commitment together to implement the plan. For the first few items, it is recommended to choose things that are reasonable and do-able at this point. That will create momentum to explore some more complex developments.

1. Review the findings from your evaluation process. What needs future development? What excites and challenges you?
2. Privately, each individual lists five areas of development (this is the time to dream big dreams).
3. Bring the group together and list everyone's areas of development, noting items chosen by more than one person. As a group, step back from the list and see if there are any items that emerge, any trends, any focus to the listing. For example, though people noted different items, there may have been much energy around issues in the precatechumenate. Exploring that further is reasonable.
4. As a group, choose five items to explore together. Many (if not all) will emerge from the listing process described above.
5. Choose one of the five items that is reasonable and do-able (i.e., start with a small victory and build some momentum).
6. Respond to the following questions for the chosen task:
   a. What do you want to accomplish (be very clear and specific about your goal)?
   b. How are things now? Be honest and concrete about things as they are now; that will help generate a momentum toward the creative future.
   c. What are the practical first steps to move from your current practice to your vision? List those first steps so you know where to begin; you can change and adjust them as you go along.
   d. What resources (books, people, skills, etc.) do you have available to you to move forward? Go beyond your immediate group and explore the resources available in your parish.
   e. What resources will you need to move forward?
   f. Who will be responsible for overseeing this plan?
   g. How will you evaluate it?
7. And now, do it!

Appendix

Correlation of United States and Canadian editions of the
Rite of Christian Initiation of Adults

* This has a different text than in US edition.

**This has a different text in the rubric than in the US edition. The ritual text itself is the same.

USA text	CAN text[1]
INTRODUCTION	
1	1
2	2
3[2]	3*
4	4
5	5
6	6
7	7
8	8
9	9
10	10
11	11
12	12
13	13
14	14
15	15
16	16
17	17
18	18
19	19
20	20

USA text	CAN text
21	21
22	22[3]
23	23
24	24
25	25
26	26
27	27
28	28
29	29
30	30
31	31
32	32
33	33[4]
34	34
35	35
PART 1	
Period of the Precatechumenate	
36	36
37	37
38	38
39	39

USA text	CAN text
40	40
First Step: Acceptance into the Order of Catechumens	
41	41
42	42
43	43
44	44*
45	45
46	46
47	47
Rite of Acceptance into the Order of Catechumens	
48	48
49	49
50	50
51	51*
52	52
53	53
54	54*
55	55[5]
56	56[6]

[1] When the Canadian text refers to another section of the Canadian text that has a different numbering than the US edition (but the parallel text), the difference is not noted.

[2] The US text refers to the US adaptations: the combined rites and the National Statutes.

[3] The Canadian text includes the anointing with the oil of catechumens on Holy Saturday.

[4] There are no decisions made by the Canadian Conference of Bishops noted here as in the US edition.

[5] The references in option B (* and **) have different texts than the US edition.

[6] There is no signing of the hands and feet as in the US edition.

USA text	CAN text		USA text	CAN text		USA text	CAN text
57	57		80	80		99	191[10]
58	58*		*Rites Belong to the Period of the Catechumenate*			100	99
59	59*					101	100
60	60		*Celebrations of the Word of God*			102	101
61	61					103	102
62	62		81	81		*Presentations*	
63	63		82	82		104[11]	103
64	64		83	83		105	104
65	65		84	84		*Sending of the Catechumens for Election*	
66	66		85	85			
67	67[7]		86	86		106	
68	68		87	87*		107	
69	69*		88	88		108	
70	70*		89	89*		109	
71	71		*Minor Exorcisms*			110	
72	72**		90	90		111	
73	73**		91	91		112	
	74[8]		92	92		113	
74			93	93		114	
Period of the Catechumenate			94	94		115	
75	75		*Blessing of the Catechumens*			116	
76	76		95	95		117	
77	77		96	96		*Second Step: Election or Enrollment of Names*	
78	78		97	97			
79	79		*Anointing of the Catechumens*			118	105
			98	98[9]		119	106
						120	107

[7] The US text includes an additional option for the dismissal (B). Thus the correlation between US and Canadian texts is A/A B/no text C/B D/C.

[8] The Canadian text includes a directive for additional rites (included in the US text in the last rubric of n. 74). Included here is the giving of salt and a religious medal as optional rites (not included in US text).

[9] The Canadian text precedes this section on the anointing of the catechumens with the title "Optional Rites During the Catechumenate," whereas in the US text, it is considered as part of the period of the catechumenate. See Canadian edition, n. 172.2.

[10] This text (adapted) appears later in the preparation rite of Holy Saturday.

[11] It is at this point in the US text that we see "optional" for the remaining rites for the period of the catechumenate.

USA text	CAN text
121	108
122	109
123	110
124	111
125	112
126	113
127	114*
128	115*
Rite of Election or Enrollment of Names	
129	116
130	117
131[12]	118*
132	119**
133	120
134	121
135	122
136[13]	123*
137	124
Period of Purification and Enlightenment	
138	125
139	126
140	127
Rites Belonging to the Period of Purification and Enlightenment	
141	128
142	129
143	130
144	131

USA text	CAN text
145	132
146	133
147	134
148	135
149	136
First Scrutiny	
150	137
151	138
152	139
153	140
154	141
155[14]	142*
156	143
Presentation of the Creed	
157	144
158	145
159	146
160	147
161	148
162[15]	149*
163	150
Second Scrutiny	
164	151
165	152
166	153
167	154
168	155
169[16]	156*
170	157

USA text	CAN text
Third Scrutiny	
171	158
172	159
173	160
174	161
175	162
176[17]	163*
177	164
Presentation of the Lord's Prayer	
178	165
179	166
180	167[18]
181	168
182	169
183[19]	170*
184	171
Preparation Rites on Holy Saturday	
185	172[20]
186	173[21]
187	174

[12]The US text includes a ritual dialogue with the community in each of the options provided.

[13]See comment on note 7.

[14]See comment on note 7.

[15]See comment on note 7.

[16] See comments on note 7.

[17]See comment on note 7.

[18]The Canadian text includes two options for the Lord's Prayer, while the US text provides only one.

[19]See comment on note 11.

[20]In 172.2, the Canadian text includes the anointing with the oil of catechumens as one of the preparatory rites for Holy Saturday. The US bishops moved this to the period of the catechumenate (see US edition, n. 33.7).

[21]In n. 173.3, the Canadian text includes directives for the inclusion of the anointing with the oil of catechumens. See note 20 above.

USA text	CAN text
188	175
189	176
190	177
191	178
192	179
193	180
194	181
195	182
196	183
197	184
198	185
199	186
200	187[22]
201	188
202	189
	190[23]
	191
	192
	193
	194
203	195
204	196
205	197

Third Step: Celebration of the Sacraments of Initiation

USA text	CAN text
206	198

[22]The Canadian bishops did not make a decision about choosing a baptismal name as the US bishops did. See US edition, n. 33.4.

[23]The Canadian text includes the anointing with the oil of catechumens, already celebrated in the US text during the period of the catechumenate (see US edition, nos. 98ff.).

USA text	CAN text
207	199
208	200
209	201[24]
210	202
211	203
	204[25]
212	205
213	206
214	207
215	208
216	209
217	210

Celebration of the Sacraments of Initiation

USA text	CAN text
218	211
219	212
220	213
221	214
222	215
223	216*
224	217**
	218[26]

[24]The Canadian text includes reference to the anointing with the oil of catechumens during the baptismal liturgy, which is not included in the US text (because of the US bishops' decision to move this ritual to the period of the catechumenate, see US edition, n. 33.7).

[25]The Canadian text includes directives on the anointing with the oil of catechumens.

[26]The Canadian text includes the anointing with the oil of catechumens after the renunciation of sin and before the profession of faith, if it has not been anticipated.

USA text	CAN text
225	219
226	220
227	221
228	222
229	223
230	224
231	225
232	226
233	227
234	228
235	229
236	230*
237	
238	
239	
240	
241	231
242	232
243	233

Period of Mystagogy

USA text	CAN text
244	234
245	235
246	236
247	237
248	238
249	239
250	240
251	241

PART II

1. Christian Initiation of Children Who Have Reached Catechetical Age

USA text	CAN text
252	242

USA text	CAN text
253[27]	243*
254	244
255	245
256[28]	246*
257	247
258[29]	248*
259	249
260	250
261	251
262	252
263	253
264	254
265	255
266	256*
267	257
268	258[30]
269	259
270	260
271	261
272	262
273	263
274	264
275	265
276	266

USA text	CAN text
277[31]	
278	
279	
280	
281	
282	
283	
284	
285	
286	
287	
288	
289	
290	
291	267
292	268
293	269
294	270
295	271
296	272
297	273
298	274
299	275
300	276
301	277[32]
302	278
303	279
304	280

USA text	CAN text
305	281
306	282
307	283
308	284
309	285
310	286
311	287
312	288
313	289
314	290
315	291**
316	292
317	293
318	294
319	295
320	296
321	297
322	298
323	299
324	300
325	301
326	302
327	303
328	304
329	305
330	306

2. Christian Initiation of Adults in Exceptional Circumstances

USA text	CAN text
331	307
332	308
333	309
334	310
335	311

[27] The US text includes reference to the optional rite of election, not included in the Canadian text.

[28] The US text includes reference to the optional rite of election.

[29] The US text includes reference to the optional rite of election.

[30] There is no signing of the hands and feet as in the US edition.

[31] The US text includes an adaptation for use in the United States: a rite of election or enrollment of names.

[32] The US text includes a blessing of oil (in section A) and a rubric for a possible blessing after the anointing (before the Laying on of Hands).

USA text	CAN text
336	312
337	313
338	314
339	315
340	316
341	317
342	318
343	319
344	320
345	321
346	322
347	323
348	324
349	325
350	326
351	327
352	328**
353	329
354	330
355	331
356	332
357	333
358	334
359	335
360	336
361	337
362	338
363	339
364	340
365	341
366	342
367	343
368	344
369	345

USA text	CAN text
3. Christian Initiation of a Person in Danger of Death	
370	346
371	347
372	348
373	349
374	350
375	351
376	352
377	353
378	354
379	355
380	356
381	357
382	358
383	359
384	360
385	361
386	362
387	363
388	364
389	365
390	366
391	367
392	368
393	369
394	370
395	371
396	372
397	373
398	374
399	375

USA text	CAN text
4. Preparation of Uncatechized Adults for Confirmation and Eucharist	
400[33]	376
401	377
402	378
403	379
404	380
405	381*
406	382
407	383*
408	384
409	385
410	386
411[34]	
412	
413	
414	
415	
416	
417	
418	
419	
420	
421	
422	
423	

[33]The US text includes this clarification: as infants "either as Roman Catholics or as members of another Christian community."

[34]What follows are optional rites for baptized but uncatechized adults, for use in the United States.

USA text	CAN text
424	
425	
426	
427	
428	
429	
430	
431	
432	
433	
434	
435	
436	
437	
438	
439	
440	
441	
442	
443	
444	
445	
446	
447	
448	
449	
450	
451	
452	
453	
454	
455	
456	
457	

USA text	CAN text
458	
459	
460	
461	
462	
463	
464	
465	
466	
467	
468	
469	
470	
471	
472	
5. Reception of Baptized Christians into the Full Communion of the Catholic Church	
473	387
474	388
475	389
476	390
477	391
478[35]	
479	392
480	393
481	394
482	395
483	396
484	397

USA text	CAN text
485	398
486	399
487	400
488	401
489	402
490	403
491	404
492	405
493	406
494	407
495	408
496	409
497	410
498	411
499	412
500	413
501	414
502	415
503	416
504	417
APPENDIX I	
505[36]	
506	
507	
508	
509	

[35]The US edition makes reference to the US adaptation of liturgical rites in Part 4 (not included in the Canadian text).

[36]The US text provides for various "combined rites" for the major steps. The only combined rite included in the Canadian edition is the "Celebration at the Easter Vigil of the Sacraments of Initiation and of the Rite of Reception into the Full Communion of the Catholic Church," which is parallel to the US edition nos. 562ff.

USA text	CAN text
510	
511	
512	
513	
514	
515	
516	
517	
518	
519	
520	
521	
522	
523	
524	
525	
526	
527	
528	
529	
530	
531	
532	
533	
534	
535	
536	
537	
538	
539	
540	
541	
542	
543	

USA text	CAN text
544	
545	
546	
547	
548	
549	
550	
551	
552	
553	
554	
555	
556	
557	
558	
559	
560	
561	
562	418
563	419
564	420
565	421
566	422
567	423
568	424
569	425
570	426
571	427[37]
572	428*
573	429

[37]The Canadian text does not include the scored version of the blessing.

USA text	CAN text
	430[38]
574	431
575	432
576	433
577	434
578	435
579	436
580	437
581	438
582	439
583	440
584	441
585	442
586	443
587	444
588	445
589	446
590	447
591	448
592	449
593	450
594	451
APPENDIX II	
595	452
596	453
597	454

[38]The Canadian text includes the anointing with the oil of catechumens, already celebrated during the period of the catechumenate in the US text.

USA text	CAN text
(CAN text only:) Other Rites for Use in Canada[39]	
Introduction	
	455
	456
	457
	458
	459
	460
	461
	462
Rite of Welcoming Candidates for Confirmation and Eucharist[40]	
	463
	464
	465
	466
	467
	468
	469
	470
	471
	472
	473

USA text	CAN text
	474
	475[41]
	476
	477
	478
	479
	480
	481
	482
	483
	484[42]
	485[43]
	486
	487
	488[44]

[41]Note that the rite here does not have a signing of all the senses. See US edition n. 423.

[42]Note the difference in the ritual text from the US edition. Here the baptized Catholic remain with the community. The US edition is silent about this.

[43] Note the difference in the ritual text from the US edition. Here the baptized candidates for reception into full communion are dismissed (as is normal with the catechumens). The US edition is silent about this.

[44]This parallels the comments in the US edition, n. 407 regarding the participation in liturgical rites.

USA text	CAN text
	489
	490[45]
	491
	492
	493
	494[46]
	495
	496
	497
	498
	499
	500
	501
	502
	503
	504
	505
	506
	507
	508
	509

[45]This "Prayers For Strength" is unique to the Canadian edition. The US edition does not include a parallel ritual.

[46]This rite differs from the US edition nos. 446ff (Rite of Calling the Candidates to Continuing Conversion) in that the Canadian ritual text specifies in n. 497 that this is not to be celebrated with the rite of election.

[39]These adaptations for use in Canada are similar to the adaptations for use in the United States, listed in Part Two, Chapter 4.

[40]Compare this adaptation with the US adaptation at US edition nos. 411ff.

USA text	CAN text	USA text	CAN text
	510[47]	NS4	
	511	NS5	
	512	NS6	
	513	NS7	
	514	NS8	
	515	NS9	
	516[48]	NS10	
	517	NS11	
	518	NS12	
	519	NS13	
	520	NS14	
	521	NS15	
	522[49]	NS16	
	523	NS17	
	524	NS18	
	525	NS19	
	526	NS20	
	527	NS21	
	528[50]	NS22	
	529	NS23	
	530	NS24	
(US Text only:) **APPENDIX III:** *National Statutes for the Catechumenate*		NS25	
		NS26	
		NS27	
NS1		NS28	
NS2		NS29	
NS3		NS30	
		NS31	
		NS32	
		NS33	
		NS34	
		NS35	
		NS36	
		NS37	

[47]See US edition, n. 407.

[48]See US editon, n. 407.

[49]This is the Canadian adaptation to respond to the same concern as in the US edition, nos. 459ff.

[50]The US edition does not include such specific guidelines for reconciliation.

Resources

CHRISTIAN INITIATION

Primary Sources

Rite of Christian Initiation of Adults (United States edition).Washington, DC: United States Catholic Conference, 1988.

Rite of Christian Initiation of Adults (Canadian edition). Ottawa: Publications Service of the Canadian Conference of Catholic Bishops, 1987.

Secondary Resources

Austin, Gerard. *The Rite of Confirmation. Anointing with the Spirit.* New York: Pueblo Publishing Co., 1985.

Ball, Peter. *Adult Believing. A Guide to the Christian Initiation of Adults.* New York: Paulist Press, 1988.

Baumbach, Gerard F. *Experiencing the Mystery. The Sacred Pause of Easter.* New York: Paulist Press, 1996.

Boyer, Mark G. *Breathing Deeply of God's New Life. Preparing Spiritually for the Sacraments of Initiation.* Cincinnati: St. Anthony Messenger Press, 1993.

Brown, Kathy and Frank Sokol, eds. *Issues in the Christian Initiation of Children: Catechesis and Liturgy.* Chicago: Liturgy Training Publications, 1989.

Bruns, William R. *Cenacle Sessions: A Modern Mystagogy.* New York: Paulist Press, 1992.

———. *Easter Bread: Reflections on the Gospels of the Easter Season for Neophytes and Their Companions.* New York: Paulist Press, 1991.

Catechumenate: A Journal of Christian Initiation (periodical). Chicago: Liturgy Training Publications.

Catucci, Thomas and Kathy Coffey: *Lenten Journey: A Resource for Christian Initiation.* Denver: Living the Good News, Inc., 1992.

———. *Lenten Journey: Resources for Children and Youth.* Denver: Living the Good News, Inc., 1992.

Christian Initiation of Adults. Liturgy Documentary Series 4. Revised edition. Washington, DC: United States Catholic Conference, 1988.

Christian Initiation of Adults. Study Text 10. Revised edition. Washington, DC: United States Catholic Conference, 1988.

Coffey, Kathy. *Children and Christian Initiation. A Practical Guide.* Denver: Living the Good News, Inc., 1995.

———. *Children and Christian Initiation. A Practical Guide to the Catechumenate.* Denver: Living the Good News, Inc., 1995.

———. *Children and Christian Initiation. A Practical Guide to Mystagogy.* Denver: Living the Good News, Inc., 1995.

———. *Children and Christian Initiation. A Practical Guide to the Precatechumenate.* Denver: Living the Good News, Inc., 1995.

———. *Children and Christian Initiation. A Practical Guide to Purification and Enlightenment.* Denver: Living the Good News, Inc., 1995.

Duffy, Regis. *On Becoming a Catholic Christian. The Challenge of Christian Initiation.* San Francisco: Harper and Row, 1984.

Duggan, Robert and Maureen Kelly. *The Christian Initiation of Children: Hope for the Future.* New York: Paulist Press, 1991.

Duggan, Robert, ed. *Conversion and the Catechumenate.* New York: Paulist Press, 1984.

Dujarier, Michel. *A History of the Catechumenate: The First Six Centuries.* New York: William H. Sadlier, 1979.

———. *The Rites of Christian Initiation. Historical and Pastoral Reflections.* New York: William H. Sadlier, 1979.

Dunning, James. *Echoing God's Word. Formation for Catechists and Homilists in a Catechumenal Church.* Chicago: Liturgy Training Publications, 1993.

Ferrone, Rita. *On the Rite of Election.* Forum Essays No. 3. Chicago: Liturgy Training Publications, 1994.

Hamma, Robert M., ed. *A Catechumen's Lectionary.* New York: Paulist Press, 1988.

Hinman, Karen. *How to Form a Catechumenate Team.* Chicago: Liturgy Training Publications, 1986.

Huels, John M. *The Catechumenate and the Law.* Chicago: Liturgy Training Publications, 1994.

Jackson, Pamela. *Journeybread for the Shadowlands: The Readings for the Rites of the Catechumenate, RCIA.* Collegeville, MN: The Liturgical Press, 1993.

Johnson, Maxwell, ed. *Living Water, Sealing Spirit: Readings on Christian Initiation.* Collegeville, MN: The Liturgical Press, 1995.

Joncas, Jan Michael. *Preaching the Rites of Christian Initiation.* Forum Essays No. 4. Chicago: Liturgy Training Publications, 1994.

Kavanagh, Aidan. *Confirmation: Origins and Reform.* New York: Pueblo Publishing, 1988.

————. *The Shape of Baptism.* New York: Pueblo Publishing, 1978.

Lewinski, Ron. *Guide for Sponsors.* Third edition. Chicago: Liturgy Training Publications, 1993.

————. *Welcoming the New Catholic.* Third edition. Chicago: Liturgy Training Publications, 1993.

Milne, Mark K. *Sunday Dismissals for the RCIA.* Collegeville, MN: The Liturgical Press, 1993.

Mitchell, Nathan. *Eucharist as Sacrament of Initiation.* Forum Essays No. 2. Chicago: Liturgy Training Publications, 1994.

Morris, Thomas H. *Walking Together in Faith: A Workbook for Sponsors in Christian Initiation.* New York: Paulist Press, 1992.

Morris, Thomas H. and Kathy Coffey. *Confirmation. Anointed and Gifted with the Spirit. Leader's Guide.* Denver: Living the Good News, Inc., 1997.

The Murphy Center for Liturgical Research. *Made, Not Born. New Perspectives on Christian Initiation and the Catechumenate.* Notre Dame: University of Notre Dame Press, 1976.

Oakham, Ronald, ed. *One at the Table. The Reception of Baptized Christians.* Chicago: Liturgy Training Publications, 1995.

Osborne, Kenan. *The Christian Sacraments of Initiation.* New York: Paulist Press, 1987.

Powell, Karan Hinman and Joseph Sinwell. *Breaking Open the Word of God, Cycle A.* New York: Paulist Press, 1986.

————. *Breaking Open the Word of God, Cycle B.* New York: Paulist Press, 1987.

————. *Breaking Open the Word of God, Cycle C.* New York: Paulist Press, 1988.

Reedy, William J., ed. *Becoming a Catholic Christian.* New York: William H. Sadlier, 1979.

Sinwell, Joseph. *Come Follow Me.* New York: Paulist Press, 1990.

Tufano, Victoria, ed. *Celebrating the Rites of Adult Initiation: Pastoral Reflections.* Chicago: Liturgy Training Publications, 1992.

————. *Readings in the Christian Initiation of Children.* Chicago: Liturgy Training Publications, 1994.

Turner, Paul. *Confirmation: The Baby in Solomon's Court.* New York: Paulist Press, 1993.

Vincie, Catherine. *The Role of the Assembly in Christian Initiation.* Forum Essays No. 1. Chicago: Liturgy Training Publications, 1993.

Wilde, James, ed. *Finding and Forming Sponsors and Godparents.* Chicago: Liturgy Training Publications, 1988.

Yarnold, Edward. *The Awe-Inspiring Rites of Initiation.* Second edition. Collegeville, MN: The Liturgical Press, 1994.

LITURGY AND SACRAMENTS

Primary Sources

Book of Blessings. Collegeville, MN: The Liturgical Press, 1989.

Lectionary for Mass. New York: Catholic Book Publishing Company, 1970.

The Liturgy Documents. A Parish Resource. Third edition. Chicago: Liturgy Training Publications, 1991.

The Sacramentary. New York: Catholic Book Publishing Company, 1985.

Secondary Sources

Baker, J. Robert, Larry J. Nyberg and Victoria Tufano, eds. *A Baptism Sourcebook.* Chicago: Liturgy Training Publications, 1993.

Duffy, Regis. *An American Emmaus. Faith and Sacrament in the American Culture.* New York: Crossroads, 1995.

Francis, Mark. *Liturgy in a Multicultural Community.* Collegeville, MN: The Liturgical Press, 1991.

Huck, Gabe. *The Three Days: Parish Prayer in the Paschal Triduum.* Revised edition. Chicago: Liturgy Training Publications, 1992.

Huck, Gabe et al., eds. *The Easter Sourcebook.* The Fifty Days. Chicago: Liturgy Training Publications, 1988.

Huck, Gabe and Mary Ann Simcoe, eds. *Triduum Sourcebook* (3 volumes). Chicago: Liturgy Training Publications, 1993.

Joncas, Jan Michael. *Catechism of the Catholic Church on Liturgy and Sacraments.* San Jose: Resource Publications, 1995.

Neumann, Don. *Holy Week in the Parish.* Collegeville, MN: The Liturgical Press, 1991.

Ramshaw, Gail. *Words Around the Fire.* Chicago: Liturgy Training Publications, 1990.

———. *Words Around the Font.* Chicago: Liturgy Training Publications, 1994.

———. *Words Around the Table.* Chicago: Liturgy Training Publications, 1991.

Searle, Mark, ed. *The Church Speaks Out About Sacraments with Children.* Chicago: Liturgy Training Publications, 1990.

CATECHESIS

Primary Sources

The Catechetical Documents. A Parish Resource. Chicago: Liturgy Training Publications, 1996.

Catechism of the Catholic Church. Washington, DC: United States Catholic Conference, 1994.

Secondary Sources
Living the Good News. Lectionary-based resources. Denver, Colorado.
McBrien, Philip. *How to Teach with the Lectionary: Leader's Guide.* Mystic, CT: Twenty-Third Publications, 1992.
Ostdiek, Gilbert. *Catechesis for Liturgy.* Washington, DC: The Pastoral Press, 1986.

SCRIPTURE RESOURCES

Boadt, Lawrence. *Reading the Old Testament.* New York: Paulist Press, 1984.
Faley, Roland James. *Footprints on the Mountain. Preaching and Teaching the Sunday Readings.* New York: Paulist Press, 1994.
Moloney, Francis J. *The Gospel of the Lord. Reflections on the Gospel Readings, Year A.* Collegeville, MN: The Liturgical Press, 1992.
———. *The Gospel of the Lord. Reflections on the Gospel Readings, Year B.* Collegeville, MN: The Liturgical Press, 1993.
———. *The Gospel of the Lord. Reflections on the Gospel Readings, Year C.* Collegeville, MN: The Liturgical Press, 1994.
O'Brien, John E. *Refreshed by the Word, Cycle A.* New York: Paulist Press, 1995.
———. *Refreshed by the Word, Cycle B.* New York: Paulist Press, 1996.
———. *Refreshed by the Word, Cycle C.* New York: Paulist Press, 1994.
Perkins, Pheme. *Reading the New Testament.* Second edition. New York: Paulist Press, 1988.
Pilch, John. *The Cultural World of Jesus, Cycle A.* Collegeville, MN: The Liturgical Press, 1995.
———. *The Cultural World of Jesus, Cycle B.* Collegeville, MN: The Liturgical Press, 1996.
———. *The Cultural World of Jesus, Cycle C.* Collegeville, MN: The Liturgical Press, 1997.
———. *Introducing the Cultural Context of the New Testament.* New York: Paulist Press, 1991.
———. *Introducing the Cultural Context of the Old Testament.* New York: Paulist Press, 1991.
Sanchez, Patricia. *The Word We Celebrate.* Kansas City, MO: Sheed & Ward, 1989.

PASTORAL ISSUES

Baranowski, Arthur. *Creating Small Church Communities.* Cincinnati: St. Anthony Messenger Press, 1996

Bliven, Edward. *Book of Catholic Prayer*. Portland, OR: Oregon Catholic Press, 1993.

Boyack, Kenneth, ed. *The New Catholic Evangelization*. New York: Paulist Press, 1991.

Brennan, Patrick. *Re-Imagining Evangelization*. New York: Crossroads, 1995.

————. *Re-Imagining the Parish*. New York: Crossroads, 1994.

Dougherty, Rose Mary. *Group Spiritual Direction. Community for Discernment*. New York: Paulist Press, 1995.

Dues, Greg. *Catholic Customs and Traditions. A Popular Guide*. Mystic, CT: Twenty-Third Publications, 1995.

Erikson, Richard. *Late Have I Loved Thee. Stories of Religious Conversion and Commitment in Later Life*. New York: Paulist Press, 1993.

Huebsch, Bill. *Vatican II in Plain English. Volume 1: The Council*. Allen, TX: Thomas More, 1997.

————. *Vatican II in Plain English. Volume 2: The Constitutions*. Allen, TX: Thomas More, 1997.

————. *Vatican II in Plain English. Volume 3: The Decrees and Declarations*. Allen, TX: Thomas More, 1997.

Hughes, Kathleen. *Lay Presiding. The Art of Leading Prayer*. Collegeville, MN: The Liturgical Press, 1988.

Killen, Patricia O'Connell and John De Beer. *The Art of Theological Reflection*. New York: Crossroads, 1996.

Lucker, Raymond et al., eds. *The People's Catechism. Catholic Faith for Adults*. New York: Crossroads, 1996.

Marthaler, Berard. *The Creed*. Revised edition. Mystic, CT: Twenty-Third Publications, 1996.

Osborn, Linda. *Good Liturgy, Small Parish*. Chicago: Liturgy Training Publications, 1996.

Smith, Ronald T. *Annulment. A Step-by-Step Guide for Divorced Catholics*. Chicago: ACTA Publishing, 1995.

Turpin, Joanne. *Catholic Treasures New and Old*. Cincinnati: St. Anthony Messenger Press, 1994.

Zwack, Joseph. *Annulment: Your Chance to Remarry Within the Catholic Church*. New York: Harper and Row, 1983.